JUGENDSTIL ART NOUVEAU

Translated from the German by Michael Heron
*Copyright © 1984 by Schuler Verlagsgesellschaft mbH, Herrsching

English language translation copyright © by Little, Brown and
Company, and by Schuler Verlagsgesellschaft mbH, Herrsching.
All rights reserved. No part of this book may be reproduced in
any form or by any electronic or mechanical means including information storage and retrieval systems without permission in
writing from the publisher, except by a reviewer who may quote
brief passages in a review.

First published in Germany by Schuler Verlag
First United States edition
Library of Congress catalog card number 85-61840
International Standard Book No: 0-8212-1607-4

New York Graphic Society books are published by Little, Brown
and Company. Published simultaneously in Canada by Little,
Brown and Company (Canada) Limited

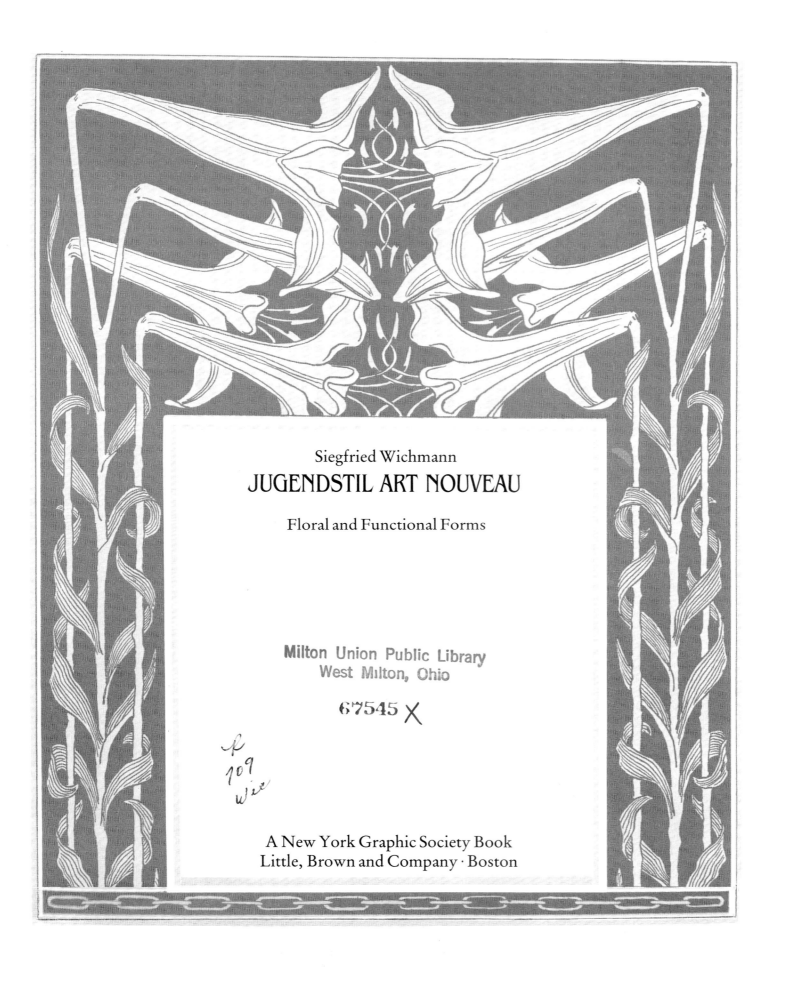

Siegfried Wichmann

JUGENDSTIL ART NOUVEAU

Floral and Functional Forms

A New York Graphic Society Book
Little, Brown and Company · Boston

Contents

Introduction

The theme is the vigorous growth of plants, not merely their image as an ornamental effect. It includes root-systems in the earth, the beautiful structure of the bark of trees and the many plant species which make the transformation to abstraction intelligible or give indications of symbolistic moods.

The cause of all this is the increasing influence of biological research on the fine arts between 1870 and 1917.

The illustrated scientific books by Ernst Haeckel and Wilhelm Bölsche were available from the early 1890s. Darwin's name was on everybody's lips and the theory of evolution, as always, was violently opposed by scientists and the Church. *Die Formenwelt aus dem Naturreiche* by Martin Gerlach, published in Vienna and Leipzig in large editions, played its part in popularizing the theory of evolution and the floral kingdom. Karl Blossfeldt took microphotographs of growing plants, which bore little relation to the traditional repeated patterns of plants. From the 1870s, there were numerous publications which dealt with the "influence of mechanical tension on the growth of plants" and many treatises were devoted to stability and the way it changed under environmental influences.

The limits of elasticity, the breaking-point of plant stems, were described (and read) in popular scientific books. Around 1900 the diffusion of scientific information reached a peak and as a result the artists of the period also became interested in it.

In this book, the word "floral" is to be understood as including marine as well as terrestrial flora. Consequently, the numerous species of sea-lilies, with their magical multi-coloured phosphorescence, are also floral, along with many others. The Protista kingdom of creatures intermediate between plant and animal, together with marine light, were themes for the symbolist poets and painters of art nouveau. The iridescence and self-illumination of the strange creatures of the sea animated French and Belgian symbolist poets to abstract hazy colours and Odilon Redon portrayed the unfamiliar creatures of the underwater world in a marine twilight. The opal, with its fine play of colour, was the fashionable stone of the period and opalescent glass encircled the first filament bulbs. Art nouveau vases "phosphoresced" above or underneath a decoration of fish-scales or snake-skin, which might also include seaweed, algae and Medusas.

Primeval and universal landscapes give an inkling of the history of creation; sectarian painters and painting sectarians create the mood in floral art nouveau. The gleaming loveliness of vitreous plants and trees, illuminated by lamps, brings something of the supernatural into the homes of the big cities, and objects from foreign lands transfigure the everyday scene. The flowing agitation of the art nouveau line heralds a fundamental concept of new forms of movement based on floral growth.

Louis Sullivan, Antoni Gaudi, Victor Horta and August Endell depict plants not statically but in their growing, changing shapes.

Scientific commentaries on the growth of plants and the changes they undergo were also studied by Hermann Obrist and transformed into symbolistically alienated forms.

The transformation followed two directions and was effected by two groups, the first that of symbolistic abstraction which has already been mentioned, the second the constructive group.

Constructions and functions are latent in all plants and animals. Here the concept "functional" is not a rigid formula, but the unlimited freedom of a more widely conceived limitation based on floral diversity. Because of external influences the stem of a bent flower is "locked" into its bending. So the bending is the form of the mechanical efficiency which the plant stem must produce if it is not to break. Highly functional prerequisites are enclosed in the bending. As a rule, straightening and rectilinearity do not mean an *increase* in functional efficiency, but they do seem aesthetically tidier and more distinct to us. This circumstance is bound up with form. When the cross-section of the stem changes, hostile external forces drive the plant to reinforce the points in danger of breaking. This is accepted by the designer who has developed through the floral phase when he chooses a smaller cross-section of wood for a chair design and has to reinforce it at the tension and pressure points.

Rectilinearity met the needs of the mechanical production of the time, at least in the processing of wood. An object with a flat base and floral decoration is just as stable as one with a flat base and no ornament. The functional question is how to hold it.

A vessel with a plant stem as handle may be more serviceable than a smooth Secession vase which slips out of one's hand.

When Van de Velde observes the shoots on a plant stem and makes use of the perception to create a practical handle, that is second-generation floralism, in other words recognizing complicated natural forces and using them functionally.

If the plant model is then suitably developed for manufacturing, the demand for serial production may be satisfied, owing to its increased usefulness.

Photographic enlargements of the process of growth in the plant kingdom gave the artists of the day an insight into constructions. The origins of modern design start where this observation begins to take effect. Nevertheless, the transitional phase is generally dependent on many other factors. The floral element taken *from* nature is not the only criterion; the prerequisite is the desire to see things in contact *with* nature. Nevertheless the mass consumer's desire to keep up appearances, guided by a habit-forming

diversity of styles, at first rejected the functional aesthetic in favour of irrational embellishment. But the functional aesthetic ultimately leads to the functional in practice, and soon the functional style was felt in all spheres of life. Fitness also plays a large part in artistic problems; design as adaptation or adaptation as design becomes a slogan.

The rejection of vigorous plant growth did not effect a successful separation. Bentwood furniture, for example, with its plant-like bending, was still connected with vegetable qualities and models through the material used to make it.

The last chapter of this book discusses the stereometric form and the square or cube.

Here a static equilibrium of surface and body is demonstrated as the highest practical form. Nevertheless, the aesthetic concerns of Josef Hoffmann are developed from contrasts, excess and deficiency. The Cartesian transformations are ultimately square systems developed from grid-like right-angled and equidistant co-ordinates.

These led, depending on the artist's aim, to a strictly proportional change – from square to right-angle. The growing forces of the plant were subject to this transformation, or they could be measured by the system of co-ordinates.

D'Arcy Thompson includes a chapter on "Mathematics and Form" in his book *On Growth and Form*. It contains conclusions characteristic of the searching, innovative mood around 1900, for Thompson also had his forerunners. I do not intend to pose the question of scientific accuracy here, but the sympathetic research which occupied itself with the inner working of floral forces, and so perceived innate functions, was not subjected to detailed aesthetic stylistic analysis.

Writings on the history of art have always referred to Ernst Haeckel in connection with discussions of art nouveau, but they have never made a really comparative analysis.

This book attempts to introduce new references and discuss aspects of art nouveau that have not been tackled before.

1 Kolo Moser, reclining nude, growing out of an iris blossom. *Ver Sacrum* I, sequence 11, p. 2. Black ink on white paper, 28.8 x 23.4 cm, *c.* 1898, J. Hummel Vienna.

The illustration is accompanied by a poem by Arno Holz:
"Seven billion years before my birth
I was an iris.
Beneath my shimmering roots
revolved another star.
On its dark waters
swam
my giant blue blossom."

The poetic words by Arno Holz refer to the theory of transformism, about which Ernst Haeckel said: "This theory, which Darwin looked on as the summit of our knowledge of nature, is usually called origin of species or the theory of derivation. Others call it the theory of transformation, or simply transformism. Both designations are correct. For this theory claims that all the different organisms (i.e. all the species of animals and plants that have ever lived and still exist on this planet) descend from a single primitive form or from a few very simple forms and that they developed from them naturally by gradual transformation."
E. Haeckel, *Natürliche Schöpfungsgeschichte*, Berlin 1879, p. 1 *et seq.*

Sieben Billionen Jahre vor meiner Geburt
war ich eine Schwertlilie.

Unter meinen schimmernden Wurzeln
drehte sich ein andrer Stern.

Auf seinem dunklen Wasser
schwamm
meine blaue Riesenblüte.

Plants and their Movement – an Art Nouveau Theme

Scientific investigations had a decisive influence on artists. Wilhelm Bölsche had discovered an explanatory formula for all non-scientists and, above all, the requisite vocabulary for publishing popular scientific books which were read by a wide public around 1904.[1]

August Endell, too, had studied Wilhelm Bölsche and remarks in his work *Um die Schönheit – eine Paraphrase um die Münchner Kunstausstellung*, 1896 (p. 16):

"Anyone who has never been delighted by the exquisite bending of the grass stalk, the marvellous inflexibility of the thistle leaf, the youthfulness of sprouting leaf buds, who has never been shaken and stirred to the depths of his soul by the unshakeable power of broken bark, the slender flexibility of the birch trunk, the great

2 August Endell, metal-work for a desk by Henry von Heiseler; c. 1896–9. 72.2 x 94.2 cm. wrought iron. House of Kirsch, Munich (see also p. 10). Private collection, south Germany.

calm of broad masses of leaves, knows nothing of the beauty of forms."[2]

Augustus Welby Pugin (1812–52), the Neogothic architect, had already encouraged the study of plants and their growth and making use of them artistically. He wanted to lead ornamentation directly back to nature. He saw not only the formal developments, but also the different phases of the growth of a plant, but Pugin was not systematic enough in his investigations. Obrist, on the contrary, had a scientific training and a memory which was receptive to the subtlest alterations in structure; he had learnt to see plants in their botanical context.[3] Accordingly, the form of movement in plants was divided into two main groups: that of growth and that of attractive movements, movements which he used artistically in the most varied forms. Touching, shaking and changing are of vital importance for the growth of the plant, for its state is never rigid. This leads to physical and mechanical processes of unrolling and rolling up, in which the spiral movement was important to Obrist, especially for his artistic experience (ill. 132).

On the problem of growth he observes: "By the growth of an organism should be understood an increase in volume taking place from inside to outside, which is generally also expressed by structural changes."

Obrist goes on to say, that "the external conditions of growth continue in the plant. Every growing plant organ finds itself originally in a developing state in which the necessary building matter is already stored." According to Obrist, there follows a period of enlargement in which the plant assumes its final size and structure. Then comes a final phase of inner development in which the elements of the substances assume a permanent state.

Obrist had also studied the morphological factors of plant growth and the process of cell-division, and tackled the morphological parallels of growth and root formation. Ill. 145 shows that the root theme had scarcely been treated artistically before and needed new forms. However, Chinese and Japanese artists had already approached the subject thousands of years ago.[4] Investigation of the root is a question that Obrist constantly posed to himself. Its peculiar outline was of particular interest to him as a potentially artistic form. The growth of the root is unlimited and underground the root continually puts forth nodulous offshoots, the younger shoots being always nearer the top than the older shoots. But the plant stem, too, was of primary artistic importance for Hermann Obrist. Intensive study of grasses, especially knotgrass species, showed him the branching, but also the bud formation under the leaf protuberances which he used as ornamental forms. In his drawings of root structures, he always saw the growth of above-ground leaf shoots in direct connection with the underground root system. Obrist also devoted himself to the growing movements of climbing plants and tendrils.[5] These have thin bud axes, whose first stem limbs extend into a kind of "bud peak" and then bend sideways. They begin to execute peculiar movements. An unusual feature is that the upper tip of the bud rotates in a circle or an ellipse. Longitudinal growth takes place along an imaginary straight line around which the climbing stem wraps itself. The tip of the bud tries to reach a support by this circular movement, which is very characteristic of climbing plants. As soon as this support is reached the end of the bud curves and grows on in a spiral. The direction is constant as a rule.

In his description of his representations of plants, which he always combined with creative artistic possibilities, the sensitivity of the plant was an important feature for Hermann Obrist. He constantly busied himself with this problem, especially with spiral growth (ill. 104). The many ways in which light influenced the growth of plants was a perpetual surprise to him. Underwater light in particular made possible the most heterogeneous plant structures, among which he was fascinated by the hybrid plant-animal organism (ill. 94).

Tendrils and climbing plants are subject to certain tactile stimuli, so that they curve on contact and the young tendril tip becomes prehensile.

Through further tactile effects and continued curvature of the tip, new windings arise, while the free part of the tendril, lying between its base and the point of attachment, climbs corkscrew-wise, yet with several changes between left-handed and right-handed. Observations about this were frequently written on his paintings and sketches and are also to be found in his *Programmatischen Schriften,* for example on a sketch *loc. cit.,* pp. 21 and 17:

A: L'inspiration, simply inspiration. L'inexplicable …/spring cliffs, summer cliffs, autumn cliffs. Theme of variation:

––– Autumn faded crinkled spiral leaves/Perhaps seed clusters.

C: External and inner forces/through which the movements and the emotions they release come into being. 1: Active, but passively endured forces: wind, water, gravity, weight, pressure, flames/smoke, clouds. 2: Active organic forces of the plant itself: growth of the bud, upward unfolding into/light and blossom, overcoming of obstruction,/climbing, breaking through, attacking, overcoming/extricating itself from thorn bushes, pebbles, etc./clasping, ensnaring, twisting round … fading, fatigue, bending in curves, sinking, falling/burdensome fruit, ––– dying in spiral windings and painful torsions.[6]

Obrist and his friends were influenced by Haeckelian principles and the illustrations of Wilhelm Bölsche. The artists drew many inspirations from Gerlach's illustrations of the natural world of forms, which Blossfeldt also liked to photograph.[7] The question was always how the plant arranges its whole organizational relations according to its assimilation system, i.e. to the qualities of the sap, inasmuch as the total form of the higher plants is dominated by the principle of developing as many large thin leaves as possible on comparatively thin supports in order to achieve the maximum benefit from the light.

The insights of the scientists are given artistic form. The pluralism of the individual form is strengthened by overlapping. The plant is made visible by "striving upwards, unfolding to light and blossoming, overcoming obstruction, climbing, breaking through, attacking, overcoming". But Obrist always sees the ambience, the "space around", when he writes "The whole a plastic movement mass, not too exclusively rocky. Close to the rocks moved buckled masses and deep holes with curves. Giant twisted strands and dry leaves richer in plant motifs from the details of your life."[8]

3 Otto Eckmann, carnation arabesque, *PAN* 1896/3, p. 216.

With the growth of the plant, the water content automatically increases and with it the pressure on the elastic cell wall of the plant. Obrist closely observed this pressure difference in the tension of the tissue. He strove to learn from the shaping power of nature herself and made Haeckel's sentence his own: "There are only three things for the creative mind: here am I, there is nature, there the object that I am supposed to beautify."

The materialistic principle dominates the artistic portrayal of plants in the *Gründerzeit*. In imitation of historical styles natural form reaches the stage of verism. In striped patterns or decorative borders, leading lines intersect wicker work-like arrangements, and an exaggerated material effect often moderates the ornamental pattern. In the repeated pattern which covers the surface, but also organizes, divides and animates it, all the things of the environment are included as models. The more it concerns itself with floral forms, the more the *Gründerzeit* style oscillates between a contemplative and a calculated composition. From it result rich techniques, modulated surfaces in agitated applications which always prefer sculptural or relief-like effects. Imitation of nature and excess of ornament are typical signs of this stylistic phase. Out of it the artists of the *Gründerzeit* develop many methods of representation in order to decorate all kinds of objects. In general, this period is characterized by efforts to combine the most antithetical styles in order to achieve effects that will give pleasure to the would-be trend-setters. In the process, the beginnings of surrealism are sometimes fore-shadowed.

The art nouveau artists adopt this conception partly in order to test and transform it. On the one hand stylistic pluralism becomes a central principle of arrangement. On the other, the *Gründerzeit* style, too, had altered the object by the liberal distribution of ornament, for example in the decoration of the body of a vase. In art nouveau the change was achieved by other means, and here scientists rendered significant services.

Obrist, basing himself on Haeckel, thought that the phenomena of movement in matter and nature happened with absolute inevitability and were conditioned by constant qualities which led to continuous reciprocal actions.

Obrist united what Haeckel* had expressed in a scientific doctrine by developing the human figure from a plant form (ill. 229). Man and plants are closely associated in a symbiosis which Obrist depicted in numerous drawings. With Haeckel, he was trying to say that the active material substrate or "stuff of life" is present in the bodies of all organisms. In growth and the movement caused by growth Obrist finds a force, to portray which can be an artistic goal for him. In contrast to the ornamental repeated pattern of the *Gründerzeit* style, the work of Obrist and Endell is an interpretation of energy processes as manifested in the force of growth. Around 1900 Obrist says (in his posthumous writings): "Whither is movement striving? Enthralling, filling up of space by division of masses, curve division, contrast direction: the towering, lying, sinking, upward striving, supporting, plunging, undulating, bending, falling, sinking, suddenly rising, curving, entwining, storing, broken, burst, stiff, opposing, embracing, striving upwards, striving away, forwards, backwards, swirling, achieves spirals through the degree of strength of the black and white, of the mass, of the degree of pressure of the line."[9]

Instead of the external conception of objects, we have the gradual emergence of the remembered image combined with contemplative inspiration. The way from illustration to sign was thus completed as early as 1900, at least theoretically.

Things become the expression of an idea. All previous outward forms are enhanced by Obrist in their figurative precision, so that the emphasized outline or its mass makes the outward image independent. The formal enhancement of his art is subject to ornamental laws which drive the variety of spiral motifs to rhythmization. The organized tension of lines in particular should and must work on the human psyche. A new relation to space and the alteration of the static structure bring movement to inert objects. Obrist unconditionally demands "dynamic energies" from the picture; the artist should "make forces visible by the strength or weakness of the medium, the colours, the light, the strength of line, hardness of form or softness of the intensity of curvature, the intensity of the bentness by strengthening of line by multiplication, crescendo, decrescendo, accelerando, ritardando, velocità, intenseness, violence, contrasts" (posthumous writings).[10]

To achieve a heightening of his representation and set himself apart from *Gründerzeit* production, Obrist demands rhythm not only of objects in motion but also of stable heavy masses, such as cliffs etc., around which the curve plays. The rhythm should increase in tempo in "long drawn out curve transformations" (posthumous writings). "Heaviness leaves its mark – bodily, cubically, stereometrically. To the point of ecstasy, more stormy, more violent, more fiery in the whirlwind! The enthusiasm, the flight, whirlpool of bliss, beyond time, beyond all eternities!" (Posthumous writings.)[10]

Consequently, the measurable units of time and the resultant short-term transformations of the object in the light/air medium are no longer worthy of representation, but rather the spirals considered as continuous, which, filled with dynamic force, signify motion not tied to time – "beyond time, beyond all eternities".

The picture with the wandering point of view wins new possibilities with the spiral motif and the upward-shooting zigzag. The goal of movement lies outside the surface of the picture or can be imagined as extended at will. So the spiral motif was no solitary phenomenon around 1900, rather it signified an active heightening of a dynamic process of movement which becomes the expression of a specific pattern of existence in its potentiated visibility.

*Haeckel, Ernst, zoologist, 1834–1919. Professor at Jena, 1865–1909. His main work, *Die Welträtsel, Gemeinverständliche Studien über biologische Philosophie* (1899), had a wide circulation and far-reaching effects in its day. There is no a priori knowledge, he says, only the knowledge of earlier generations, gained by experience, which has become constitutional by inheritance. Philosophy, too, must be based on the principle of evolution. We can no more imagine a "first beginning" for matter and motion than we can imagine a final end. The acceptance of a God guiding world events must be rejected. Haeckel summed up his doctrine under the name of monism. (From Heinrich Schmidt's *Philosophisches Wörterbuch*, Stuttgart, 1869.)

4 Arthur Hennig, trees and bushes, oil on canvas, 1912, 110 x 111 cm. Private collection, Munich.

8 Louis Comfort Tiffany,
two tulip-shaped ornamental
glasses (Favrile glass), c. 1897.
Left: slender triangular form
with three pinched-in folds at
the lip. Twisted green,
yellow, red and white internal
glass fibres. Decoration:
petals. 37.5 cm. Right: stem
with swelling, with tulip
blossom and foot; whitish
rim. Technique as above.
Decoration: calyx sepals.
35.8 cm. Bavarian National
Museum, Munich. Inventory
no. SW 16,15.

9 Louis Comfort Tiffany,
candlestick, triangular stem
rising from a double-leaved
base, with six jagged floral
stars (greater plantain), fire-
gilded bronze, marked at
edge of base "Tiffany Studio,
New York, 11, 648". 45.5 x
21.5 cm. Bavarian National
Museum, Munich. Inventory
no. SW 95.

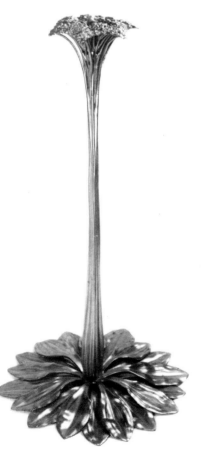

10   Louis Comfort Tiffany, ornamental glass, *c.* 1910. Jack-in-the-pulpit (the cuckoo-pint, *Arisaema*). Gleaming yellow glass with iridescent reflections and yellowish-green stem. Calyx with shimmering gold and iridescent surface. Crackle around the lobed rim. Marked "L.C.T.Y. 3263". 44.5 cm. Bavarian National Museum, Munich. Inventory no. SW 8.

Favrile glass allows the designer to make the growth of the bud or fully opened flower visible by changing the form. It has been established that the plant first flowers under the influence of light. This assimilation of light and specific substances continuously forms organic substances out of inorganic compounds such as water and carbon dioxide, and so contributes to maintaining life. Light in its essentially life-giving form is absolutely indispensable to the plant. Art nouveau artists transformed light into an iridescent self-illumination of the plant. Lighting by electric bulbs also contributed to their aim of shaping plants artistically by emphasizing the significance of their growth, colour-giving qualities and light reflection. Tiffany had observed that tensions are set up inside plant stems. He deliberately made swellings in his glass stems or made them conspicuous with twisted glass fibres, which would normally be purely decorative, but in his glass designs were intended to bring out the growing tissue tension. The still upright position of plant stems in Tiffany's designs is always rendered in a highly floral and vegetal way.

11   Martin Gerlach, wild vine-leaves. Plate 17 in his *Formenwelt aus dem Naturreiche* (Vienna and Leipzig, 1904).

12   Three-fold screen designed and executed by Zago Emillio, 1901. Autumnal vine-leaves, coloured grapes, traces of a reddish colour on the leaves, partially treated with wax mordant, carved linden-wood. 161 x 119 cm. Decoration: garland of vine-leaves with bunches of grapes. Private collection, Munich.

13   France, lamp in the shape of intertwined poppy heads, cast chased bronze, *c.* 1902. 78 x 39.5 cm. Austrian Museum of Applied Art, Vienna. Inventory no. 867. Gerlach's model sheets, which illustrated the world of natural forms, were also often used as models by the Tyrolean school of carving. On the basis of scientific research, a scrupulous examination of botanical assumptions was undertaken and these were mainly confirmed by photography. Karl Blossfeldt and Martin Gerlach are two important figures in this field who used photography to establish the special properties of plants by enlargements and special lighting effects, for the purposes of artistic creation. As a result, Karl Blossfeldt was appointed an assistant lecturer at the Royal Museum of Industrial Art (Königliches Kunstgewerbemuseum), Berlin. The plant was looked on as the foundation of the forms of applied art. In his teaching, Blossfeldt primarily considered plants as the model for tectonic forms. This was also a concern of Ernst Haeckel, as he often made clear in his lectures.

14 Bozen Technical School, wall bracket, massive pear-tree wood, treated with reddish-brown wax mordant, carved. Decoration: flowering tulips among leaves in three-dimensional relief. Height 35 cm, width 40 cm, depth 19 cm. Austrian Museum of Applied Art, Vienna. Inventory no. W.I. 484.

15 Bozen Technical School, small wall bracket, spruce, treated with reddish-brown wax mordant, tulip blossoms and leaves issuing from the stem, 1901. Height 13 cm, width 23 cm, depth 9.3 cm. Austrian Museum of Applied Art, Vienna. No inventory number.

16 Franz Železny, large wall bracket, pear-tree wood tinted with coloured wax mordant, c. 1900. Decoration: rose branches; rear wall *trompe l'oeil* water surface. Height 43 cm, width 110 cm, depth 28 cm. Austrian Museum of Applied Art, Vienna. Inventory no. H 958.

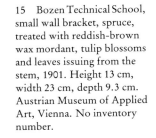

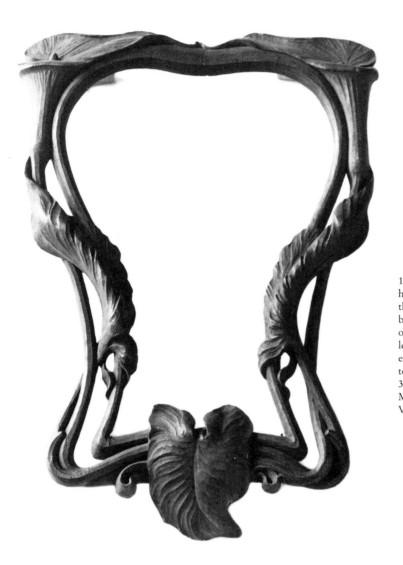

19 Bozen Technical School, hand mirror, handle carved in the round, consisting of bindweed stems, at the edge of the mirror two bindweed leaves, with one flower on either side and a bud at the top. Tinted pear-tree wood. 39.2 x 22.6 cm. Austrian Museum of Applied Art, Vienna. Inventory no. W.I. 485.

20 Wallern Technical School, bracket with irises. Decoration: irises carved in the round climb from a bunch of leaves and support the curved bracket top, profiled at the edge. Soft wood with walnut veneer, lightly tinted with wax mordant. Height 40.2 cm, width 40 cm, depth 26.4 cm. Austrian Museum of Applied Art, Vienna. Inventory no. W.I. 351.

17 House of Portois and Fix, Vienna, armchair, arms continuing into back, fluted like flower stems. Decoration: cyclamen motif on the chair back, carved in the round on the front side, front legs with bud-like swellings, rear legs curved polished, *Steinholz* (sawdust mixed with magnesium oxide and magnesium chloride) with matt finish. Height 76.5 cm, width 58 cm, depth 49 cm. Austrian Museum of Applied Art, Vienna. Inventory no. 2874.

18 Bozen Technical School, mirror frame, linden-wood matted with wax; the motifs carved in the round are taken from the Calla. Symmetrically arranged leaves twine round the sides of the frame: below, open leaf. 44.5 x 29 cm. Austrian Museum of Applied Art, Vienna. Inventory no. W.I. 221.

21   Delft vase with big-bellied body drawn in below. At shoulder height three protruding cylindrical openings after Islamic models. Hard, glazed and iridescent body. Decoration: fishes among brown seaweed and alga stems. Height 22.7 cm, diameter at base 7.7 cm. Marked at foot "E. Bodart, Delft" and distinctive sign. Private collection, Munich.

23   Juriaan Kok, two-handled vase, 1903. Quasi- or eggshell porcelain. Decoration: lily buds and flowers with leaves. Marked with trademark and year. Executed by J. Schellink. 19.5 cm. Bavarian National Museum, Munich. Inventory no. S.W. 30.

24   Juriaan Kok, four-sided vase with two unemphatic handles, 1903. Quasi- or eggshell porcelain. Decoration: clematis tendril with flowers, leaves and buds. Marked with trademark and year. 20.7 cm. Bavarian National Museum, Munich. Inventory no. SW 31.

22   Th. A.C. Colenbrander, orchid vase, c. 1903. Flat, separated round base, body of two cones running into each other, beaker-like mouth, earthenware, streaming glaze, black, whitish-grey and brown. Height 13 cm, diameter 4.4 cm. Bavarian National Museum, Munich. Inventory no. SW 176.

25   Juriaan Kok, pot with lid, 1904. Quasi- or eggshell porcelain. Decoration orchid flowers. Marked with trademark and year. 13.6 cm. Bavarian National Museum, Munich. Inventory no. SW 34.

The Dutch ceramists Colenbrander, Kok and van de Hoef created a delightful decoration which coalesced with the functional form of the pot body. Juriaan Kok (1861–1919), as Director of the Rozenburg Faience Factory at The Hague, developed the so-called quasi- or eggshell porcelain. He exhibited his ceramics for the first time at the Universal Exhibition of 1900 in Paris and had an instant success. "Everything about this porcelain is astonishing and individual, the mass, the forms, the painting", was the verdict of the contemporary press.

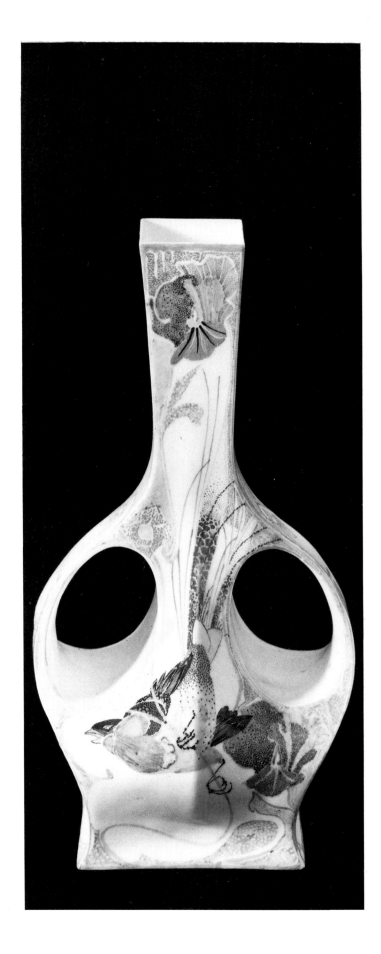

26 Juriaan Kok, two-handled vase, square base, slightly pinched four-sided body, handles at the shoulder rising upwards and turning into a four-sided neck. Quasi- or eggshell porcelain. Decoration: pansies and sparrows among leaves. Marked with trademark and year. Executed by J. Schellink, *c.* 1903. 17.8 cm. Private collection, South Germany.

27 Ornamental bottle-shaped vase, 1904. Quasi- or eggshell porcelain. Decoration: mating birds among flowering poppies. Marked under base with trademark and year. Executed by W.P. Hartgring. 30.3 cm. Bavarian National Museum, Munich. Inventory no. SW 32.

These vases are thin-walled and light as a feather. Handles grow out of the vessel's surface and, instead of the usual round pottery shape, angular but curved bodies are created which have markedly pinched shoulders and necks. The covers of vessels and bottles have mottled rings which allow the silhouette to rise to its culmination. The painting pays scrupulous attention to achieving a uniform value in the colouring. The bizarre walls are covered as if with a filigree network of birds of paradise (ill. 27). They are reminiscent of Javan batique designs, which is understandable, because Holland was closely connected with Indonesia in its colonial days. But East Asian pictures, which bring birds and plants into a mutual relationship, also determined the composition and individual form of Juriaan Kok's works.

28 Juriaan Kok,
sugar bowl on square, slightly
incurved base, four-sided
body bellying out, slightly
fluted at the corners, slightly
recessed towards the upper
square rim, square lid with
broad flat edge, four-sided
pointed top, tip interrupted.
Quasi- or eggshell porcelain.
Marked with trademark and
year. Executed by J.
Schellink. Height 13 cm.
Bavarian National Museum,
Munich. Inventory no. SW 34.

29 Juriaan Kok,
eggshell porcelain from the
Rozenburg Faience Factory
at The Hague. Teapot,
spherical body on flat base,
curved broadly based spout,
slightly arched lid with ring,
flat handle attached to the
shoulder. Decoration:
orchids. Marked with
trademark and year.
Executed by J. Schellink.
Height 13 cm. Bavarian
National Museum, Munich.
Inventory no. SW 33.

30 Juriaan Kok,
three coffee-cups and saucers,
c. 1904. Cups of octagonal
design slightly tapering at the
base, broadening out calyx-
like at the mouth. Shallowly
arched saucer on round centre
with octagonal rim. Quasi- or
eggshell porcelain.
Decoration: orchids. Marked
with trademark and year.
Executed by J. Schellink.
Height of cup 6 cm, diameter
of saucer 12.8 cm. Bavarian
National Museum, Munich.
Inventory no. SW 35–37.

31 Juriaan Kok,
three cups and saucers, cup
on a round base becoming
broader and octagonal at the
lip, handle forming
parallelogram broadly
attached at top and bottom,
shallow saucer on flat centre
with octagonal rim. Quasi- or
eggshell porcelain.
Decoration: orchid flowers
and foliage. Marked with
trademark and year.
Executed by J. Schellink.
Height of cup 5 cm, diameter
of saucer 13 cm. Bavarian
National Museum, Munich.
Inventory no SW 41–43.

32 Juriaan Kok,
teapot, c. 1904. Spherical
body on flat base, curved,
broadly based spout, slightly
curved lid with ring handle,
flat handle attached to the
shoulder, quasi- or eggshell
porcelain. Decoration:
orchid flowers. Marked with
trademark and year.
Executed by J. Schellink.
Height 13.6 cm. Bavarian
National Museum, Munich.
Inventory no. SW 38.

33 Juriaan Kook,
sugar bowl on square, slightly
incurved base, four-sided
big-bellied body, slightly
fluted at the corners, slightly
recessed towards the upper
square rim, square lid with
broad flat edge, four-sided
pointed top, tip interrupted,
quasi- or eggshell porcelain.
Decoration: orchids. Marked
with trademark and year.
Executed by J. Schellink.
Height 13 cm. Bavarian
National Museum, Munich.
Inventory no. SW 39.

34 Juriaan Kook,
cream jug on square base with
bevelled corners, big-bellied
body, recessed shoulder,
slightly outward curving neck
turning into a high lip on one
side and a handle on the
other. Quasi- or eggshell
porcelain. Decoration:
orchids. Marked with
trademark and year.
Executed by J. Schellink.
Height 9 cm. Bavarian
National Museum, Munich.
Inventory no. SW 40.

35 Rörstrand Porcelain Factory, Sweden, vase with short neck recessed from belly, wavy mouth, glazed white porcelain, *c.* 1902. Decoration: climbing foliage-plant, calyx incorporated with upper wavy rim, marked on base with trademark "KL" (green stamp – 3 crowns). 26 cm. Private collection, Munich.

36 Nils Erik Landström, vase with flat base, *c.* 1900. Cylindrical body, narrowing slightly towards the base, shoulder with short recessed neck, white-glazed painted porcelain. Relief decoration: larch twigs with small cones. Design: Nils Erik Landström, green stamp at the foot "Rörstrand" with 3 crowns, below "NL", also incised distinguishing sign and no. 15263. 26.5 cm. Private collection, Munich.

37 Rörstrand Porcelain Factory, Sweden, low vase with wavy rim, flat base with bellied body, *c.* 1900. Decoration: climbing Alpine violets in slightly broken up relief, over-topping the rim. White-glazed painted porcelain. Height 12 cm, diameter 16.5 cm. Private collection, Munich.

Naturalistic Japanese ornament is not the only decisive feature of the period; the monochrome vessel wall with structural glazes of Chinese origin also invites the exploration of a multiplicity of surface treatments and new ceramic forms. From 1889 a periodical which had recently become celebrated, *Le Japon Artistique,* published in Paris by Samuel Bing, showed Japanese and Chinese pottery shapes which demonstrably stimulated art nouveau ceramists.

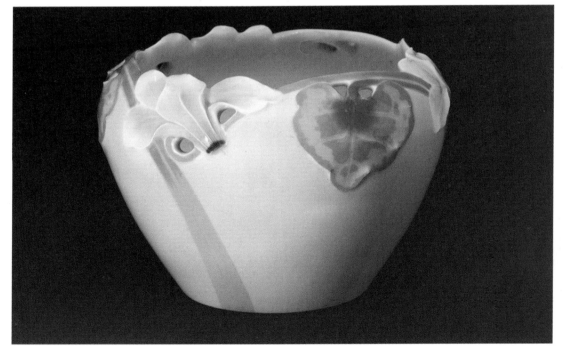

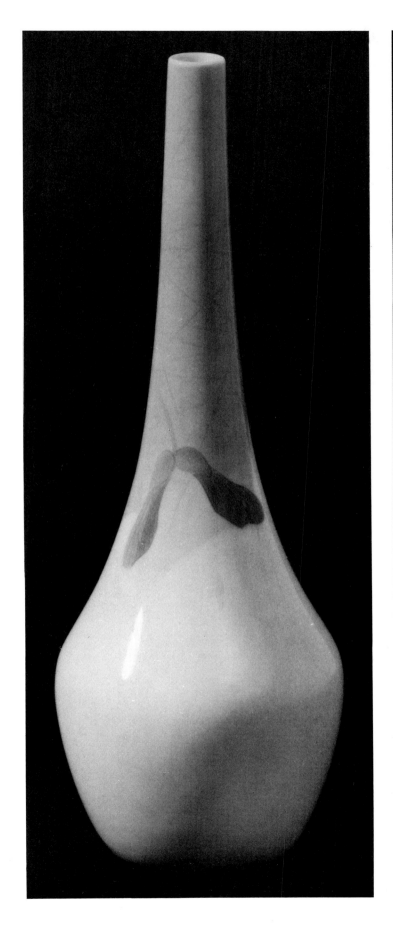

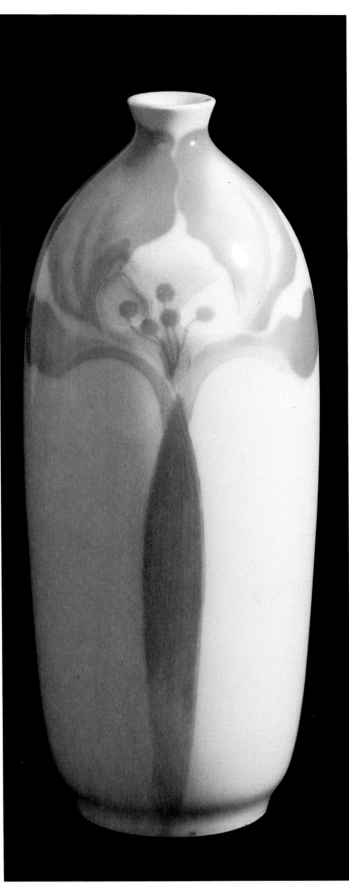

38 Rörstrand Porcelain Factory, Sweden, vase with flat base, club-shaped body with long narrow neck and straight rim. Decoration: sycamore seeds and spider on a thread, white-glazed painted porcelain, marked on base with trademark. 20.7 cm. Bavarian National Museum, Munich. Inventory no. SW 55.

39 Rörstrand Porcelain Factory, Sweden, vase with flat base, cylindrical body, slightly arched shoulders and short recessed neck, white-glazed porcelain, painted in colour. Decoration: iris plant. Marked on base with trademark. 22 cm. Bavarian National Museum, Munich. Inventory no. SW 55.

40 Josef Maria Olbrich
design for a tulip lamp, *c.*
1902. 1 Sketch after tulip
blossoms, 2 clustering for
lamp, lampstands. Design for
the Musiksaal in Darmstadt.
Pencil and black ink on paper,
27.6 x 21.4 cm (not
reproduced in full).
Kunstbibliothek,
Jebenstrasse, Berlin OZ 224 (I).

41 Emile Gallé,
ornamental lamp in the shape
of a flowering tulip, *c.* 1900.
Carved wood base, flashed
glass with oxides sealed in
during fusion, engraved
leaves on the orange part of
the shade. Marked on the foot
"Emile Gallé". 65.2 cm.
Kunstmuseum, Düsseldorf,
collection Prof. Hentrich.

42 Josef Maria Olbrich
design for a wall lamp, side
view, black and green ink,
marked above: "Wiener
Stadtbahn, light in the
entrance hall". 16.4 x 21.3
cm. Schreyhl, 1972 (10068),
Kunstbibliothek, Jebenstrasse,
Berlin. K. 5660 b/50 a.

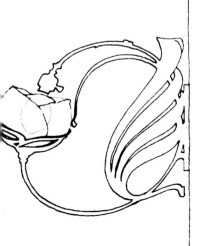

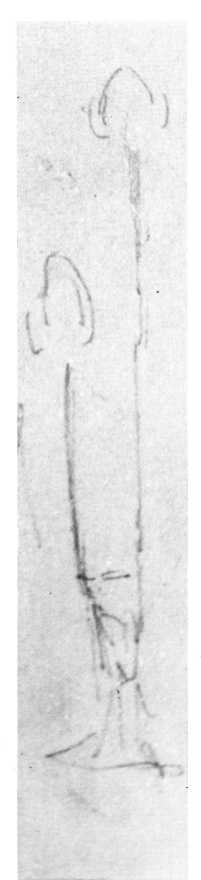

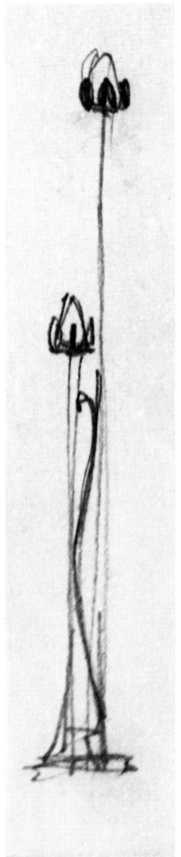

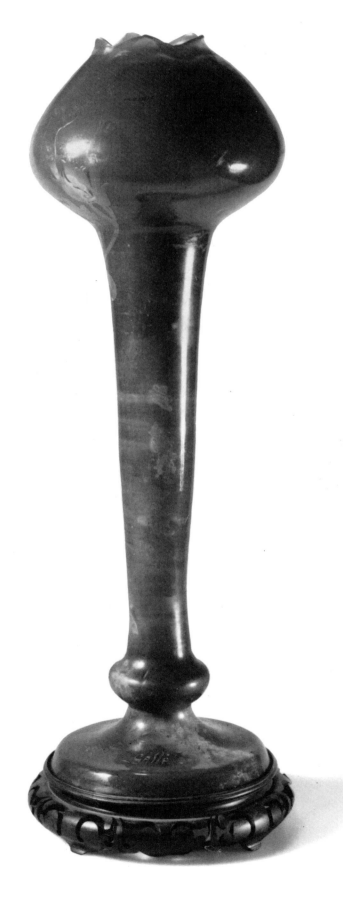

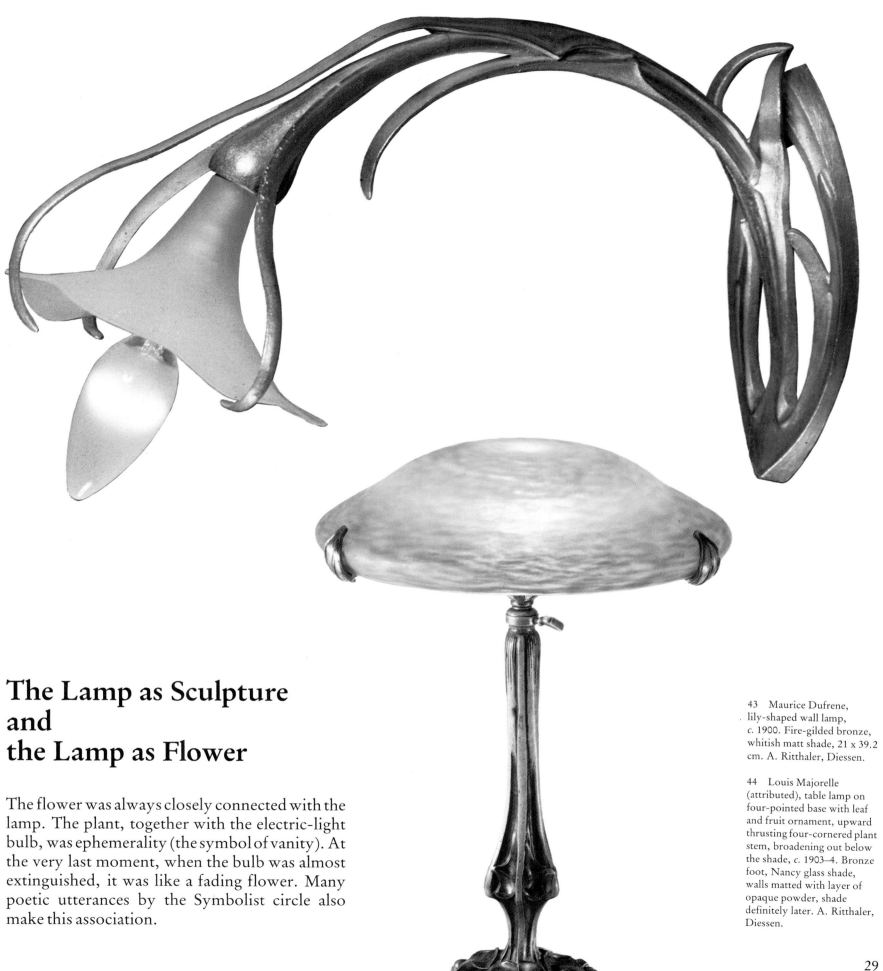

The Lamp as Sculpture
and
the Lamp as Flower

The flower was always closely connected with the lamp. The plant, together with the electric-light bulb, was ephemerality (the symbol of vanity). At the very last moment, when the bulb was almost extinguished, it was like a fading flower. Many poetic utterances by the Symbolist circle also make this association.

43   Maurice Dufrene, lily-shaped wall lamp, *c.* 1900. Fire-gilded bronze, whitish matt shade, 21 x 39.2 cm. A. Ritthaler, Diessen.

44   Louis Majorelle (attributed), table lamp on four-pointed base with leaf and fruit ornament, upward thrusting four-cornered plant stem, broadening out below the shade, *c.* 1903–4. Bronze foot, Nancy glass shade, walls matted with layer of opaque powder, shade definitely later. A. Ritthaler, Diessen.

29

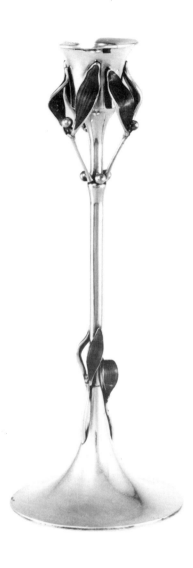

45 Georg Adam Scheidt, Vienna, candlestick, on a foot rising into a cone, *c.* 1899. Plant stems with leaves and blossoms, silver and green enamel. Height 22.5 cm. Württemberg Landesmuseum, Stuttgart.

Another feature is that the flower can assume many shades of colour under different kinds of illumination by external light. For example the colours of tulip leaves and water-lilies were studied under light in relation to water and air and it was recognized that the change in colouring depended on an illumination which could also be achieved by electric light. The lamp became a floral object which played a substitute role in the houses and flats of the big cities. It reflected nature in an altered and yet nostalgic way which stemmed from symbolism and bore the stamp of the *Gründerzeit.*

Another form of the symbolization of the lamp is the female figure (ills. 71, 72). And it was precisely in the symbolistic tendency of art nouveau that it acquired a decisive value. It is the fairy, the nymph, but also the hybrid creature intermediate between winged woman and floating dancer. The irrational illumination, the discoloration and hence the otherness of stiff materials, such as fabrics, which now enclose the lamp-shade sculpturally and ornamentally, those are the changes later made use of by surrealism. A great interest was taken in variety shows and the dancer Loie Fuller (ill. 71) sent society, especially artists, into ecstasies with her illuminated veil dances. The figure of Fuller which is found in many lamps shows how deep the effect of the combination of electric light and expressive movement was. Floralism combined with the female figure into an image. Thus it was possible for a female figure to be interwoven with a tree which spread its top above the lamp (ill. 72). So the association of vigorous floral forms and exaggerations of the human figure is a phase which could be transposed over and above surrealism to abstraction. To begin with, flowers had a decisive effect on the important artists of the Munich and Darmstadt art nouveau schools. Nevertheless a combination of everyday use and creative form and colouring was created in the lamp, with its highly individual illumination and intrinsic sculptural value.

Banal everyday life was enhanced by an atmospheric "lighting" experience, which was then accepted by the electric lamp industry, resulting in many commissions for craftsmen, artists and architects in order to meet the heavy demand.

Around the turn of the century, the art of making coloured lamps reaches its absolute zenith. Entirely new structural forms and new technical refinements were largely responsible for its far-reaching effects. The discovery of new glass techniques helps to give practical form to the elementary, but also hybrid, concept of art nouveau and *Jugendstil.* A remarkable and irresistible magic emanated from objects of kaolin, quartz and many other ingredients.

In 1904, the art critic Felix Poppenberg wrote as follows about an exhibition of lamps: "Then there are stylized solar discs, ears-of-corn formations, jagged clusters of rays like bushes, reminiscent of the deep-sea organisms from Haeckel's *Kunstformen der Natur.* And related to them are those varieties with sea-star motifs and the delicate crepon-crinkled foliage as exhibited by the branches of the miniature trees in the wonderland of the ocean floor.

"Colour symphonies roll and swell. Lamp-shades are completely flooded with subtle nuances of colour. Immersed in the changing gleam, they stand there, a faint pink and saffron-yellow aura hovering over them, like the shades of the most delicate border of cloud in the fading dawn.

"And the ambience of the ocean light is created, full of mother-of-pearl iridescence; purple-violet, canary yellow and lilac pink are sketched in delicate variations; precious stone and gleaming enamel appear with pomegranate and amaranth hues, resplendent as the mottled red and yellow chrysanthemum, the Japanese heraldic banner.

"Other flowers stand and look at you. Callas with their exuberantly arched calyxes like the mouth of a tuba grow out of massive bases on thick stems. And gladioli, with their narrow sickle-shaped leaves and the climbing shoots of violet and red flowers. The tall stems of the amaryllis tower up as impressively as candelabra, but their bells are delicately shaded like fragile chiffon flounces."[1] And in another passage: "Every efficiency factor here not only fulfils its function, but is simultaneously the spontaneous expressive accent of this composition based on reciprocity and mutual interaction. Just like the patterning on Tiffany glass. The cloudy bluish grey shimmers forth, as do the budding green, the pear-coloured glaze, the creamy yellow, the vanishing pink of the glass in the floating ground of vases and bowls."[2]

The poetic art of glass gains an ever increasing influence. Museums acquire Tiffany lamps and vases from Bing in Paris for as much as 40,000 U. S. Dlrs. an item. Certain neo-Impressionist shades of colour in Tiffany's lustrings betray the conformist colour sense which painters and artistic craftsmen also choose. In his book *Glasarchitektur,* conceived in 1909 and published in 1914,

Paul Scheerbart proposed that the walls of houses should be made of Tiffany Favrile glass. He writes: "The famous American Tiffany, who introduced the so-called Tiffany glass, did much to promote the glass industry; he developed coloured clouds in glass. The loveliest effects are possible with these clouds, and from them house walls acquire a brand-new charm which nevertheless puts ornamentation into the background, but does not render it impossible in special places."[3]

Scheerbart, who made fun of his own fantasy, not dreaming that his exaggerations would actually become reality, continues his description of the future and foresees that one day Tiffany glass would be used to make glass bricks.

"The so-called glass brick then forms the material for the walls which may easily become one of the most interesting specialities of glass architecture.

46 Eduard Foehr, candlestick, *c.* 1900. Climbing plant, stem on flat base, with leaves on upper part, open iris as candle socket. Cast, chased and engraved silver. Height 28 cm. Württemberg Landesmuseum, Stuttgart.

50   Louis Majorelle,
two table lamps in the form of
bluebells. Height 50.2 cm,
diameter 19.8 cm.

51   Daum Brothers,
table lamp. Decoration: birch
leaves and crocuses. Height
33 cm, diameter 13.2 cm.

52   Fernand Dubois
(attributed), table lamp in the
form of a snowdrop. Height
47.2 cm, diameter of foot 22.3
cm.

53   Muller Frères,
mushroom table lamp.
Decoration: mushroom
lamellae. Height 67.2 cm,
diameter 26.7 cm.

54   Daum Brothers,
table lamp. Decoration: wild
vines. Height 36.2 cm,
diameter of shade 19 cm.

55   Louis Majorelle
(attributed), table lamp.
Decoration: ears of wheat.
Height 68.2 cm, diameter
13.2 cm.

56 Louis Comfort Tiffany,
table lamp with broad dome-
shaped glass shade, in
opalescent and Favrile glass,
c. 1900–2. Decoration:
flowering apple-tree with
leaves. Bronze base with root
system rising from it. Height
76 cm, diameter of shade 63.5
cm. Bavarian National
Museum, Munich. Inventory
no. SW 102.

57   Louis Comfort Tiffany,
table lamp (in the manner of
P. Handel). Decoration:
narcissi. Height 71 cm,
diameter of shade 50.5 cm.

58   A. Florquin
(attributed), table lamp in the
form of a branch, shade with
opaline glass. Height 55 cm,
diameter of shade 26.2 cm.

59 Louis Comfort Tiffany, table lamp, in form of mushroom-shaped spider web. Height 47.2 cm, diameter of shade 38 cm.

60 Louis Comfort Tiffany, table lamp. Decoration: dogwood belts. Height 60 cm, diameter of shade 46 cm.

61   August Cain, candlestick, *c.* 1898. Tulip with flower and bulb, stem enlarged by leaves in the round, below the bulb three frogs as caryatids. Fire-gilded bronze. Height 24.5 cm. Signed on the bulb: "A. Cain". A. Ritthaler, Diessen.

62   Maurice Bouval (attributed, probably school of), table lamp in the form of a luxuriant poppy blossom. Twisted stem with poppy heads, filigree base, glass shade coloured in molten state, wavy rim, powdered colour decoration in the manner of Daum. Fire-gilded bronze. 42 x 23.8 cm. Influenced by Louis Majorelle, glass shade from the 1920s. Private collection, Munich.

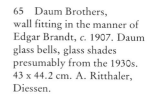

65 Daum Brothers,
wall fitting in the manner of
Edgar Brandt, *c.* 1907. Daum
glass bells, glass shades
presumably from the 1930s.
43 x 44.2 cm. A. Ritthaler,
Diessen.

66 Daum Brothers,
lampshade, *c.* 1906 or later.
Glass coloured in the molten
state, etched and polished.
Decoration: leaves and round
berries in a typically
silhouette effect. Marked on
shade: "Daum Nancy". 40.5
cm. Bernhard Maler,
Munich.

63 Workshop of Ludwig
Vierthaler,
in the manner of Jean Dampt,
c. 1899. Wall fitting of
exuberant flowers and leaves,
brass, painted several times.
73 x 45 cm. Private collection,
South Germany.

64 Workshop of Ludwig
Vierthaler,
seven-lamp chandelier. E.
Ehrenböck and L. Vierthaler
worked for M. Hondepine
(dealer in metal goods) in
Paris. The Hondepine
distributing organization also
employed some small casting
and chasing workshops in
Alsace. Ehrenböck was
Hondepine's brother-in-law.
(Documentation about this in
preparation.)

67 Workshop of Ludwig
Vierthaler,
after Jean Dampt, wall fitting
or ceiling candelabra in the
form of white lilies, *c.* 1898.
Leaves in the round on the
stem, brass, painted several
times and engraved. 82 x 30.5
cm. Private collection, South
Germany.

68 Plate 33 from
Martin Gerlach,
*Formenwelt aus dem
Naturreiche*, Vienna and
Leipzig, 1904. Martin
Gerlach took his own
photographs, but he also
accepted work by Karl
Blossfeldt.

69 *(Opposite)* Louis
Chalon,
candelabra in fire-gilded
bronze, *c.* 1898. Decoration:
three arms with butterflies
facing inwards, below, more
butterflies perched close
together above the umbel.
81.2 x 61.5 cm. Coll. Werner
Ott, Cape George, Canada.

70 Candelabra in the form
of two butterflies facing each
other on a ring, Belgium, *c.*
1900 (copied in Gerlach's
Formenwelt, Plate 33).
Patinated bronze. Width 54.2
cm, diameter 40 cm. Private
collection, Munich.
Ernst Haeckel remarks; "The
eighth and last order of
insects and at the same time
the only ones with mouths

that can actually suck are the
butterflies (Lepidoptera).
This order appears in several
morphological aspects as the
most advanced division of
insects and so was the latest to
develop."
Hermann Obrist steeped
himself in Haeckel's writings
and he also made many
drawings after the individual
forms of insects. In the

second half and at the end of
the 19th century the insect
became an essential theme for
art nouveau, depicted by
artists as surreal, yet also as
extremely real. The insect
which swarms round a
glowing lamp provided the
artist with a reference point
for ornamenting the lamp
with large insects. There are
many examples; in the

symbolism of the turn of the
century, they acquire a new
emphasis on their actuality in
this world. The Darwinian
theory of natural selection
was now taken for granted by
natural scientists, and artists
were the first to regard the
theme as absolutely topical
and worthy of
representation.

71 *(Opposite)* Raoul
François Larche,
the veil dancer Loie Fuller,
bronze statuette, *c.* 1900.
Hollow casting, engraved and
fire-gilded; in the veils
swirling above the head an
electric lamp (see detail,
right). Workshop: Sio
Decauville (Edmond-
Gustave). 46 x 27.2 cm.
Bavarian National Museum,
Munich. Inventory no. SW 81.

72 *(Opposite)*
Eduard Thomasson
(brother of Hippolyte, 1881–
1924, Paris), table lamp, *c.*
1902. Fire-gilded cast chased
bronze. Decoration:
reclining girl on ivy branch
(detail below). 30.2 x 19.7
cm. Private collection,
Munich.
After studying at the Ecole
des Arts Décoratifs in Paris,
Thomasson was first active as
a sculptor and later as a craft
designer, the table lamp
coming from the middle
period of his creative activity.
Thomasson was in no way
inferior to Raoul Larche.
About 1900 the sculptor had
developed the classical theme
of Daphne in the bay-tree
into a standard model. The
floral process, together with
the female body, could be
stylized as the concept
"Femme-Fleur". The
materials of the smooth fire-
gilded body and the
engraved floral foliage led to
contrasts which were
enhanced by the illumination
of the lamp.

73 Richard Riemerschmid,
three-legged occasional table
with brass top and supports,
1900. Stained walnut. Made
for Liberty & Co., London.
78.3 x 41.5 cm. Statuette,
Raoul François Larche (ill. 71).

74   Philip Handel, stained-glass window with flowering tree, New York, c. 1901. 168 x 101 cm, with frame 178 x 111 cm. Coll. Werner Ott, Cape George, Canada.

75   Martin Gerlach, *Formenwelt aus dem N[...]che*, Vienna and Leipzig, 1904, Plate 15 (detail): apple blossom.

76   Poster by Leopold Stolber for the XXIII Secession Exhibition, Vienna. 98 x 67.5 cm. Private collection, Munich. Stolber tried to transform the three-dimensional blossoms into a surface decoration by juxtaposing parallel rows of flat flowers and forming them into a compositional schema, which is typical of the ornamental effect of floral art nouveau. The decorative element of the flowering tree in the production of the stained-glass window also acquires an important positional value. Thus the firm of Philip Handel produced high-quality windows which mark a peak in the conception of floral art nouveau. In 1885, Philip Handel and Adolph Eyden founded the firm of Eyden and Handel, Glass Decorators, in Meriden. In 1893 Philip Handel became the sole proprietor and as from 1903 the firm was called The Handel Company Inc. Handel reached his zenith with his stained-glass windows, which are far more important than his table lamps. The firm was noted for its first-class technicians, whom Handel had carefully cultivated for many years. The east Asian influence, adopted from Japanese painted screens, is striking. The feeling reflected by the window is combined, in the floral development of the time, with a mastery of composition that gives the artistic statement a focal importance.

77 Wilhelm Stoiber, swimming fish. The style lays emphasis on the alternative abbreviation of the subject matter, which, against the simplified underwater landscape, creates the engraving. Illustration from *Ver Sacrum*, 5th year, p. 83.

August Endell and Hermann Obrist acquired a profound knowledge of the underwater world after reading Ernst Haeckel's 17th lecture, *Stammbaum und Geschichte des Pflanzenreiches*. On p. 410, Haeckel observes: "The first class of seaweeds, the primordial seaweeds, could also be called primordial plants, because they embrace the simplest and least developed of all plants. And in particular the oldest of all vegetable organisms, which were the origin of every other plant … In spite of their extremely simple composition of identical or very slightly differentiated cells, the seaweeds exhibit an extraordinary multiplicity of different forms. On the one hand, they include the simplest plants, lowest on the evolutionary scale, and on the other hand highly developed and individual forms." Hermann Obrist and August Endell took an interest in the peculiar forms of the underwater regions and they found there countless forms which had never been seen before. This especially affected those artists at the turn of the century who had taken an interest in the scientific contributions of Wilhelm Bölsche and Ernst Haeckel, influenced by these

Geological and Submarine Motifs and Themes

In the course of the 19th century all species of the animal kingdom were investigated and classified and the numerous subdivisions of species were scientifically extended.

Haeckel began to apply the theory of evolution, as reformed by Darwin, to the whole field of morphology (the science of form) in the most comprehensive way. As a result he came to natural philosophical conclusions which reached their peak around 1900, after many researchers had developed popular scientific systems based on Haeckelian premises. The division of the whole organic world into three main kingdoms – animal, Protista and vegetable – effected a classification which even the layman could understand.

Ernst Haeckel spoke about the purpose of his researches; his goal was to bring the art forms of nature to life for the mass of interested people: "The main purpose of my *Kunstformen der Natur [Art Forms of Nature]* was aesthetic. I wanted to make accessible to wider educated circles the wonderful treasures of beauty which are hidden in the depths of the sea or are only visible under a microscope because of their minute size. But I combined this with the more scientific purpose of giving an insight into the extraordinary structure and specific organization of these forms."[1] Thanks to Darwin, the morphology and especially the historical development of organisms was a field which also concerned the interested layman. In the 19th century, the ramifications of morphology and the history of organic evolution were a sphere which involved the artist through the medium of scientific illustrations. Hermann Obrist, for example, was not principally interested in the plants themselves, but in their original forms. These appeared as completely new and made visible a realm which primarily comprised the submarine world, or root growth in the earth, and gave the artist an all-embracing picture. And so in the art of the 19th century, especially in applied art, we find that the actual primeval form appeared on the one hand as a hitherto unknown abstract form, yet on the other hand led to abstraction in the different language of images. Darwin's and later Haeckel's opponents contributed to the popularization of the subject, in which the public, too, took a special interest.

words of Haeckel's: "And yet even these richly varied submarine seaweed forests off the coasts of Europe give only a faint idea of the colossal forests in the Sargasso Sea, those vast banks of seaweed which cover an area of some 40,000 square miles and which intimated to Columbus on his voyage of discovery that land was near. Similar but much more extensive forests of seaweed grew in the primordial seas, presumably in dense masses, and the way in which countless generations of these ancient seaweeds died in succession is attested by, among other things, the great Silurian alum shales of Sweden, the peculiar composition of which essentially originated from those submarine masses of seaweed."

(Ernst Haeckel, *Schöpfungsgeschichte,* Berlin, 1879, p. 403 *et seq.*)

Wilhelm Bölsche, a German supporter of Darwin, had found a popular scientific pictorial base in his numerous books through which he reached a wide readership and was able to expound the history of evolution to a large and interested public.[2] Around 1900, artists had reacted to the multiplicity of forms, and this incredible richness inspired much artistic creativity.

A tendency towards stereotyped pictorial patterns characterizes both the high quality and the trivial pictorial reproduction of symbolist art nouveau. For artists and poets alike, the attempt to extend the visible things of the age or make them representable at all was decisive. It is interesting to see how the environment is extended to the boundary zones as it acquires a "hybrid" illumination. Near and far can be seen and experienced together, just as the wide-angled totality can be seen close up in contrast. Universal landscapes in a cosmic atmosphere are also seen segmentally. New themes, such as the underwater scenery with its dim light, ambience of waving seaweed and *nostalgie de la mort*, strive

78 Emile Gallé, four-handled vase, big-bellied with wavy neck, colourless crystal, 1890 or earlier. 14.5 x 19 cm. Decoration: floating micro- and macroplankton, Chlorophyceae in various forms, *Fucus spiralis* and *Chondrus crispus,* different groups of algae, with threadlike branching thalli. The moonfish *(Mola mola)* in the underwater light and sand snails, mainly *Hydrobia ulvae* and *Buccinum undatum.* Coloured relief enamel decoration, gilding and fused in gold and silver; partly incised. Marked on base "E. Gallé, Nancy". Private collection.

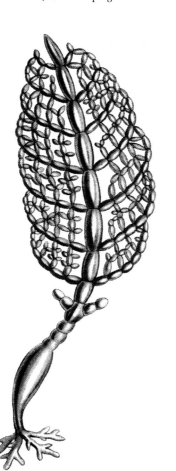

for strangeness. In the realm of objects the fossil is as much a subject in its arrangement or surface structure as root systems and cortical masses. Geological stages, too, and heightened atmospheric phenomena are depicted.

Musicians must also be mentioned along with the painters, illustrators, craftsmen and poets. Close contact can be shown between all creative artists. In Paris, London and Brussels there were close relations between painters and craftsmen and the poets and writers of the period. Mystic Utopias and genuine socialism were often closely connected – viewpoints which were represented pictorially by the Rosicrucians, the School of Pont Aven and the Worpsweder painters, among others. A combinational art was coming into being that searched for a group direction in order to follow a communal goal. The style remains faceted; the flight from reality is stronger than the topical everyday viewpoint.

The theme of the underwater landscape was simultaneously real and strange. The most heterogeneous colours and forms led to a fairy-tale atmosphere which the seaweed and algae alone were enough to create. Ernst Haeckel described the underwater flora and the many hybrids penetratingly:

"We distinguish five different classes in the main class of seaweeds or algae … The first class of seaweeds, the Archephyceae, can also be called the first plants (Protophyta), because the latter comprise the simplest and most elementary of all plants and in particular the oldest of all vegetable organisms which originated all the other plants. Joining the first plants or first seaweeds as a second class, are the group of green seaweeds or green algae. Like the majority of the former, the green seaweeds as a whole are coloured green, by the same colouring agent, or chlorophyll, which makes the leaves of all the higher plants green. Apart from a large number of lower seaweeds, the majority of freshwater algae belong to this class, the common *Conferva* and green *Eudorina,* and the light-green sea lettuce *Ulva* which looks like a long thin lettuce leaf. In addition, numerous microscopically small algae which, assembled

into a dense mass, spread a light-green slimy coating over the water …

"In the third class, that of the brown or black seaweeds, the main class of algae reaches its highest degree of development. The characteristic colour is generally a more or less dark-brown, sometimes changing to olive-green and yellowish-green, at others to brownish red and black. Here belong the largest of all seaweeds, which are also the longest of all plants, the colossal giant seaweeds, among which *Macrocystis pyrifera* on the Californian coast reaches a length of 400 feet. Another member of the class is the free-floating *Sargassum* (gulf-weed) which forms the floating meadows or banks of the Sargasso Sea. Although each one of these great seaweed trees is composed of many millions of cells, it nevertheless consists at the beginning of its existence, like all the higher plants, of a single cell, a simple egg.

"The fourth class of seaweeds, that of red or pink seaweeds, is less important. Admittedly a great wealth of different forms develops from this class. But most of them are much smaller than the brown algae. Otherwise, they are in no way inferior to the latter in perfection and differentiation of the external form, indeed surpassing them in many respects. They include the most beautiful and decorative of all seaweeds which are among the most attractive of plants because of their delicate threads and division of their leaf bodies, and their pure and delicate red colouring. The characteristic red colour is sometimes a deep purple, sometimes a burning scarlet, sometimes a delicate rose-red, passing to violet and blueish purple, or brown and green colours in wonderful splendour."[3]

In the period of European symbolism around 1900, the things of the external world acquire, through scientific research, a value which they characteristically have in dreams or in manifestations during meditation. The antitheses in works of art are partially determined by the artistic medium. They become experience through the new vision of the environment. A decisive feature is that not only the artist, but also the observer takes an active part in the pictorial process. So the behaviour of the observer seems to assume an importance as a transmitter of new pictorial experiences in the age of symbolism. In many fields the reflection of atmospheric feelings determines the sense of reality imposed by nature and opposes this conception to the traditional vision of the *Gründerzeit* time. The result is a bringing together of absolute opposites into a hybrid combination. A subjective process now takes place in the observer that mainly stops him from confirming what is currently accepted as attractive. Screening from the effect of reality is not produced solely by the strangeness of the object; its siting in unknown or unusual places also gives the observer the freedom to complete the scenario as he wishes.

In most cases he cannot think through the ideas kindled by the work of art, so that a part of the symbolical theme must remain undeciphered. This "unknown" which keeps the observer guessing is a significant attraction. Fragments of reality or static objects shown as floating or discoloured or deliberately transformed in other ways give the artist that liberty and hence attraction which is accepted by the beholder and which ensured his keen interest in the phenomenon of symbolism in the period around 1900.

The jelly-fish, for example, acquires a new value in aesthetics. It is no longer the symbol of deliquescence or gelatinous shapelessness. It stimulated Ernst Haeckel to write his second great monograph, because he experienced in the flowerlike beauty of jelly-fish bodies a quite new magic. A great many artists made statements about the beauty of the jelly-fish around 1900.

August Endell and Hermann Obrist, to mention only two artists, chose the multiple forms of the jelly-fish as a stimulus to new laws of form. Hermann Obrist pursued a morphology of organisms, as he studied the inner and outer structure of animal and plant bodies and rejoiced in their beauty, admired their diversity and was amazed by their functionalism. Contemporaries especially admired the diversity and the strange

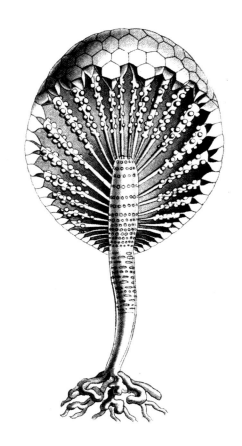

movement and growth of the various forms of organisms. In particular, the past provided enough knowledge to establish certain imaginative reconstructions which were adventurous and strange. As his sketches show, Obrist was a close and careful observer of nature and went to work in the same way as Ernst Haeckel. Haeckel had rightly remarked:

"The genuinely empirical scientists who believe in promoting science only by the discovery of new facts can achieve as little in that way as the purely speculative philosopher, who believes he can dispense with the facts and construct nature out of his own ideas. They become fantastical dreamers or at best exact copying machines of nature. Basically, the actual situation which has now arisen means that the genuine empiricists are satisfied with an incomplete and unclear philosophy not even known to themselves, while the genuine philosophers content themselves

sea-bottom, some floating at various depths, others swimming on the surface. Only a very few live in fresh water (e.g. *Gromia, Actinophrys, Actinosphaerium*). Most of them have hard shells of calcium oxide or silica arranged in the most decorative way, which are well preserved in their fossil state. Notwithstanding this primitive structure, the Foraminifera alone exude a hard shell, mostly of calcium oxide, which exhibits a great diversity of decorative structures.

Generally, decorative and often tree-like forked spines radiate from the surface of the spheres. At other times the skeleton consists solely of a silica star and is then mostly composed of twenty spines distributed according to an established mathematical law and united at a common central point. In the case of other Radiolaria the skeleton forms ornamental, many-chambered casings, as with the Polythalamia. There is indeed no other group of organisms which has developed such a wealth of widely differing basic forms and such geometric regularity, combined with the most decorative architectonics, in their skeletal structures."

Bornetella capitata (Siphoneae), Plate 64, no. 11, in Ernst Haeckel, *Kunstformen der Natur*, Leipzig, 1899.

with an equally impure and incomplete empiricism. The goal of science is the production of a complete architectonically arranged fabric of teachings."[4]

To contemporaries the art forms of nature made up the so-called *Zweckästhetik* (functional aesthetic) which had become known by numerous exhibitions and publications. Felix Poppenberg refers to an exhibition which is interesting for this investigation and writes:

"There is such a functional aesthetic in nature, too. A special section of the stimulating Dresden Exhibition of 1906 offered ample opportunity for studying how, in the structure of animals, the functional organs mostly have a decorative effect as well. For example, in the movement of mussels and snails, in coral stems, in crystallizations, in the glass sponges and their veining and in the openwork patterns of calcareous sea creatures an ornamentation is shown that is not mere decoration but always expresses a living principle, a function, a natural process. So now applied art, too, should strive towards ornament as an essential characteristic, to use inner qualities as informative hieroglyphs, not as a dead appendage that seems to have been dragged in by the hair."[5]

August Endell describes how the adoption of this functional aesthetic in everyday artistic life took place:

"The starting point for my work was the embroideries of Hermann Obrist, in which I got to know for the first time free organically discovered, not externally composed, forms. At first I studied purely as a psychologist and aesthetic theorist until I was gradually convinced that it must be possible to achieve strong and living effects in architecture and applied art exclusively through freely invented forms. After many experiments and a series of practical works, I was sure of myself and began work systematically in this way.

"Concurrently, there was a constant testing of new combinations, and research into their way of working. For example, if one sees angular emergent veins on the bark of a tree, which go vertically upwards, separate and join up again with their neighbour, then this principle of common climbing, separating and re-uniting will be investigated in every conceivable variation in large sketches, to see how it works."[6]

Form and Movement in Glass

Artistically speaking, especially in the glassmaker's art, movement is introduced into shapes by a pronounced division of the vessel's body. At first this structural element was indicated by the baluster motif. Balusters dominated glass forms from the beginning of modern times to the end of the 19th century. The art nouveau and *Jugendstil* period first began to break up and do away with the baluster motif. To that end, new forms or a new vision had to be found, and here natural scientific publications provided the answer.

One of the most important steps in the fashioning of vessels and lamps, which produced the most innovative features, was the adoption of floral basic forms, which emanate from growing vegetable, lobular and heterogeneous structures. Under the influence of Haeckelian research into natural form, designers realized that the most stimulating models for new elementary forms were to be found in precisely that field.

In fact, the heterogeneous natural forms, which artists discovered for themselves and saw for the first time, had incalculable effect within formal structure. Twists, folds, curls, limp hanging flaps and buds were reproduced in glass and led to a deviation from conventional forms on to which organic natural forms were, so to speak, grafted. We clearly see how the traditional glass form is set in motion by the floral movement of the mouth, how it begins to swing until it loses its specific individuality of shape in the flow of movement. The lobular turned-down edges seem to be lightened; the conventional bowl shape is eliminated by the distortion of the body, the hanging-down mouth and asymmetrical bases supporting the body. The special character of the glass mass is carried *ad absurdum* by frosted glass decoration and naturalistically applied individual forms. The peak is reached with flattened conventional spherical forms in which the volumes are so altered that they are scarcely recognizable. Naturalistic landscapes, which give the object a more conclusive character than that of mere decoration and are to be understood as landscapes opening in every direction, are painted on these distorted objects.

Directly emerging floral adjuncts are applied to otherwise conventional vessel shapes. The clearly articulated body acquires a fan-shaped wavy application with lustre glaze giving a streaming effect. Thus a body without a historical model is created, one which has no object for comparison (ill. 86).

Even clearly articulated forms from the Pallme-König glassworks may be alienated by iridescent lustre decoration, producing a tangled effect. Here the actual production process is carried to excess. The molten mass is arbitrarily cut into with pliers, the neck is as if torn out, individual parts project above the indefinable vessel body. The wall in its heterogeneous instability seems to be laced in by thread-glass. This novel, eccentric enhancement of form was introduced by François Rousseau, who had already experimented in the 1880s with squeezing and distorting cylindrical glass bodies quite arbitrarily, with splitting the glass mass by craquelure and fusing on extravagant rough-surfaced elements.

Louis C. Tiffany, too, subjected his products to this rough-surfaced transformation process, although he improved it by refined treatment. In his lava vases (ill. 83) he forms original structures which can summon up associations of anthropomorphism by broadening and narrowing thread applications. Tiffany reached the high point of floralistic intensification in his Jack-in-the-Pulpit glass (ill. 10). The broad lobate structure with tilted calyx standing on an onion-

shaped base has achieved an original effect which, enhanced by the force of plant growth, goes even further and by the iridescent, lustring decoration of the solidifying process on the surface achieves abstracting effects, which lie beyond an imitation of nature and lead to an enhancement of the glass formation. After this hectic wave of transformation, introduced by *Jugendstil* and art nouveau, artists were reminded of the old values and so began to treast glass anew as a translucent medium in its vitreous structure (ills., pp. 146-7). These creative processes essentially indicate that a tradition has to be eliminated and overcome. The stimulus of historical and ethnological models kindles personal conceptions. The classical amphora shape is repeatedly used by Daum, but is made different by excessive elongation of the neck into a tube. Daum tries to disregard and go beyond antique models, but the same efforts are also evident in the Schneider Manufactory. The amphora is interpreted florally, it acquires lanceolate leaves, the forms are stilted in a hybrid manner and adorned with coloured decoration in the *fin de siècle* style. The omission of handles and a certain variation by Schneider is intentional.

The abundant adoption of Asiatic vessel forms is evident in all the glassworks. The gourd motif (ills., pp. 99-103), which played a significant role in Asia, was lavishly used by Daum. He brought naturalistic, almost veristic structural characteristics to the surface, only to difference them again through the glass medium. The bottle gourd in its double construction is just one of the objects imitated from Asian forms. Emile Gallé, for example, uses the pagoda form, which he elevates by a wooden base (ill. 212), or by imitating decorations taken from Japanese woodcuts. Lalique also chooses the gourd shape (ill. 5); he establishes it by the frosted glass technique and so achieves a new exemplary effect, inasmuch as both decoration and vessel are given equal importance. Fish decoration was also adopted from Japanese models (ill. 215) and even Louis Tiffany imbeds his water-lily motif in the vitreous bodies like an aqueous material (ills. 79, 82).

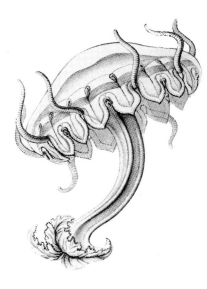

Large jelly-fish, *Palephyra primigenia*, Plate 18, nos. 3–5 in Ernst Haeckel, *Kunstformen der Natur*, Leipzig, 1899.

79 Louis Comfort Tiffany, vase, clear glass, partially flashed, polished, cut and engraved, 1916 or later. Decoration: water lily leaves and stems. Marked on base: "T. 2625". 11.5 cm. Bavarian National Museum, Munich. Inventory no. SW18.

The so-called submarine decoration inspired many artists, painters and above all craftsmen. Glass designers in America and Europe, in particular, occupied themselves with the underwater kingdom. Ernst Haeckel remarks in his *Schöpfungsgeschichte, op. cit.,* p. 293: "In all living bodies, without exception, a certain amount of water is combined with solid matter in a quite specific manner and from this characteristic combination of water and organic matter arises that end state, neither hard nor fluid, which is of the greatest importance in explaining the origin of life." Underwater life, the picture of the underwater world which was depicted around 1900 in a manner never seen before, includes all the hermaphroditic types of life; these are in essence one of the fields which partially demonstrate the Darwinian and Haeckelian theory.

80　Underwater scene, polyps, umbrella jelly-fish, ctenophores and corals. Plate VII in Ernst Haeckel, *Schöpfungsgeschichte*, Berlin, 1879, p. 465. Hermann Obrist's collection of examples also contained this illustration, which inspired him in his drawings of the submarine landscape. 22 x 14.5 cm. Private collection, South Germany.

81　*Salacia polyastrica* (Siphonophora), Plate 7, no. 3 in Ernst Haeckel, *Kunstformen der Natur*, Leipzig and Vienna, 1904. According to Haeckel, a "delightfully ornamented" jelly-fish – a jelly-fish in the whiplash line of art nouveau. Haeckel writes in his *Schöpfungsgeschichte*, p. 462: "From the class of umbrella jelly-fish a third class of stinging creatures, that of the brilliant siphonophores, developed. They are swimming colonies of Medusas which have assumed an amazingly different form through a kind of division of labour."

82　Louis Comfort Tiffany, low vase, slightly separated base, arched body joining the shoulder, recessed neck, lustred interior ranging from honey-colour to gold, exterior flashed with colourless layers. Decoration: among the thick colourless layers, floating underwater blossoms with seaweed-like stems and leaves, whitish-pink to yellow-green-ochre and brown-ochre. Marked on base: "L.C. Tiffany". 14.3 cm. Private collection, Munich.

83　Louis Comfort Tiffany, vase in the lava technique, *c.* 1898. Glass coloured black in the molten state. Decoration: black overlaid many times. Gold-silver-copper-red-green-blue iridescent underwater stem of a siphonophore or brown seaweed. Marked on base: "6840 L.C. Tiffany Favrile". 12.8 cm. Bavarian National Museum, Munich. Inventory no. SW 5.

84 Jelly-fish, *Pelagia perla*. Detail from Plate 98, no. 5, in Ernst Haeckel, *Kunstformen der Natur*, Leipzig and Vienna, 1904.

85 Josef Verlik (glass), Georges Despret, design and silverwork. Vase, spherical body, the arched shoulder turning into a bellied neck with swollen turned-up rim, flashed and etched ceramic-like glass. Violet glass with dove-blue to beige flashes. Foot, chased silver ivy leaves rising up to the vessel wall. 19 cm. Bavarian National Museum, Munich. Inventory no. SW 52.

54

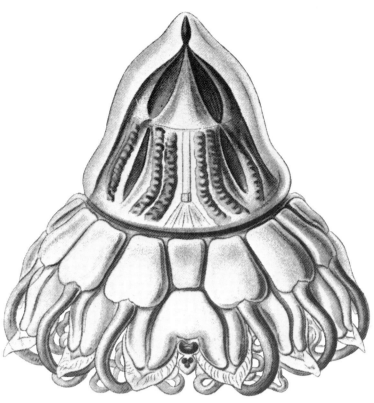

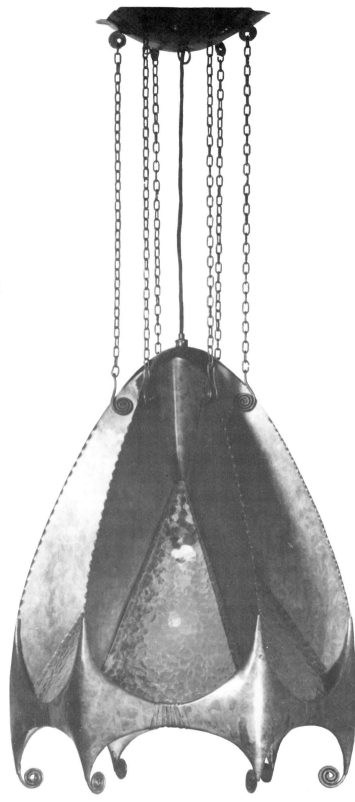

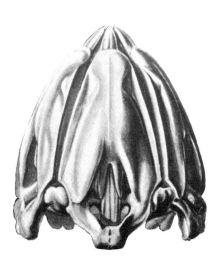

86 Pallme-König glass factory in Steinschönau and Kosten (Bohemia). Vase, recessed foot ring, irregular bell-shaped body, rim with two deep incisions, lobe-like, turned-down, compressed sides, tips fused on, yellow-green transparent glass, reddish-brown glass fibres. Decoration: irregular rectangular network on all sides. 28 cm. Bavarian National Museum, Munich. Inventory no. SW 23.
The new forms intensify into abstruse structures and levels and open the way to new possibilities in glass because of their unusual formation. Jelly-fish-like creations originate which could have been stimulated by Haeckel's research into underwater fauna.
Here too the mushroom model is technically decisive, both in form and colour, for the silhouette. Glass acquires tactile qualities; a material imitation of the exotic mushroom growing in the darkness replaces the representation of blossoming beauty.

87 Pallme-König glass factory in Steinschönau and Kosten (Bohemia). Inkwell, with three protrusions from a circular plan that gradually merge with the neck of the vessel at the shoulder. It is closed by a flattish floral pewter lid. 6.3 x 12.2 cm. Bavarian National Museum, Munich. Inventory no. SW 24.

88 *Periphylla mirabilis* (Peromedusa) from the east coast of New Zealand. Detail from Plate 38, no. 2 in Ernst Haeckel, *Kunstformen der Natur,* Leipzig and Vienna, 1904.

89 Josef Maria Olbrich (attributed), candelabra in the form of a floating octopus or perhaps *Periphylla;* before 1900. Other possible models are certain forms of the sea cucumber, an underwater animal, which Ernst Haeckel impressively illustrated several times in his plates. Hanging candelabra of chased copper, with glass insertions. 110 cm. Private collection, Vienna.

90 *Sphaerechinus longispinus* (Echinidea), Aristotle's lantern. The popular name inspired the designer to use the Echinidea as a candelabra shape. Plate 60, no 11, in Ernst Haeckel, *Kunstformen der Natur,* Leipzig and Vienna, 1904.

91 Hermann Obrist, submarine fissure (second version), *c.* 1899. Obrist was influenced by *Kunstformen der Natur,* Plate 52. Pencil on parchment paper. 30.3 x 11.8 cm. Private collection, Munich.

92 Ernst Haeckel, *Kunstformen der Natur,* Leipzig and Vienna. 1904. Plate 52 (detail). Hartshorn fern from tropical swamps.

About 1900 the submarine landscape began to influence the fine arts to an increasing degree. Hermann Obrist was not the only artist to depict it. In E. Gallé's numerous glass vessels, too, underwater scenery and underwater light are an essential feature of his early work. Starfish, octopus, jelly-fish and the organisms between animal and plant had not yet been investigated as thoroughly as they were in Haeckelian theory (also diffused by Wilhelm Bölsch in his popular science books). Although perfectly realistic, the underwater landscape contained the germ of surrealism which the art of the time steered along new paths to abstraction.
These assumptions went back to Haeckelian research. Thus natural form and artistic form were realized in accordance with Haeckel's intention and goal. Ernst Haeckel had found impressive words in his lectures. This is what he had to say in his book *Die Schöpfungsgeschichte,* which was partly compiled from individual lectures: "We obviously draw the most reliable conclusions about the genealogy of the animal kingdom (as about that of the vegetable kingdom) from comparative anatomy and ontogeny. In addition, paleontology gives extremely valuable information about the historical succession of many groups."

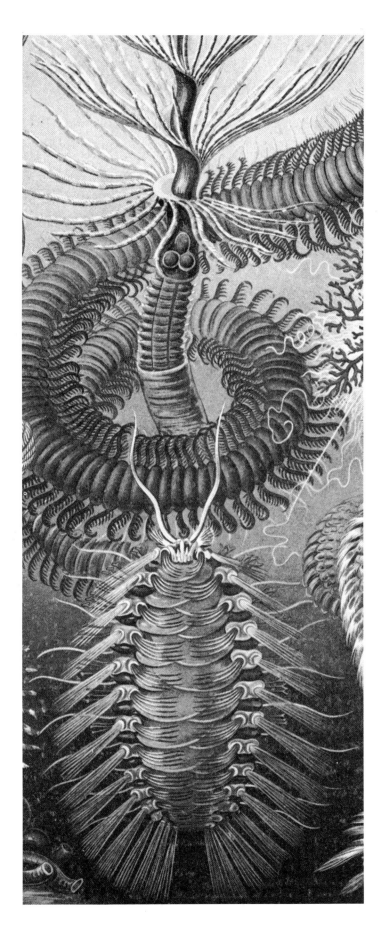

93   Various bristle-worms (Chaetopoda). Plate 96, nos. 3, 6, from Ernst Haeckel, *Kunstformen der Natur*, Leipzig and Vienna, 1904. The large numbers of marine worms, which had by no means been fully investigated, frequently stimulated Haeckel to continue the theories of evolution which elaborated after Darwin. The species of the Polychaeta class, with their insect-like form, must also have influenced Hermann Obrist. In the adjoining picture we see how the notched articulation of the worm bridges the cleft in the sea. From this grew the so-called "Fire flower" which Obrist constructed of seaweed and the tentacles of the jelly-fish. Obrist creates not only new formal references, but also new contents which, alien to all known human possibilities, demonstrate the more abstruse aspects of natural form. Thus the path to an alienating conception of art was traced.

94   Hermann Obrist, Fire flower IV, charcoal over pencil on parchment paper, *c.* 1899. 289 x 130 mm. Further details about Fire flower III are in Siegfried Wichmann, *Hermann Obrist, Wegbereiter der Moderne*, Nr. 34 in the catalogue of the exhibition at the Villa Stuck, Munich, 9 March 1968. Private collection, Munich.

The underwater fauna with their animal forms surprised Hermann Obrist. He was occupied with this problem for a long time, particularly with the geometric and linear arrangements which emerged in the forms of snails and mussels. Obrist commented on the mussel form: "Dynamic: make energies, powers visible by the strength or weakness of the centre, intensity of curvature. Intensity of curvature through strengthening the line by multiplication ..." Hermann Obrist's concern was a strongly expressive art based on intensified curvature of the linear summation and the expressive line.

95 Hermann Obrist, revised reproduction from his collection of models; illuminated cross-section of snail shell. 120 x 160 mm. Private collection, Munich.

96 Detail of Plate 44 in Ernst Haeckel, *Kunstformen der Natur*, Leipzig and Vienna, 1904. The Haeckelian art forms, as he formulated them, found a tremendous response among many creative artists around 1900. *Kunstformen der Natur* introduced artists to brand-new fields which obviously could not have been considered worthy of depiction before. Hermann Obrist steeped himself in the Haeckelian literature and he must also have been close to Darwin in his ideas. It can be shown that Obrist left behind him countless reproductions after *Kunstformen der Natur*. He also made many drawings from it, and forms from this work were a welcome aid to him for many years.

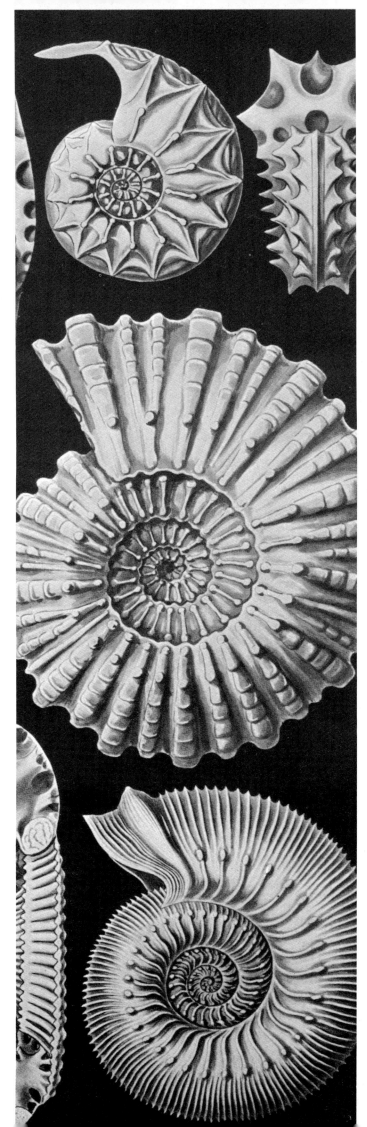

97 Hermann Obrist, *Werden und Vergehen* (detail), *c.* 1899. Inscribed above in pencil by the artist: "*Werden und Vergehen,* Karus star – compared to Pentacrinus! 209 – Nautilus – pompilius – inwardness. 241, below right: mysterious form – crystals – druse – 87. Dendrite, 86 – Infiltration! – Zonaria – pavonia! – 141." Pencil on white linen paper, 25.5 x 16.9 cm. State Graphics Collection, Munich.

98 Fritz Endell (1873–1955), *Fantastic discovery – spirals.* Coloured woodcut after Hermann Obrist, colour print on Japanese paper. 26 x 11.7 cm. State Graphics Collection, Munich.

99 Hermann Obrist, *Fantastic mussel,* charcoal over pencil, on transparent paper, *c.* 1895. 27 x 16.1 cm. Further information about the drawing in Siegfried Wichmann, *Hermann Obrist, Wegbereiter der Moderne,* Villa Stuck Exhibition Catalogue, Munich, 9 March 1968, no. 34. State Graphics Collection, Munich.

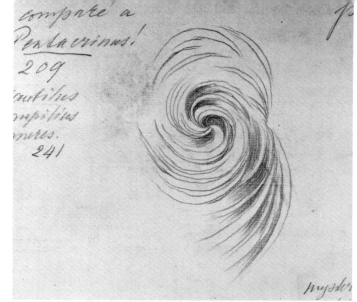

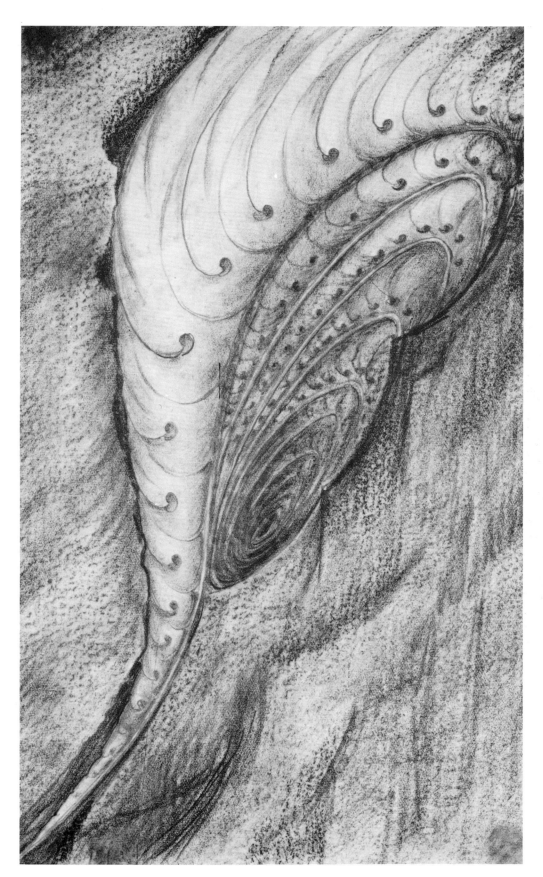

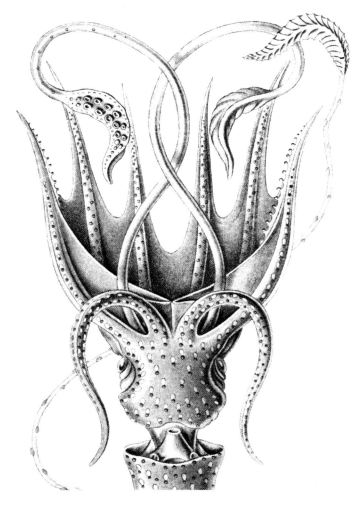

100 August Endell, bookcase. Side panels with curved lower quarter, widening and projecting above. Decoration: octopus tentacles overlapping the edge. Matt elm, height 179 cm, width 120 cm, depth 35 cm. Bavarian National Museum, Munich. Inventory no. SW 103.

101 *Bipinnaria asterigera* of the family Amphoridea. Plate 95, No. 11, in Ernst Haeckel, *Kunstformen der Natur*, Leipzig, 1899. *Above:* decapod *Histioteuthis*

Rüppellii Verny, Plate 54, No. 2, in the same work.

102 August Endell, stucco frieze for the Goudstikker house (2nd story), Munich, 1899 (detail). From H. Obrist's collection of examples, privately owned, Munich 1896. Original photograph after the no longer extant object. Sophia and Mathilde Goudstikker were the owners of the Hofatelier Elvira. The frieze shows variations of an octopus, which Endell had undoubtedly found among Haeckell's illustrations.

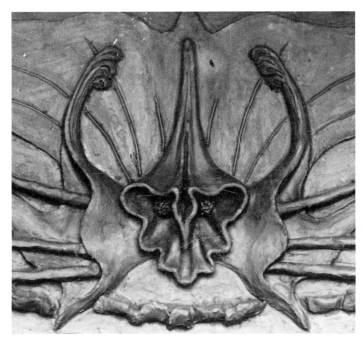

103 August Endell, bookcase, detail opposite.

104 Fire flower III, charcoal over pencil on white cardboard, *c.* 1899. 3.73 x 1.21 cm. See S. Wichmann's catalogue *Hermann Obrist, Wegbereiter der Moderne,* Munich, 1968, no. 47. State Graphics Collection, Munich.

105 August Endell, stucco frieze (detail) shown at VIIth International Art Exhibition, 1897, in the Munich Glaspalast. Contemporary photograph from Hermann Obrist's collection of examples. Both representations show the polychaete worm, a marine organism which Ernst Haeckel had observed closely.

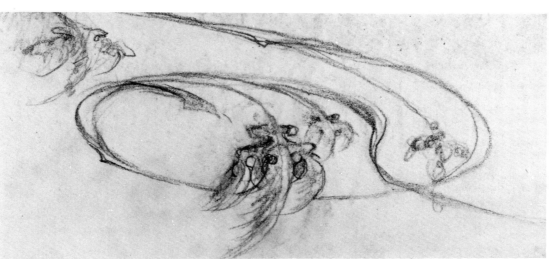

106 Hermann Obrist, pinnate grass, *c.* 1899. Pencil on transparent paper fixed to cardboard, 9.5 x 16.1 cm. Similar sketches on parchment. State Graphics Collection, Munich.

107 August Endell, façade of Hofatelier Elvira, 15 Von-der-Tann-Strasse, Munich, 1896–7 (detail). The building was destroyed in 1944.

108 August Endell, reception room in the Hofatelier Elvira, Munich, with view of staircase (inset) copied from Ernst Haeckel, *Kunstformen der Natur* (1899), no. 52. The stucco wall ornament derives from the shapes of octopus, seaweed and marsh fern.

109 Ernst Haeckel, *Kunstformen der Natur,* Leipzig-Vienna, 1904, Plate 52 (lst edit. 1899), and other publications going back to 1879. *Platycerium,* the hartshorn fern, one of the Filicinae or tree ferns. Strikingly decorative forms on branches and stems of tropical swamp trees.

Blossfeldt, and Haeckel's *Kunstformen der Natur.* The austere underwater floral decoration characteristic of Endell was influenced by the photographs of Karl Blossfeldt (1865–1932). He arranged these with designs by Charles Ricketts and Charles Shannon. After 1890, the periodical *The Dial* was circulated to German art

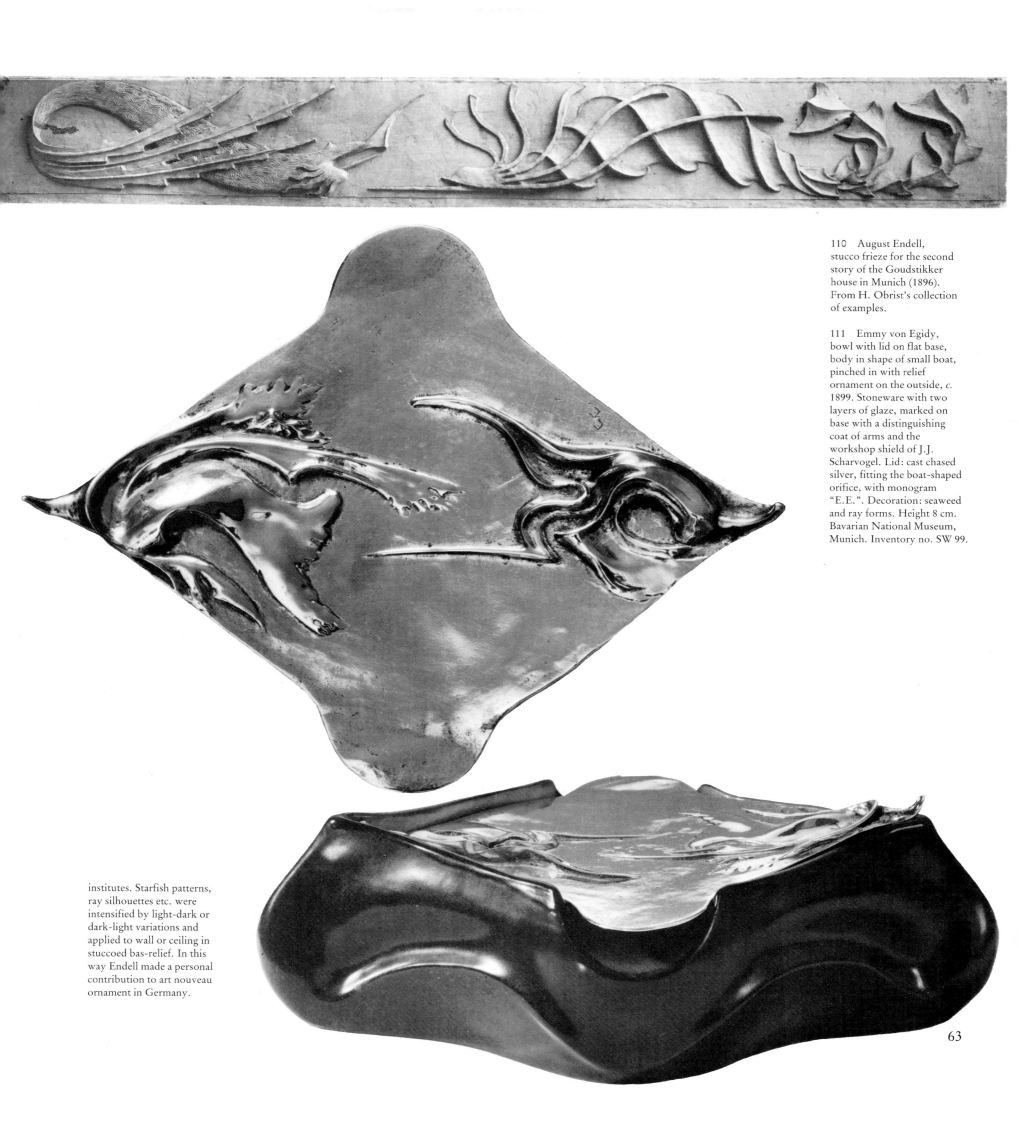

110 August Endell,
stucco frieze for the second
story of the Goudstikker
house in Munich (1896).
From H. Obrist's collection
of examples.

111 Emmy von Egidy,
bowl with lid on flat base,
body in shape of small boat,
pinched in with relief
ornament on the outside, c.
1899. Stoneware with two
layers of glaze, marked on
base with a distinguishing
coat of arms and the
workshop shield of J.J.
Scharvogel. Lid: cast chased
silver, fitting the boat-shaped
orifice, with monogram
"E.E.". Decoration: seaweed
and ray forms. Height 8 cm.
Bavarian National Museum,
Munich. Inventory no. SW 99.

institutes. Starfish patterns,
ray silhouettes etc. were
intensified by light-dark or
dark-light variations and
applied to wall or ceiling in
stuccoed bas-relief. In this
way Endell made a personal
contribution to art nouveau
ornament in Germany.

63

112 Hermann Obrist, large wall hanging with flowering tree, *c.* 1896. Satin-stick, partly underlaid, and stem stitch in rust-brown, yellow and light green silk on brown silk rep. 321 x 210 cm. Executed by Berthe Ruchet. The New Collection, State Applied Art Gallery, Munich. In 1895 Hermann Obrist added an embroidery workshop to his house in Munich. It produced needlework that was extremely individualistic for the period. Even before 1895, Obrist found inspiration for his embroideries in the works of Ernst Haeckel. Berthe Ruchet worked for Obrist as an embroiderer from 1893–4 until the end of 1900. From 1895 to 1896 the embroideries were not all executed but they continued until 1900. Obrist undoubtedly used models for his embroideries from Ernst Haeckel's work *Natürliche Schöpfungsgeschichte.* This "needle painting" made a great impression on anyone with artistic talent, as Georg Fuchs wrote in *Pan,* 1896, 5:

"The Flowering Tree. The broad trunk rises in majestic splendour, sending out widespread branches on both sides. It stands there in state, bedecked with golden blossoms. A current of growing power seems to pulse through trunk and branch in a steady rhythm and to palpitate in the outermost green tips and most delicate yellow calyxes, a single great beat of growth, a dithyramb to spring, and exultant 'Let it be!' And yet, what sublime calm, what quiet celebration, what pure heavenly splendour! The candle flicker of the sprouting buds and young flowers, this gentle resplendence, these premonitory darkenings between the nobly unfurled branches, this glimmer in the still half-hidden green of the leaves ... May the spirit of Hermann Obrist bring German applied art to fruition in such a way that we can once again say of it: 'A flowering tree!'"

113   Hermann Obrist, large wall-hanging with alpine violets ("whiplash" according to Fuchs: *PAN* 1896), *c.* 1895, signed at bottom right "H.O." (monogram). Satin-stitch in goldish-yellow silk on green-blue-grey wool. 119.5 x 183.5 cm. Executed by Berthe Ruchet. City Museum, Munich.

114   From Ernst Haeckel, *Kunstformen der Natur*, Leipzig and Vienna, 1904. *Below:* Plate 64, No. 6 *Caulerpa macrodisca* (Siphoneae) from the coral reefs of the Celebes. *Below, left:* detail from Plate 62, *Canna* (Nepenthaceae).

65

115 Plate 31 in Ernst
Haeckel, *Kunstformen der
Natur,* Leipzig, 1899.
Radiolaria, marine protozoa.
From 1878 Haeckel produced
numerous portfolios with
woodcuts, including *Das
Protistenreich,* "a popular
survey of the forms of
elementary organisms",
(Leipzig, 1878).
As natural scientist and artist,
Obrist was influenced by
Haeckel's monistic theory
and became a member of the
Monistic Society, to which he
gave lectures. An important
role was also played by Ernst
Haeckel's *Natürliche
Schöpfungsgeschichte,* which
appeared in 1878–9 and was
then republished in 1890 in an
eighth revised and enlarged
edition. Obrist, Endell and
the pupils of the Debschitz
school, among others, also
used illustrations from the
Schöpfungsgeschichte as
models for pictures. Obrist
selected illustrations from
Kunstformen der Natur
(1899) and especially from
Haeckel's earlier
publications, and definitely
made continuous artistic use
of them until about 1914.
Obrist's fountain for Krupp
von Bohlen at Essen is proof
that the sculptor identified
himself with the *Kunstformen
der Natur.* In 1913 the
fountain was set up in Essen
on the Margarithenhöhe and
in 1914 in the side court of the
Werkbundtheater in
Cologne. In the nineties
Obrist made many individual
drawings of details of the
fountain and under the
influence of the Haeckelian
world of deep-sea forms he
followed the original design
concept through until the
fountain was completed.

116 Hermann Obrist,
large fountain for Krupp von
Bohlen, Essen, 1913,
composed of forms of
Radiolaria (deep-sea
organisms). Decoration:
above, Radiolaria, below,
octopus and jelly-fish forms.
Chiselled and cut Treutling
marble. 630 x 390 cm. 1900–
c.1910.

117 Plate 93 in Ernst
Haeckel, *Kunstformen der
Natur*, Leipzig, 1899.
Rhizopoda or Myromycetes.
Detail of ill. 112.

118 *Die Kunstformen der
Natur*, published by E.
Haeckel in 1899, was
preceded and prepared by a
large number of publications.
The books contained many
illustrations, for example *Das
Protistenreich* (28 woodcuts),
1878, *Das System der
Medusen* (atlas with 40
plates), 1879, *Die Tiefsee-
Medusen* (atlas with 32
plates), 1881, *Report on the
Radiolaria* (62 plates), 1887,
*Natürliche
Schöpfungsgeschichte* (20
plates), 1890. The
illustrations in these works
influenced Obrist in his study
of the natural sciences, purely
from the point of view of their
artistic form. Haeckel wrote
in his book *Natürliche
Schöpfungsgeschichte*, 1879,
p. 329: "The great majority of
Protista, the monera,
amoebae, Myxomycetes,
Rhizopoda, Infusoria etc., in
short nearly all the primitive
organisms which we include
in the Protista kingdom
between the animal and
vegetable kingdoms,
propagate themselves
exclusively by *asexual* ways.
And among them is one of the
classes of organisms richest in
forms, indeed even in some
ways the richest of all, in that
every possible basic
geometric form is
incorporated in it. That is the
wonderful class of
Rhizopoda, which includes
the calcium-shelled
Thalamophora and the silica-
shelled Radiolaria."
(Cf. the XVIth lecture.)
These Rhizopoda frequently
served Obrist as an
inspiration for artistic forms.

67

119 Gertraud von Schnellenbühel, table lamp, *c.* 1902, formerly in the possession of Hermann Obrist. Three clusters of spirals curving out from the central stem, silver-plated brass. 48.4 cm. City Museum, Munich.

120 Detail from Plate 70, No. 1 in Ernst Haeckel, *Kunstformen der Natur*, Leipzig, 1899. *Astrophytum darwinianum* (Ophiodea).

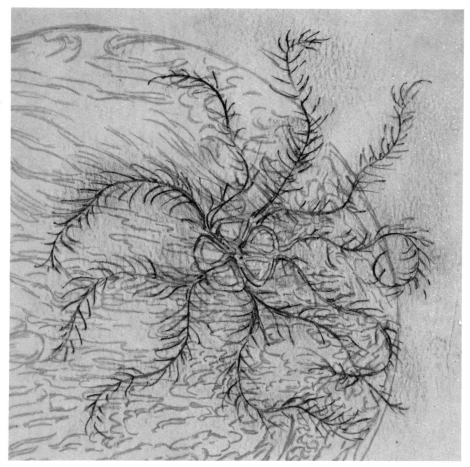

121 Hermann Obrist, embroidered tablecloth, executed by Berthe Ruchet (not exhibited).
Gertraud von Schnellenbühel was a pupil of August Endell. She adopted his natural philosophy and she represented her lamps as a summation of equiangular spirals. This corresponded to the researches of Haeckel and Thompson. Thompson observed: "The many specific qualities of equiangular spirals are closely connected with each other. The successive radii are proportional" – a circumstance from which tension and solidity can be deduced. Obrist expressed his views about spirals: he believed that everything in life is constructed on the principle of the spiral. In this he follows scientific findings, for even the spiral path of an insect corresponds to the spiral forms of nature; they are not merely flexible structures, their curvature is inherent in their evolution.

They *have* to grow into it. That tallies with the view of Thompson, who made important observations about growth and form. The study of form in the animal and vegetable kingdoms may be merely descriptive, but it can also be analytic. Hermann Obrist always made analytical statements about form, in that he put forward an order which was contemplative and artistically served Obrist as an inspiration for artistic forms. Private collection, Munich.

122   Plate IX in Ernst Haeckel, *Schöpfungsgeschichte*, Berlin, 1879. Second-generation starfish.

123   Hermann Obrist, drawing after starfish II and transformation into an embroidery pattern. Pencil and crayon on transparent paper. 13.2 x 19.5 cm. Private collection, Munich.

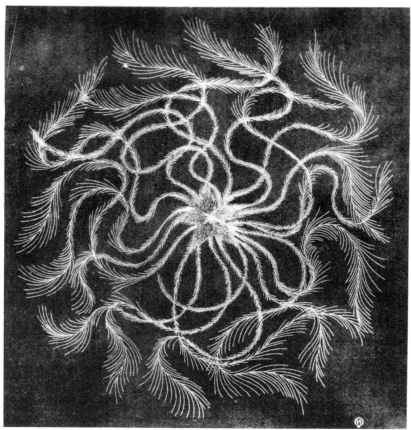

124   Hermann Obrist, drawing after starfish I and transformation into a flower. *Cf.* Ernst Haeckel, *Natürliche Schöpfungsgeschichte*, Berlin, 1879, Plate IX. Pencil and crayon on transparent paper. 14 x 15.7 cm. Private collection.

125 Plate 49 in Ernst Haeckel, *Kunstformen der Natur*, Leipzig and Vienna, 1904. Sea anemones (Actiniae). They are soft and muscular, and therefore suitable for structural alteration. Haeckel describes them as "wonderfully iridescent" and that is how Massier reproduces them here. The sea anemones are closely related to the wood mushroom, differing from it only in containing a small amount of chlorophyll.

126 Clement Massier, vase, *c.* 1900. Iridescent earthenware with modelled parts attached, pre-incribed drawing, painted. Decoration: mushroom in a brier, partly in the round. Signed "Clément Massier, Golfe Juan" (in his own handwriting). Height 35.4 cm, diameter at base 29.3 cm. Acquired from the artist by Henry van de Velde in 1900. Bavarian National Museum, Munich. Inventory no. SW 53.

127 Paul Jeanneney, barrel-shaped receptacle with lid and mushroom lamellae in the round, before 1897. Stoneware with ochre-brown reduced glaze. 16.5 x 15 cm. Flat wooden lid with mushroom knob. Private collection, Munich.

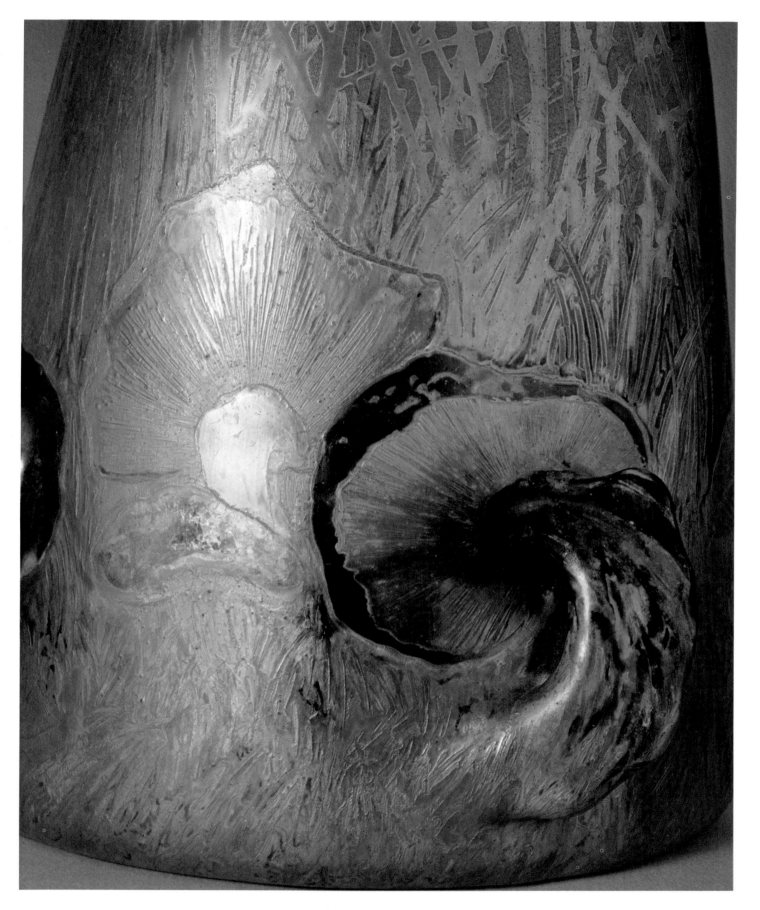

Mushrooms and toadstools differ only from algae in having no chlorophyll, and were thought at that time to belong to the same botanical group. Mushrooms excel all other classes of the vegetable kingdom in their wealth of forms and the variety of their habitats. That was a constant stimulus to artists around 1900. Sea anemones may often look very like mushroom forms. In his illustrations, Ernst Haeckel repeatedly referred to coral forms and sea anemones. The submarine fauna became an endless source of shapes which artists were inspired to elaborate in a magical and unique underwater light in their designs.

Ernst Haeckel observed in his *Schöpfungsgeschichte*, 1879, p. 417: "The first class of Thallophyta, the mushrooms (fungi) are often erroneously called toadstools and thus confused with genuinely animal toadstools or sponges. Of course they partially exhibit close relationship to the most primitive algae. The Phycomycetes actually differ from the previously mentioned Siphoneae through the absence of chlorophyll. But on the other hand all genuine mushrooms have so many peculiarities and deviate so much in their manner of feeding from all other plants that they should be accurately allotted to the Protista kingdom." Wilhelm Bölsche used this statement on many occasions, and diffused it through his books of popular science so that artists, too, could study these specialized scientific researches. That led to a new interest in the vegetable kingdom, which had not been thought worth representing before.

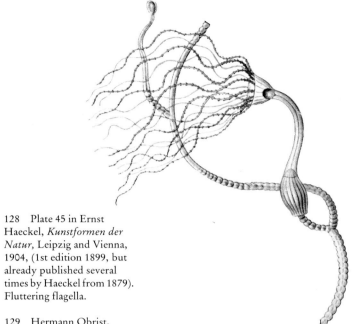

128   Plate 45 in Ernst Haeckel, *Kunstformen der Natur,* Leipzig and Vienna, 1904, (1st edition 1899, but already published several times by Haeckel from 1879). Fluttering flagella.

129   Hermann Obrist, smouldering plant, *c.* 1899, inscribed by the artist in pencil, below left, "the white/ wages (?) oaks (?) have (?) dry/deal". Pencil on transparent paper, page from sketchbook. 27 x 19.5 cm. See also S. Wichmann, *Hermann Obrist, Wegbereiter der Moderne,* Munich 1963, no. 37. State Graphics Collection, Munich.

130   Plate 13, no. 3 in Ernst Haeckel, *Kunstformen der Natur,* Leipzig and Vienna, 1904, (1st edition 1899, but already published several times by Haeckel from 1879). *Codonocladium candelabrum* (Flagellata).

131   Hermann Obrist, study after an orchid blossom, inscribed by the artist in pencil *"Pour la Coquille",* executed in pencil on transparent paper. See also S. Wichmann, *Hermann Obrist, Wegbereiter der Moderne,* Munich, 1968, no. 3. State Graphics Collection, Munich.

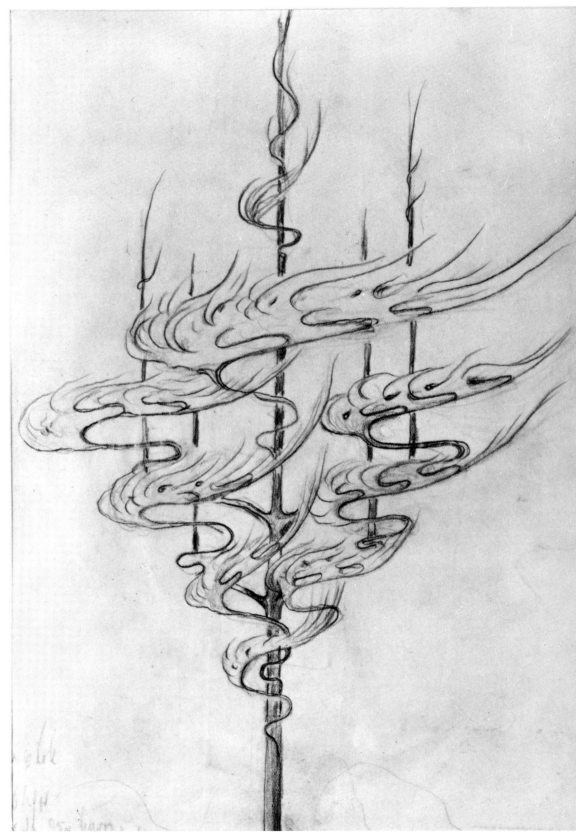

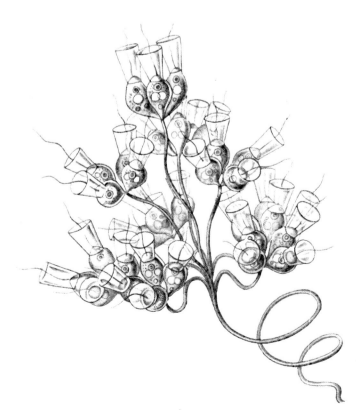

132 Karl Blossfeldt, *Wunder in der Natur*, Leipzig, 1942, p. 4. *Dipsacus laciniatus*, slit-leaved teasel. The illustrations are taken from the work *Urformen der Kunst*. Blossfeldt took these photographs in the 1890s and the first edition of the book was published by Ernst Wasmuth Verlag, Berlin, in 1929. Hermann Obrist was also familiar with Karl Blossfeldt's photographs and he included many of them in his collection of examples.

133 Hermann Obrist, primordial plant inspired by the slit-leaved teasel, *c.* 1899–1904. Pencil and crayon on transparent paper, 21.1 x 12 cm. Private collection, Munich.

134 Karl Blossfeldt, *Wunder in der Natur*, Leipzig, 1942, p. 23, *Acer rufinerve*. Sycamore shoots magnified ten times, after a print, *Urformen der Kunst*, Berlin, 1929, and *Wunder der Natur*, Leipzig, 1942.

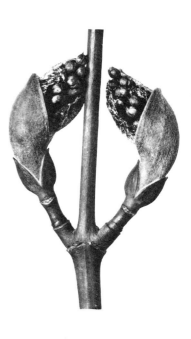

135   Johann Loetz Witwe Glass factory, detail of ill. 141. Vase in the form of a stylized tree stump on a round base. Upper half of the neck with slanting twisted swellings and three asymmetrically placed knotholes. Clear glass, blueish, silvery and matt gold lustring. 44 x 16.3 cm. Private collection, Munich.

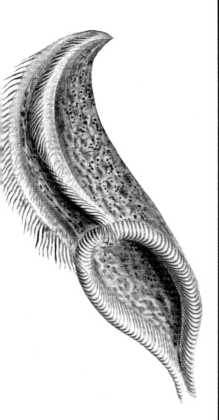

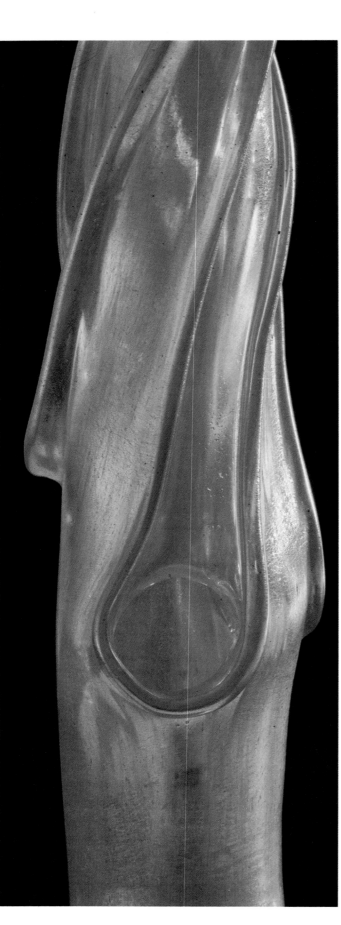

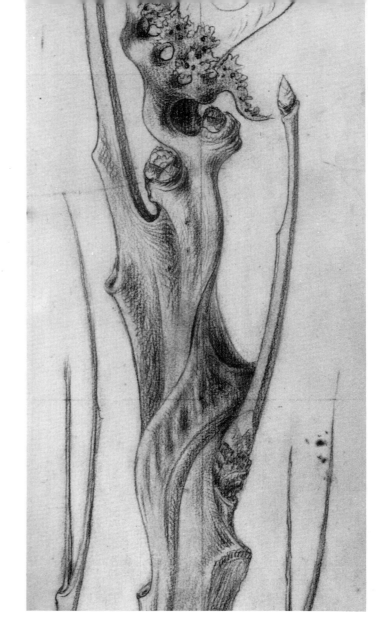

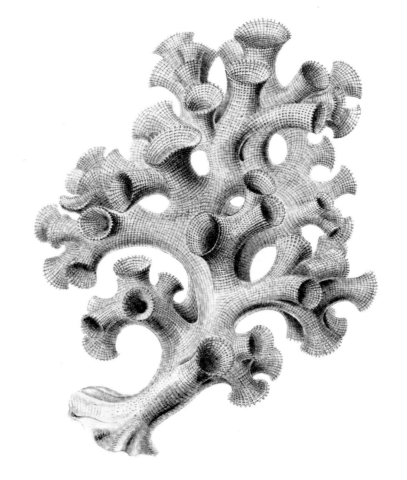

136   Plate 62 from Ernst Haeckel, *Kunstformen der Natur*, Leipzig and Vienna, 1904. Detail of Canna plant (Nepenthaceae).

137   Hermann Obrist, twisted branch with twig and fire flower (detail), *c.* 1899. Pencil on white paper, 68.9 x 18.7 cm. See also S. Wichmann's catalogue, *Hermann Obrist, Wegbereiter der Moderne,* Munich, 1968, no. 7. Private collection, Munich.

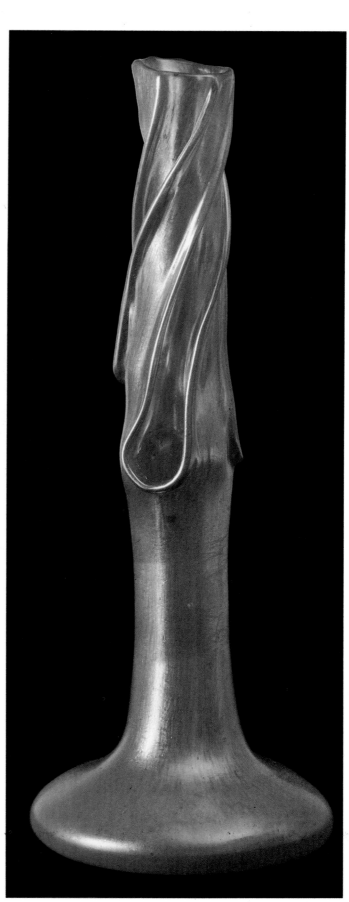

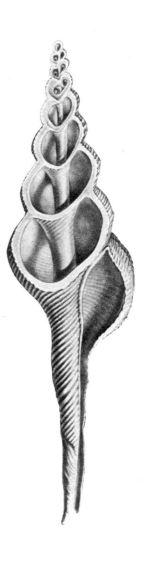

138 Plate 35, no. 1 in Ernst Haeckel, *Kunstformen der Natur,* Leipzig and Vienna, 1904, *Farrea Haeckelii* (Hexactinellae).

142 Plate 29, no. 15 in Ernst Haeckel, *Kunstformen der Natur,* Leipzig and Vienna, 1904. *Tetracoralla,* four-branched stony coral.

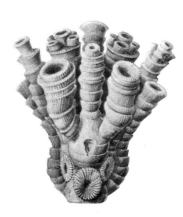

139 Frederick Carder, Corning, vase with three tubes, marked under the foot "Aurene 2744". Manufacturer, Steuben Glassworks, Corning, N.Y. Three bamboo shoots on a flat disc, blue glass, flashed with greenish, silvery lustring. "Cobalt Papillon". 15.8 cm. Frankfurt a.M., London, New York, Knut Günther.

140 Johann Loetz Witwe glass factory, vase in form of a stylized tree stump. See illustration of detail opposite.

141 Plate 53, in Ernst Haeckel, *Kunstformen der Natur,* Leipzig and Vienna, 1904.

75

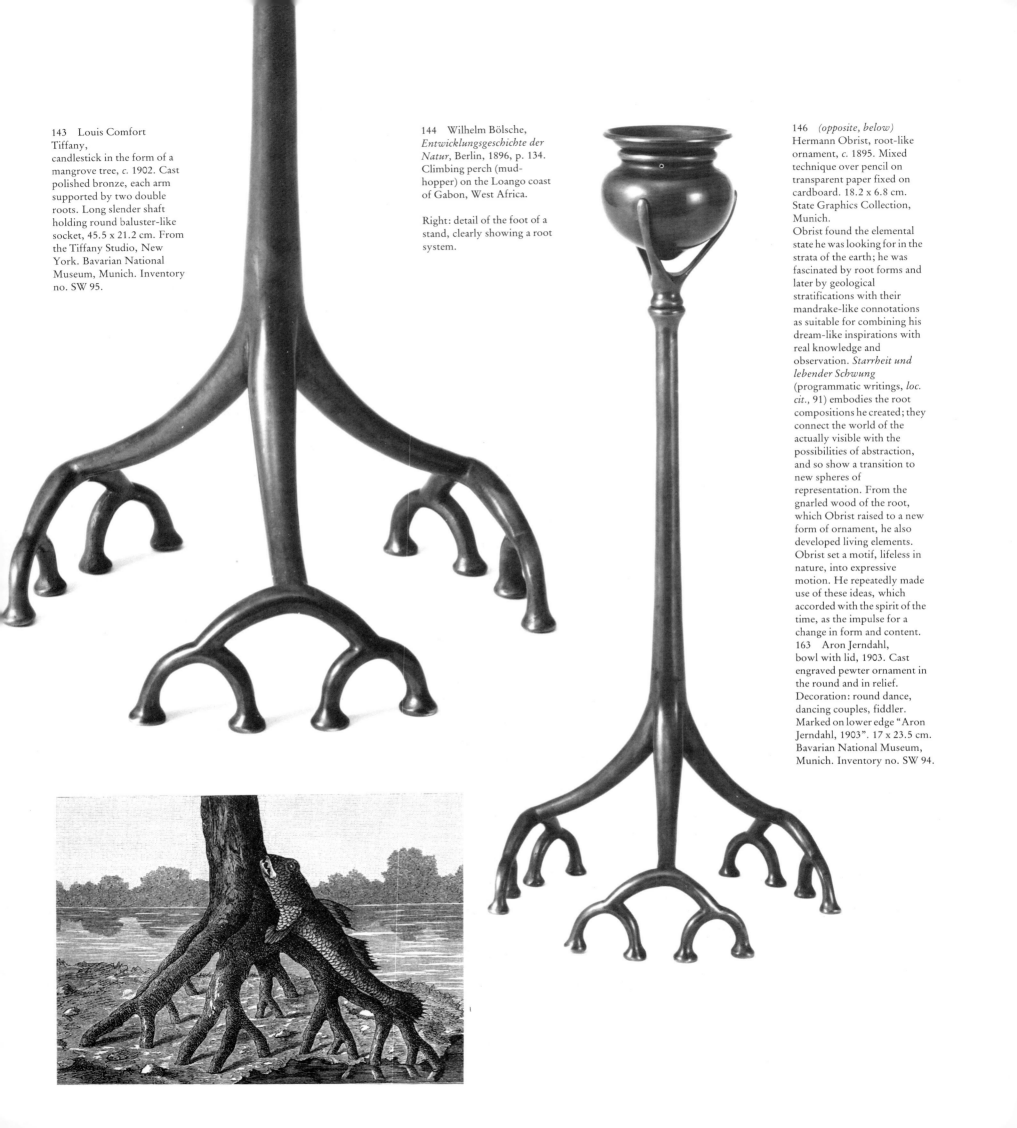

143 Louis Comfort
Tiffany,
candlestick in the form of a
mangrove tree, *c.* 1902. Cast
polished bronze, each arm
supported by two double
roots. Long slender shaft
holding round baluster-like
socket, 45.5 x 21.2 cm. From
the Tiffany Studio, New
York. Bavarian National
Museum, Munich. Inventory
no. SW 95.

144 Wilhelm Bölsche,
*Entwicklungsgeschichte der
Natur,* Berlin, 1896, p. 134.
Climbing perch (mud-
hopper) on the Loango coast
of Gabon, West Africa.

Right: detail of the foot of a
stand, clearly showing a root
system.

146 *(opposite, below)*
Hermann Obrist, root-like
ornament, *c.* 1895. Mixed
technique over pencil on
transparent paper fixed on
cardboard. 18.2 x 6.8 cm.
State Graphics Collection,
Munich.
Obrist found the elemental
state he was looking for in the
strata of the earth; he was
fascinated by root forms and
later by geological
stratifications with their
mandrake-like connotations
as suitable for combining his
dream-like inspirations with
real knowledge and
observation. *Starrheit und
lebender Schwung*
(programmatic writings, *loc.
cit.,* 91) embodies the root
compositions he created; they
connect the world of the
actually visible with the
possibilities of abstraction,
and so show a transition to
new spheres of
representation. From the
gnarled wood of the root,
which Obrist raised to a new
form of ornament, he also
developed living elements.
Obrist set a motif, lifeless in
nature, into expressive
motion. He repeatedly made
use of these ideas, which
accorded with the spirit of the
time, as the impulse for a
change in form and content.
163 Aron Jerndahl,
bowl with lid, 1903. Cast
engraved pewter ornament in
the round and in relief.
Decoration: round dance,
dancing couples, fiddler.
Marked on lower edge "Aron
Jerndahl, 1903". 17 x 23.5 cm.
Bavarian National Museum,
Munich. Inventory no. SW 94.

145 Hermann Obrist,
tray table on four floral stems
rising from roots, *c.* 1898.
Massive veneered bog oak,
height 72 cm, length 76 cm,
width 45.5 cm. Bavarian
National Museum, Munich.
Inventory no. SW 122.
Table top and tray on four
incurving legs which hold an
open wooden receptacle
between them at the foot. The
legs consist of root-like
structures; the thickenings
show the twists and turns of
roots in the earth where they
have to overcome resistance.
A quadripartite support
which holds the table top
grows from roots. They
correspond to the stem
structure of plants, which
bend slightly under the
weight of their upper parts.
Obrist was interested in
tension, and the
representation of this tension
and stress in plant stems. He
undertook several
investigations in this field and
described them
penetratingly. Obrist was
also familiar with the natural
philosophical representations
of d'Arcy Thompson, who
dealt with the stress and
bearing forces of plant stems
while preparing his book *On
Growth and Form.* He wrote:
"The biological importance
of this principle is mainly
obvious in the mechanical
construction of the stems of
reed and straw or any other
typically cylindrical stem.
The material of which the
stem consists is weak and can
scarcely withstand pressure,
but some parts of the stem
show a very strong tensile
stress" (p. 278 *et seq.*).
The tensile stresses are again
to be seen in combination
with the different pressures
which can be exerted on a
plant stem. The thickenings
prevent them from breaking.

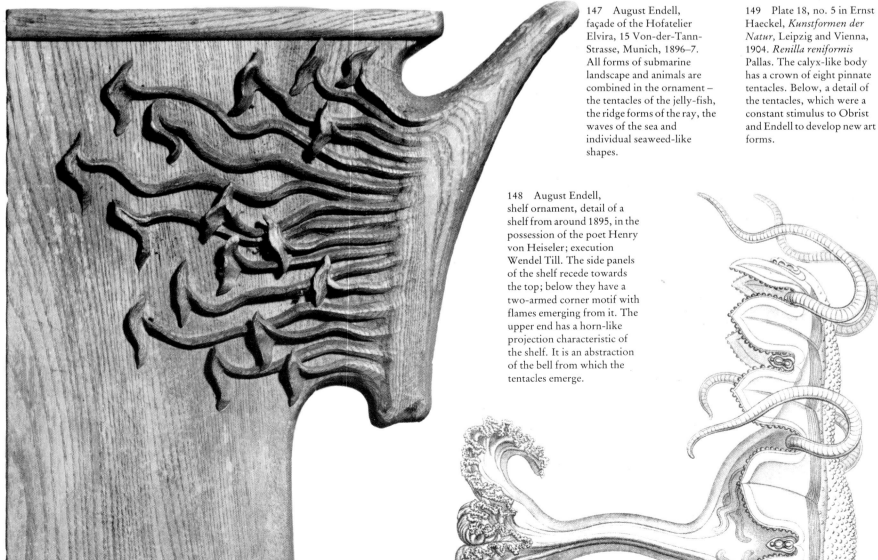

147 August Endell, façade of the Hofatelier Elvira, 15 Von-der-Tann-Strasse, Munich, 1896–7. All forms of submarine landscape and animals are combined in the ornament – the tentacles of the jelly-fish, the ridge forms of the ray, the waves of the sea and individual seaweed-like shapes.

149 Plate 18, no. 5 in Ernst Haeckel, *Kunstformen der Natur,* Leipzig and Vienna, 1904. *Renilla reniformis* Pallas. The calyx-like body has a crown of eight pinnate tentacles. Below, a detail of the tentacles, which were a constant stimulus to Obrist and Endell to develop new art forms.

148 August Endell, shelf ornament, detail of a shelf from around 1895, in the possession of the poet Henry von Heiseler; execution Wendel Till. The side panels of the shelf recede towards the top; below they have a two-armed corner motif with flames emerging from it. The upper end has a horn-like projection characteristic of the shelf. It is an abstraction of the bell from which the tentacles emerge.

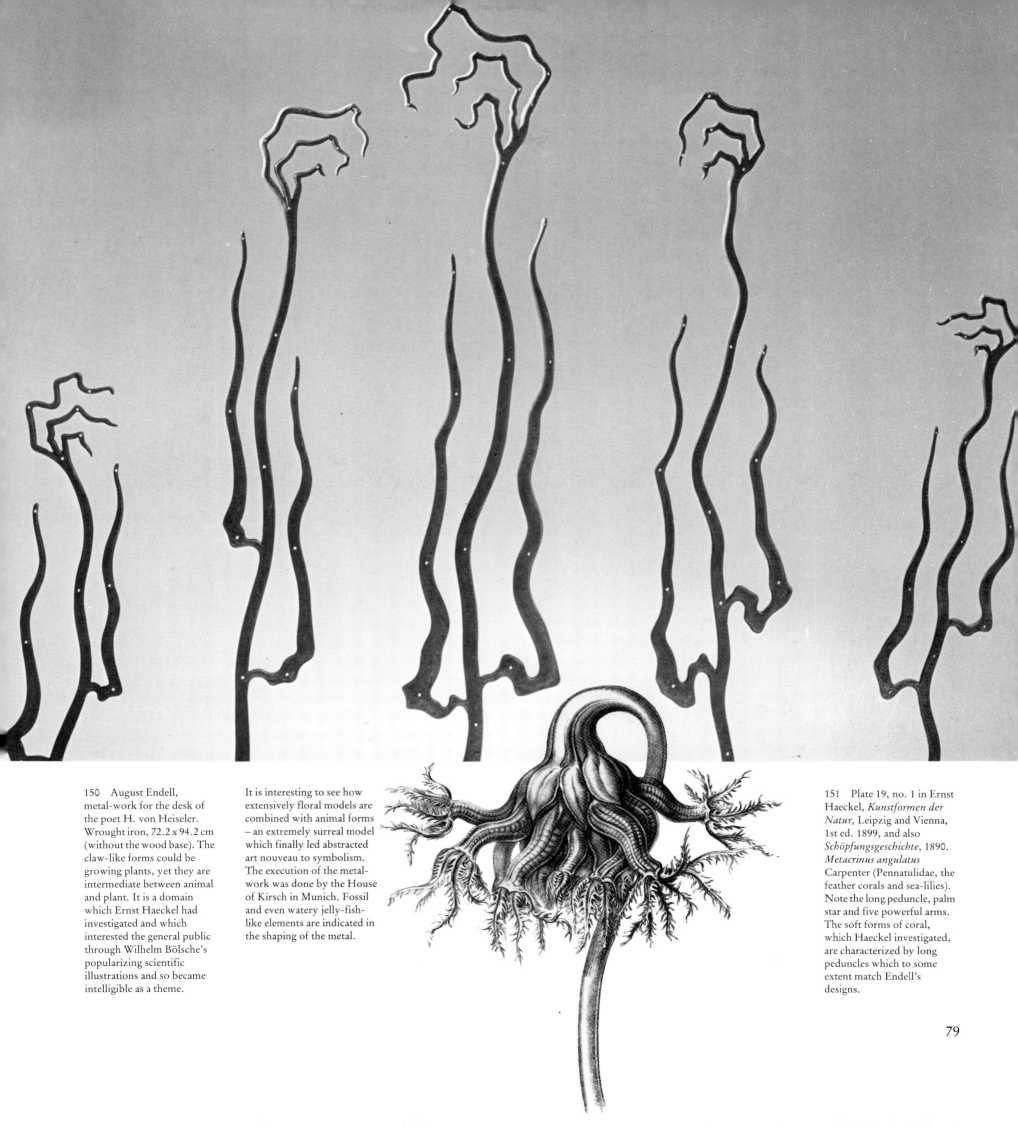

150 August Endell, metal-work for the desk of the poet H. von Heiseler. Wrought iron, 72.2 x 94.2 cm (without the wood base). The claw-like forms could be growing plants, yet they are intermediate between animal and plant. It is a domain which Ernst Haeckel had investigated and which interested the general public through Wilhelm Bölsche's popularizing scientific illustrations and so became intelligible as a theme.

It is interesting to see how extensively floral models are combined with animal forms – an extremely surreal model which finally led abstracted art nouveau to symbolism. The execution of the metal-work was done by the House of Kirsch in Munich. Fossil and even watery jelly-fish-like elements are indicated in the shaping of the metal.

151 Plate 19, no. 1 in Ernst Haeckel, *Kunstformen der Natur*, Leipzig and Vienna, 1st ed. 1899, and also *Schöpfungsgeschichte*, 1890. *Metacrinus angulatus* Carpenter (Pennatulidae, the feather corals and sea-lilies). Note the long peduncle, palm star and five powerful arms. The soft forms of coral, which Haeckel investigated, are characterized by long peduncles which to some extent match Endell's designs.

152 August Endell,
detail of the chair illustrated
opposite. August Endell
transferred irregular mussel-
like structures to his abstract
forms, which he introduced
into the furniture of his early
period. The abstruse forms of
sea animals stimulated him, as
did floral foliage which he
could transform into his own
structural forms. Thus Endell
left the world of Renaissance
forms and embarked on a new
kind of expression, tending to
abstraction, in which the
acceptance of
anthroposophical theories is
implicit.

153 August Endell,
detail of bookcase for Sophia
and Maria Goudstikker in the
Hofatelier Elvira in Munich.
The bookcase no longer
exists.

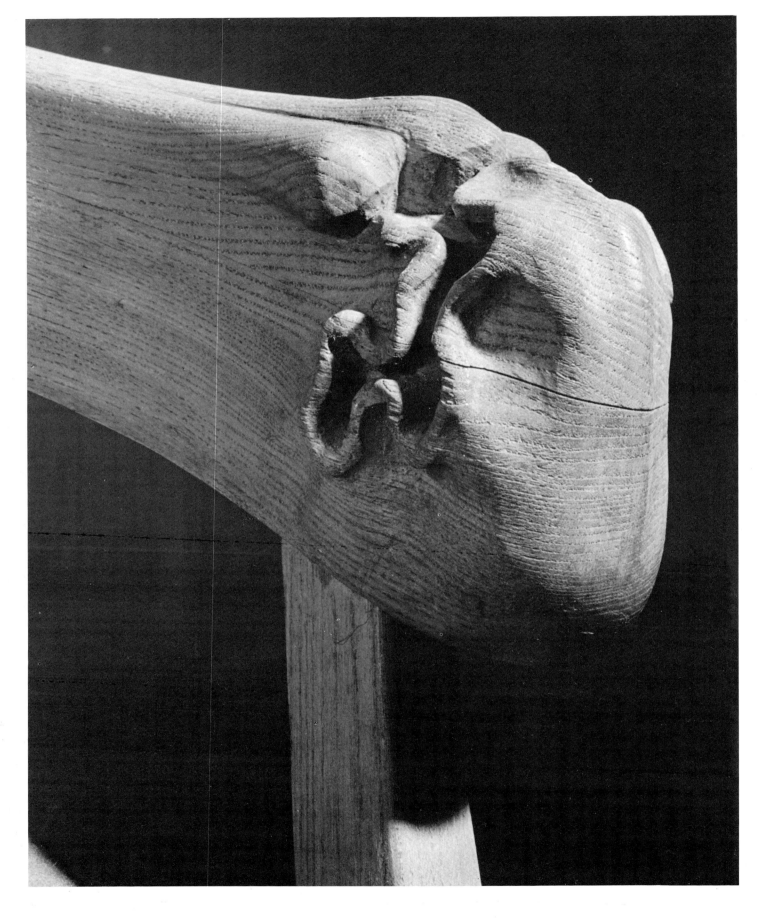

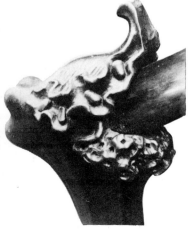

154 Hermann Obrist, abstracted flower in the shape of a bell or a prone human figure, *c.* 1899. Marked below right on the underside of the cardboard "III, 15" in pencil. Pencil on transparent paper, 7.9 x 13.9 cm on cardboard base. State Graphics Collection, Munich.

In these drawings Obrist's aim of combining vegetable forms with the representation of the human body is clearly discernible. In the process he moves in two directions. He makes Hellenistic-seeming female figures grow out of calyxes. Then again he uses human physiognomy, abstracting and transforming it into a vegetable structure.

Hermann Obrist, who discovered Haeckel's theory of nature for himself, also influenced August Endell. Indeed, it can be said that the basic forms of Endell's ornament were inspired by Obrist.
The commission for and execution of the Fotoatelier Elvira in Munich and collaboration with Bernhard Pankok, Richard Riemerschmid, Hermann Obrist and Henry van de Velde for the Thieme family (not only Heiseler) gave him the stimulus and above all the artistic impulse to conceive new furniture forms around 1896. Endell developed a hybrid style between Far Eastern analogies and a new 'root cult'. The wood that grew in spite of the earth's resistance and the forces of wind and weather had aroused his interest; his

pictorial conception was dominated by freshly stripped animal skins, opened out rays or jelly-fish tentacles, coupled with Chinese dragon symbols.

155 Detail from Plate 55, no. 12 in Ernst Haeckel, *Kunstformen der Natur*, Leipzig and Vienna 1904. *Tridacna squamosa,* giant clam (Acephala).

156 August Endell, desk chair (detail opposite), 1896. Semi-circular chairback, arms terminating in mussel motifs or spongy joints and gristly volutes; elm, seat covering. Design R. Riemerschmid. Height 85 cm, depth 55 cm. Bavarian National Museum, Munich. Inventory no. SW 104.

157 Wilhelm Bölsche, *Entwicklungsgeschichte der Natur*, Berlin, 1896, 2 vols., p. 289. Shell of auger snail.

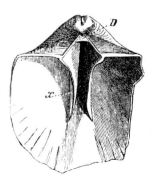

58 Hermann Obrist,
Burning gorge, c. 1895. Mixed
technique over pencil on
white cardboard. 14.7 x 10.6
cm. State Graphics
Collection, Munich.

59 A. Bigot,
Ornamental plate with a
salamander creeping through
a pond. Stoneware, running
glazes: green-black and
yellowish-brown, shining
green-blue in the centre. 23.3
cm. See also p. 228.

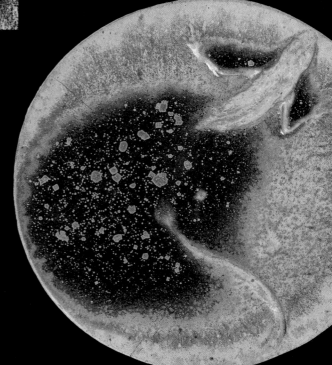

160 Clément Massier, ornamental plate, earthenware with iridescent streaming glaze, incised and painted, *c.* 1900. Decoration: butterflies in flight (after Japanese models) before bare, leafless trees. Marked on base "Clément Massier, Golfe Juan. I. Levy". 20.5 cm. Bavarian National Museum, Munich. Inventory no. SW 54.

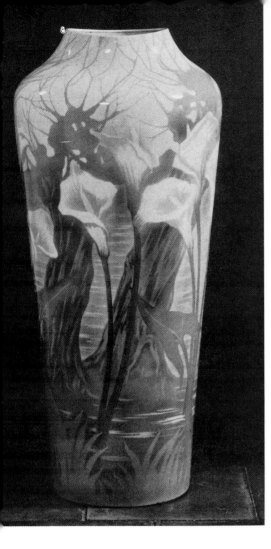

161 Louis Levallois, tall vase, slightly recessed high shoulder, broadening out like an inverted cone from a flat base, 1903. Decoration: marsh Calla in front of white willow flowers. 112 cm. State Porcelain Manufactory, Nymphenburg, Munich.

162 Engelbert Kayser, two jugs, 1898. Basic oval form. Semi-circular handles issuing from the bellied body, slanting projecting spout. Decoration: abstract relief. Kayser pewter. Height 20 cm, diameter 11.8 cm, width 16 cm. Bavarian National Museum, Munich. Inventory nos. SW 97, 98.
Kayser hints at flower panicles, but carries the specific form in a different abstract direction.
The twilit river bank landscape on the large Nymphenburg vase, ill. 161, is just as credible as the dancing figures on a pewter vessel *(opposite)* at first glance. But seen side by side with the object, it changes into the reverse, a process

reminiscent of romantic irony. The contrast between the flat ornament and the plastic body arises from the heightened tension, but it is simultaneously an attraction for the spectator.
It is striking that in nearly all floral works, the division between primary form and ornament increased after 1895. The small craft object now became an important work of art, as with the East Asian peoples. The art nouveau artists, who mostly came to handicrafts from painting, wanted to raise the status of handicrafts as opposed to the predominance of easel-painting and architecture. Obrist said about this: "The problem is to wipe out the difference between the fine arts and applied art which has existed for so long." In other words, every form of expression, if it is new and has quality, is justified.

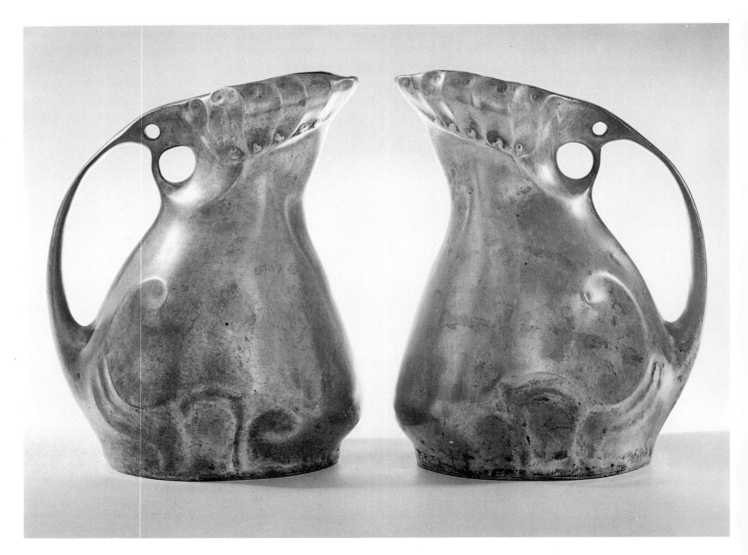

163 Aron Jerndahl, bowl with lid, 1903. Cast engraved pewter ornament in the round and in relief. Decoration: round dance, dancing couples, fiddler. Marked on lower edge "Aron Jerndahl, 1903". 17 x 23.5 cm. Bavarian National Museum, Munich. Inventory no. SW 94.

Aron Jerndahl tried to distance the body of the vessel by incorporating into the surface human figures in a swirling rhythm. The rhythmic movement is clearly visible and, with the backward and forward and bowing movement of the figures, suggests the element of water. Here too the beginnings of an alienated atmosphere are indicated. August Endell, who took unusual pleasure in forms and colours seen close to, was also drawn to recreate things seen in dreams, just as Obrist attempted to give form to 'the profusion that had never been seen before'. His conception of form at first exhibits floral motifs, as if under a lens; a combination of closeness to reality and remoteness from reality begins to open up. His furniture contains knobbly and root-like forms, as well as forms of snails and mussels. The things in dreams, about which Endell repeatedly spoke, he clearly realized in the Elvira façade (147). In general terms it can be said of the florally dependent works that their enhanced naturalism loses value, because it is no longer used in meaningful places. But this indicates nothing more than a move away from the imitation of nature.

164 Julius Zitzmann, vase, arched semi-circular foot, amphora-like body, projecting shoulder, elongated neck, lustred blown glass. Decoration: lanceolate bent back leaves fused on to the shoulder. 15.7 cm. Bavarian National Museum, Munich. Inventory no. SW 21.

165   Wilhelm Bölsche,
*Entwicklungsgeschichte der
Natur,* Berlin, 1896, p. 128.
Above and right: caterpillars
and chrysalis of a bombycid.

166   *(Opposite)*
Wilhelm Bölsche,
Entwicklungsgeschichte,
Berlin, 1896. Examples of
camouflage: stick insect and
leaves (p. 118) and praying
mantis (p. 119, detail).

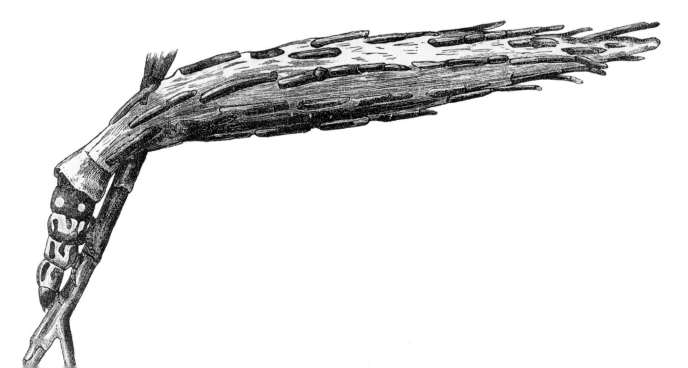

167 Emmy von Egidy, nocturnal landscape with budding branch and insect, *c.* 1899–1900. Marked below right with monogram "E.E." Mixed technique on cardboard. 4.5 x 10.5 cm. Bavarian National Museum, Munich. Inventory no. SW 183.

The tendency to picture patterning distinguishes high-quality pictorial reproduction in the field of symbolism. Decisive for the painter, and also for the poet, is the attempt to enlarge visible objects or simply to make them portrayable. Then it becomes interesting to see how the environment is enlarged to its limits, inasmuch as it acquires a uniform lunar atmosphere. Far and near can be seen and experienced together, as can the wide-angled totality seen close to, as a contrast. Even universal landscapes in a cosmic atmosphere are subject to a limited segmental insight. New themes, such as the dimly lit underwater landscape with its waving seaweed ambience and its connotations of the death-wish, strive to achieve separateness. When it comes to objects, the fossil in its composition or surface structure is a pictorial model on the same footing as root systems and cortical masses. Geological strata and exaggerated atmospheric phenomena are also depicted.

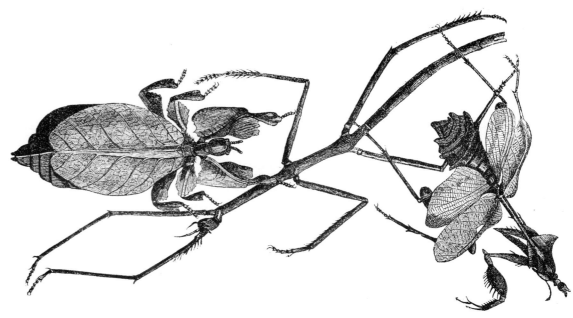

168   Hans Schmithals, composition of a dragon motif in the middle of a rotating cosmic landscape, *c.* 1900. Mixed pastel technique with gold. 47.5 x 109 cm. City Museum, Munich.

169   Hans Schmithals, composition (glacier pinnacles), *c.* 1900. Pastel on paper. 115 x 75 cm. Bavarian National Museum, Munich. Inventory no. SW 180.

170   Detail from Plate 13 in Martin Gerlach, *Formenwelt aus dem Naturreiche,* Vienna and Leipzig, *c.* 1902. Crystallization in polarized light.

171   *(Opposite, bottom)* Wilhelm Bölsche, *Entwicklungsgeschichte der Natur,* Berlin, 1896, p. 7. Various forms of fission fungi.

172 Hans Schmithals,
'Dance of the bacilli', *c.* 1900.
Pastel on paper fixed to
wrapping paper. 54.2 x 40.3
cm. Bavarian National
Museum, Munich. Inventory
no. SW 182.

Hans Schmithals appended
the following text, after Ernst
Haeckel, to this composition:
"The original gaseous state of
the rotating cosmic bodies
gradually passed through
progressive cooling and
compression, into a molten
aggregate. Through the actual
process of compression, great
masses of heat were released
and thus the rotating suns,
planets and moons soon
formed glowing balls of fire,
like gigantic molten drops of
metal, radiating light and
heat. Through the
concomitant loss of heat the
molten mass on the surface of
the fiery balls was
compressed again and a thin
solid crust came into being
which enclosed a molten
core. In all these processes
our mother earth would not
have behaved very differently
from the other astronomical
bodies." The artists of the art
nouveau movement around
Hermann Obrist in Munich
took a lasting interest in this
cosmological gas theory,
which Ernst Haeckel
propounded on p. 287 of his
book *Schöpfungsgeschichte.*
Wilhelm Bölsche, too,
concerned himself with the
natural history of the creation
of the universe and presented
these complicated processes
in the form of popular
science. This made it possible
for the layman, too, to learn
about these scientific
phenomena.

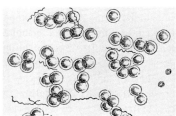

173 O. Lelièvre, crystallized quartz in silver mounting. Decoration: head of Poseidon crowned with bulrushes; at the opposite edge, female nude with floating hair. Height 5.7 cm, depth 9 cm, width 7.2 cm. Bavarian National Museum, Munich. Inventory no. SW 91.

174 Ludwig Habich, nereid. Cast engraved patinated bronze, marked with the artist's monogram. 13 x 10.2 cm. Bavarian National Museum, Munich. Inventory no. SW 90.

175 Jean Garnier, blotter, 1897. Cast engraved gilded bronze. Decoration: scallop and seaweed above and among waves. Marked "J. Garnier". Height 7.5 cm, length 13.5 cm, width 7 cm. Bavarian National Museum, Munich. Inventory no. SW 92.

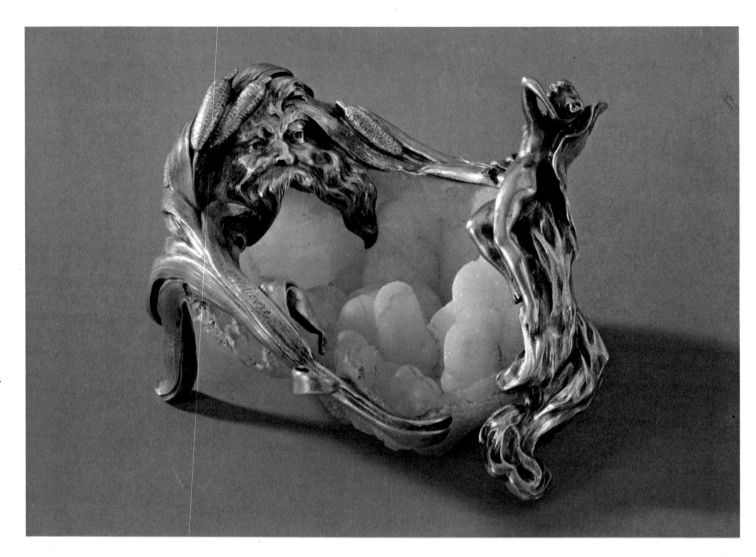

176   Plate 54, no. 4 in Ernst Haeckel, *Kunstformen der Natur,* Leipzig and Vienna, 1904. *Octopus vulgaris* Lamarck (Octolenae).

177   Rupert Carabien, siren with octopus, 1900–1. Cast polished bronze, signed "Carabien" above the base. 29 cm. Private collection, Munich.

178   Plate 55, no. 12 in Ernst Haeckel, *Kunstformen der Natur,* Leipzig and Vienna, 1904, *Tridacna squamosa,* giant clam (Acephala).

179   August Endell, title vignette for the publication *Um die Schönheit,* 1896. This dealt with August Endell's art exhibition in Munich in 1896, and was published by Emil Franke (Franke und Haushalter) Verlag, Munich, 1898.

180 Probably workshop of René Lalique or Manuel Orazi in co-operation with August-François Gorguet. Combs and hairpins in horn and gilded silver, with opals, moonstones, star sapphires and pearls, *c.* 1900. From left to right: 6.5 cm, 13 cm, 16.5 cm, 8 cm, 13 cm, 16.2 cm, 12.6 cm. Private collection, Munich.

181 Plates 29 and 110 in Karl Blossfeldt, *Urformen der Kunst,* Berlin, 2nd ed. 1929 (photographed in 1906).

To achieve a harmonization of various materials, to combine artificially made opal glass with genuine opals in a unity, was the concern of Lalique, who represented nature and art in competition and so embodied a principal theme of art nouveau, which found its zenith in his magical glass. The *Flying Elf (opposite)* in iridescent light is characteristic of another branch of art nouveau themes. Floating, gliding, falling hybrid beings are intensified by the transparency of the material. The winged woman belongs to the *fin de siècle* group of occult themes and motifs. Waxed stones after Far Eastern models are a centre of interest. The ornamental comb as a fashion accessory was given very original forms by art nouveau jewellers, especially the French. Ladies wore exceptionally beautiful combs in their high-piled hair, in the Japanese style. Hair accessories were a sign of status in Japan.

182 René Jules Lalique, brooch, Paris, 1902. Moth, gold and enamel. Signed. 4.3 x 8.5 cm. Coll. S. Wichmann, Cape George, Canada.

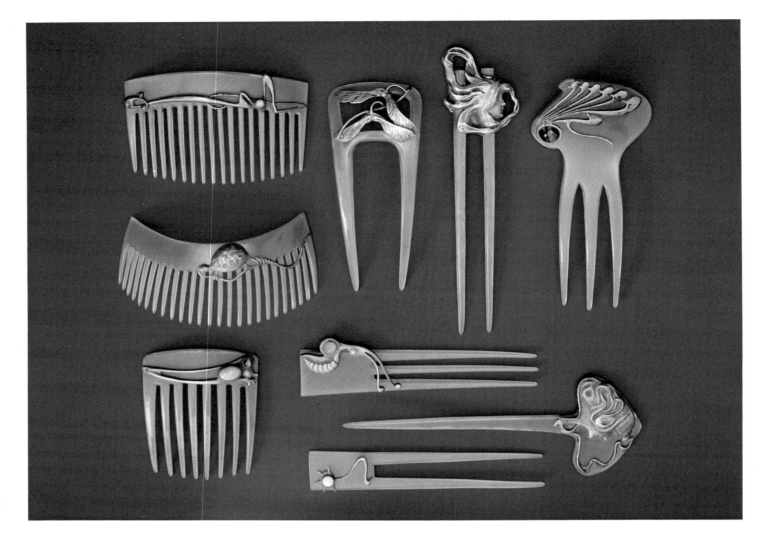

183   European silver ornaments. *Left to right and top to bottom:* Designed by M. Olbrich, belt fastening with grotesque Babylonian head, *c.* 1900. Carved and engraved white metal with red and white agate. Height 7.2 cm.

Belt fastening with mistletoe decoration, *c.* 1900. Open work in the manner of a Japanese ornamental sword plaque or tsuba. Height 6.3 cm.

Brooch, *c.* 1900. Maple seeds set with two green onyxes. 18.2 cm.

Ludwig Habich, brooch, *c.* 1902. Two mermaids in chased silver, stone setting turquoise. Marked "G.T.W." Height 2.5 cm.

Bernhard Hoetger, brooch. Prowling lion. Chased silver with lapis lazuli. Executed by Ernst Riegel. Mark and distinguishing coat of arms. 6.9 cm.

Martin Mayer, Mainz, pin-cushion. Girl's head with floating hair. Chased silver. 4.7 cm.

Case cover, chased silver, metal-work. Decoration: swan and lily. 12 cm.

Case cover, chased silver, metal-work. Decoration: thistle leaf. 12.2 cm.

Evald Nielsen, small round box, amber and metal-work, 1908. Decoration: buds and fruit. 7 cm.

E. Linzeler, small round box, chased silver. Interior gilt. Master stamp "EL". 4.6 cm.

Martin Mayer, belt fastening, *c.* 1903 Cast, chased and engraved silver, partially gilt. Decoration: snakes among branches. Amethyst in the mouth. 5.5 x 8.3 cm.

Martin Mayer, small box. Chased silver, interior gilt. Decoration: seed-pods of the Judas tree. 4.9 x 4.6 cm. Private collection, Munich.

93

184 Wilhelm Lucas von Cranach, comb with abstract floral motif, *c.* 1900. Horn, enamel, brilliants, emeralds, rubies, pearl. 14.2 x 7.5 cm. Private collection.

185 Georges Fouquet, comb with abstract wave and seaweed ornament, *c.* 1905. Horn, enamel, opals. 18 x 8.1 cm. Private collection, Munich.

186 Plate 69, no. 1 in Ernst Haeckel, *Kunstformen der Natur*, Leipzig and Vienna, 1904. *Hexacoralla*, six-armed stone coral (detail); *Turbinaria transformis* Haeckel, beaker-like stem from which a second, smaller one issues.

187–192 *Opposite, left to right:*

187 Bruno Möhring, pendant with chain, Flora under pansies, *c.* 1900. Cast gold with *pliqué à jour* enamel, flowers in opaque enamel with small brilliants; reverse side elaborated. 5 x 2.8 cm.

188 Karl Kast, mistletoe brooch, *c.* 1906. Gold with four pearls, two rubies and three emeralds. 4 x 5.2 cm.

189 German (Pforzheim), chestnut leaf with buds, *c.* 1900. White gold, four baroque pearls, enamelled. Monogram and mark. 4 x 5 cm

190 Vienna, Secession style (design: Koloman Moser), cufflinks, *c.* 1905. Chased gold, lapis lazuli, 2 x 2 cm. Bavarian National Museum, Munich. Inventory nos. SW 68, 69, 74, 73.

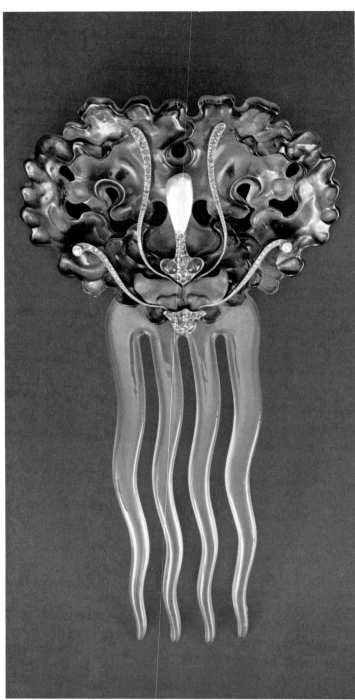

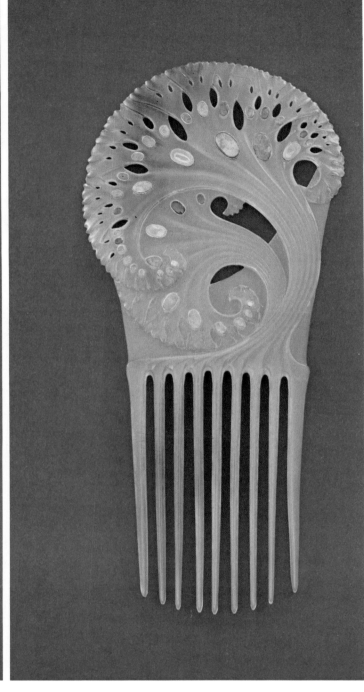

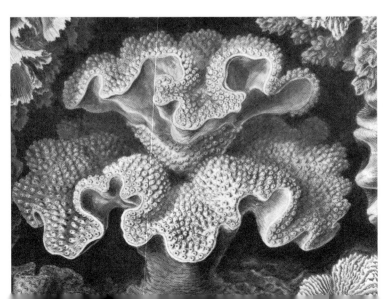

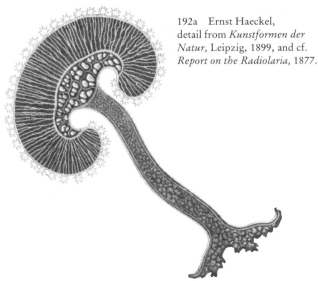

192a Ernst Haeckel, detail from *Kunstformen der Natur*, Leipzig, 1899, and cf. *Report on the Radiolaria*, 1877.

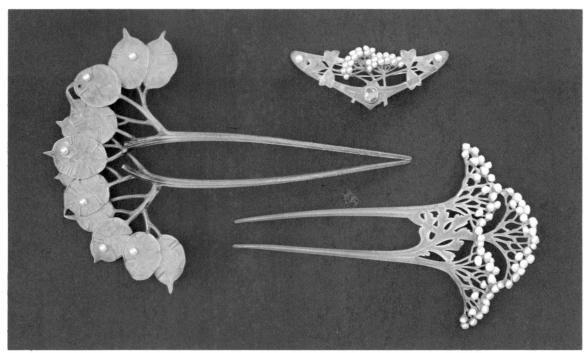

191 The firm of Otto Weber, pendant, *c.* 1902. Three sycamore seedlings in gold, mounted with three rubies, with greenish translucent glass foot fused on. 3.5 x 4 cm.

192 Georg Klimt (attributed), bracelet with symbolic female figure, *c.* 1900. Gold with a sapphire and small brilliants. 2 x 2.5 cm. Bavarian National Museum. Inventory nos. SW 78, 70.

193 Karl Blossfeldt, *Urformen der Kunst,* Berlin, 2nd ed. 1929, p. 36. Photograph taken in 1906.

194 Lucien Gaillard, *left:* comb with *Caesalpinia,* 1905. Horn and pearls. 15.5 x 11.1 cm.

195 Comb and brooch with mistletoe berries and leaves, *c.* 1903. Horn, pearls and gold topaz. 13.2 x 8.2 cm and 2.8 x 6.7 cm. Private collection, Munich.

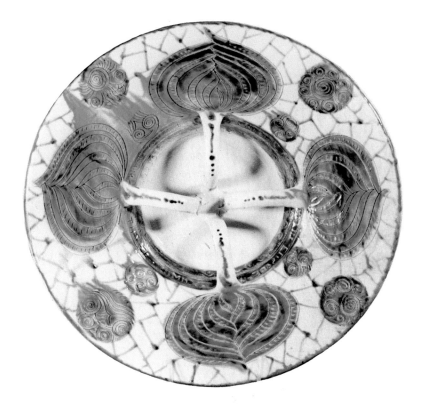

196 Hermann Gradl (Royal Bavarian Porcelain Manufactory, Nymphenburg), plate with side bowl for bones etc, 1904–5. Porcelain with painting over glaze; two pieces of the 'modern' fish service. Diameter 24 cm, length 18.5 cm. Marked on underside with impressed mark, diamond-shaped shield and trademark in blue under the glaze. Private collection, Munich.

197 Theo Schmuz-Baudiss, vase with abstract carnation design, c. 1898–1900. Flat foot ring, slightly bellied cylindrical body with wavy lip and two handles developed from leaves. Ceramic, 22.5 x 11.2 cm, signed on the edge with monogram. Private collection, Munich.

198 Elisabeth Schmidt-Pecht, ornamental plate with leaf decoration and stems in the round, c. 1900. Inscribed on the upper surface "Mich machte schlecht und recht Elisabeth Schmidt-Pecht"; also distinguishing coat of arms. Height 8.5 cm, diameter 40.5 cm. Private collection, Munich.

199 Maria Kirscher (presumably the designer), narrow-necked vase, after 1903. Handles issuing from the middle and merging with the flattish moulded base; Loetz glass coloured red in the mass. 23.2 cm. Private collection, Vienna.

In its structure the glass shows the successful use of branch-like handle forms, which are over-emphasized by the bronze mounting in the adjoining vase by O. Eckmann (200).

200 Otto Eckmann,
vase in bronze mounting (by
Otto Schulz, Berlin), c. 1901.
Narrow ring stand, broad
body with recessed
shoulders, long elogated neck
with slightly projecting lip,
marked with monogram
"OE" on the foot stand of the
bronze mounting; stoneware
glazed in the *sang-de-boeuf*
style. 52.2 x 28 cm. Private
collection, Munich.
The exuberant floral element,
whether in the metal mount,
the painted decoration or the
plastic applications, achieves
a stronger recapitulation and
a recession in the inner
surfaces of the body as
opposed to the swelling plant
form of the first phase.

201 Michael Thonet, umbrella-stand in the form of a snake coiling upwards. Beechwood, brownish matt, ochre to orange-coloured with applied gold leaf; 87.5 x 50.2 cm. Model no. 11411. Private collection, Munich. A piece of beech about 5 metres long is shaped into a snake, the wood describing a serpentine spiral. The umbrella-stand is, in form and technical execution, an example of Thonet's bending technique, developed over many years, and used here for that reason. In the 1870s the 'coiled snake' was a sought-after object.
At the end of the 1880s there was little demand, but about 1900 the umbrella-stands

were modified and once again produced in greater numbers. The changes involved the lion's claws, the snake's upright tail, the entirely new gilding of the scales and the colour scheme of the serpentine coiling of the snake's body. Beechwood bent into serpentine coils meets the needs of art nouveau ornamentation.

202 *(Opposite, left)* Louis Comfort Tiffany, vase in the form of a rose-sprinkler. Spherical body with slender, curved neck and orchid-like lip. Favrile glass, iridescent gold-green in the lower part, in the upper part snake-scale decoration, iridescent blue, with greenish-gold lustre. 36.8 x 13.2 cm. Private collection, Munich.

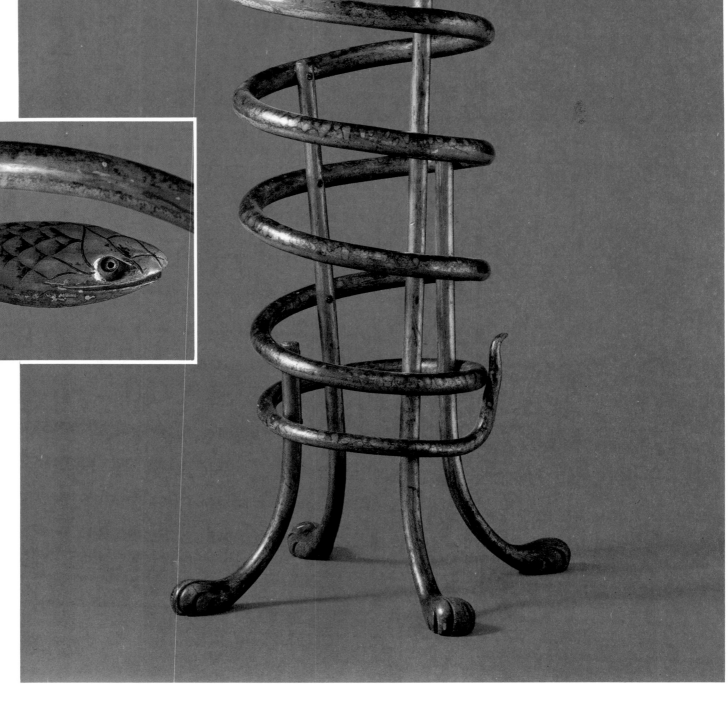

203 Louis Comfort Tiffany, vase in the form of a rose sprinkler, *c.* 1900. Spherical body with slender curved neck, snake's mouth and snake-like lip. Favrile glass, in the lower part iridescent gold, semi-opalescent with green and gold lustre. 37.7 x 11.5 cm. Signed underneath the base. Private collection, Munich.

204 Rose sprinkler, after Tiffany. Spherical body with very slim, arched neck; above the bulging ring the small lip-opening is like a snake's head. Coloured blue glass. Decoration: iridescent gold in the form of peacocks' feathers. 36 x 13.5 cm. Venice, Murano. Private collection, Munich.

205 Persia, 18th- or 19th-century rose sprinkler. Spherical body with burl ribs, curved neck with bulging ring and snake-like mouth towards the lip. Coloured yellow glass, slightly iridescent. 28.5 x 7.5 cm. Private collection, Munich.

206 Powell, Whitefriars Glass Factory, London, vase in the form of a rose sprinkler. Spherical body with slender, curved neck and snake's mouth opening. Pink glass coloured in the mass, slightly iridescent, with whitish feathery decoration. J. Powell went to New York in 1897 and worked for L.C. Tiffany. 34.2 x 7.2 cm. Private collection, Munich. The extra-European influences bring strongly alienating and even surreal structural elements to the floral conception of international art nouveau.

207 John Ruskin
(Ruskin Pottery, West
Smethwick, England), vase
with wood base, 1905–8.
Porcelain-like body, height
15.3 cm. (base 6.2 cm).
Bavarian National Museum.
Inventory no. SW 58.

208 Leopold Bauer,
vase with stand after East
Asian model; iridescent glass,
pewter mount. Height 13.5
cm, width and depth 10 cm.
Private collection, Vienna.

209 Adrien Emile
Dalpayrat,
vase in the form of a gourd
(after East Asian model), *c.*
1898. Glazed stoneware,
flashed red, green and white.
Signed with a distinguishing
mark. 23 cm. Bavarian
National Museum, Munich.

210 Porcelain Factory,
Delft, cylindrical ornamental
vase. Stoneware with
iridescent streaming glaze.
Mark on the base. Height
29.5 cm, diameter at base 10
cm. Bavarian National
Museum, Munich. Inventory
no. SW 59.

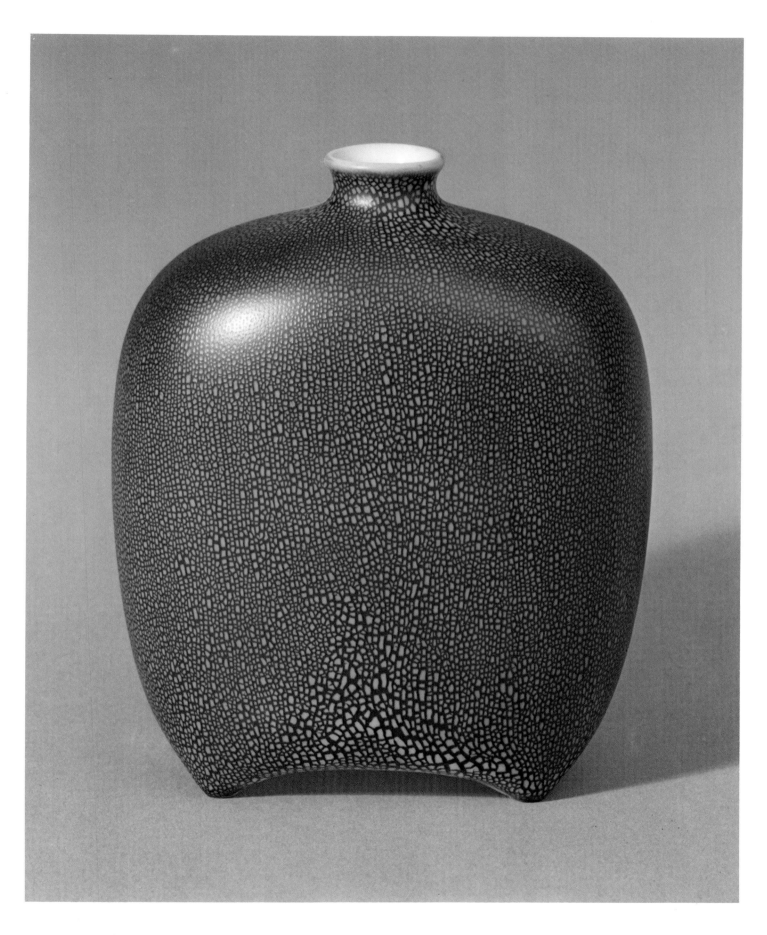

211 Christian Valdemar Engelhardt (Copenhagen Porcelain Factory), ornamental vase, *c.* 1897, with narrow neck and four feet, which are only indicated. After Chinese model (Engelhardt was in China in 1904). Porcelain, blue "snakeskin" reduction glaze. Trademark, serial number and year. Marked on base "VE". 16.2 cm. Bavarian National Museum. Inventory no. SW 56.

In the field of adoptions, analogies and copies, the Porcelain Factory at Copenhagen made an important contribution to European art nouveau pottery forms and surface treatment. In the hands of Christian Valdemar Engelhardt, monochrome blue glaze after models of the Chinese K'ien Lung period (1735–96) acquired a hitherto unknown virtuosity. Arnold Krog (1856–1931) had already laid the foundations for this technique in Copenhagen. Reduction glaze, which resembles snakeskin, shows the masterly skill of the "glazing chemists" of the art nouveau period. The radiant blue pot wall exemplifies, both technically and artistically, the same quality as related objects of the high cultures of the Far East.

212 Emile Gallé, vase with pagoda-shaped lid, 1892. Polished crystal with metal oxide inclusions. Slight vertical ribs in the manner of Chinese rock-crystal work. Original wood base. Marked on gummed label "Durant". Marked under foot "Emile Gallé 1892". 26.8 cm. Bavarian National Museum. Inventory no. SW 29.

213 Emile Gallé, round vase, recessed foot and neck with enamel and gold overlay. Decoration: spiral and wave ornament, marked on foot "Gallé". Height 7 cm, diameter of base 4 cm. Bavarian National Museum. Inventory no. SW 2.
Emile Gallé (1846–1904), who worked in Nancy, was one of the most important art nouveau glassmakers. As a designer of furniture and ceramics, he was simultaneously active as botanist, chemist and author. At the Universal Exhibition of 1878, Emile Gallé exhibited for the first time enamelled and cut glass with ornamental motifs that betrayed Islamic, but even more Asian, stimuli. As models for his vase decoration, he used Japanese botanical handbooks which he probably acquired from the Japanese botanist and painter Tokouso Takasima, who stayed in Nancy from 1885 to 1888. In 1890, Gallé began mass production and seven years later developed the celebrated *marqueterie de verre*, a technique which develops the decoration from partially fused multi-coloured glass. The rich enlivenment of the transparent crystal glasses is typical; corresponding to semi-precious stone vessels they exhibit many different influences.
Gallé spent 1878 in London, where he frequently visited the Victoria and Albert Museum. There he saw the East Asian jade vases, the glass snuff bottles and above all the skilled craft work of the Far Eastern high cultures. These objects had an

overwhelming effect. Here Gallé discovered the foundation for an understanding of the formal surface structure of Chinese jade objects. The traditional symbolic effect of minerals and stones and their structure, which were ascribed to the raw material in every century in the Far East, were readily grasped by a receptive Gallé. The School of Nancy under Emile Gallé successfully worked out meaningful connections between decoration and structural form in glass of the 1890s. Glass vases of that time can still, together with their incised inscriptions, communicate varying moods and feelings. Many are the indications given by shape and ornament, and all can be determined iconographically.

214 Eugène Rousseau, vase on original Chinese base, *c.* 1885. Crystal with inclusions, treated irregularly (as if it was the form found in nature), in the manner of rock crystal with inclusions. 17.2 cm. Bavarian National Museum, Munich. Inventory no. SW 1.

215 Ernest Baptiste Leveillé, vase with leaping carp, after Japanese brush beakers, *c.* 1895. Crystal enamelled with gold ornament, glass blown and polished cold. Height 29.2 cm, diameter of base 11.8 cm. Private collection, Munich.

Reacting to stimuli from China and Japan, Gallé made the irregular natural form of precious and semi-precious stone the basis of his glass shapes. The important vase in the form of an East Asian presentation vessel shows the structure of a calyx and a mineral growing through it; it conveys the poetic magic of that Chinese cult concept to which magical powers were ascribed. As an autonomous work of art of great individual value, the vase became the centre of art nouveau's "glassy period".

216 Daum Brothers, narrow-necked vase, *c.* 1903–05. Flashed glass with multi-coloured powder fused in and after the melt, approximately triangular base with elongated neck. Entwining decoration, blackberry twigs with leaves and berries in low relief (after Japanese pattern-book). Marked on wall "Daum Nancy" with cross of Lorraine etched in relief. 89.9 cm. Bavarian National Museum. Inventory no. SW 101.

217 Amphora-shaped vase, in the style of the Cristallerie Schneider, Epinay-sur-Seine, later than 1914. Flashed glass with polychrome powder fused in the melt and after. Decoration: entwining leaf tips with needle etching; glossy polish. Marked on foot "Le verre français". 30 cm. Bavarian National Museum. Inventory no. SW 20.

218 Emile Gallé, vase, *c.* 1900. Flat base, broad foot, body drawn in towards the centre, enlarging again above, irregularly incised rim, glass flashed several times in blue-ochre and yellow. Decoration: water-lilies in relief above the water-level with leaves stretching upwards. Marked on wall "Gallé". Height 37.8 cm, diameter of base 16.2 cm. Private collection, South Germany.

219 Emile Gallé, vase, 1904 or later. Arched foot, compressed club-shaped body, whitish glass flashed several times with violet and ochre-brown. Marked on foot "Gallé". Height 49 cm, diameter of foot 13 cm. Private collection, South Germany.

In addition to Emile Gallé, the brothers Daum in the eastern French town of Nancy also gained a world-wide reputation. The characteristic feature of Daum manufacture was serial production, for the etched wares show countless variations. The contrast between the rough ground

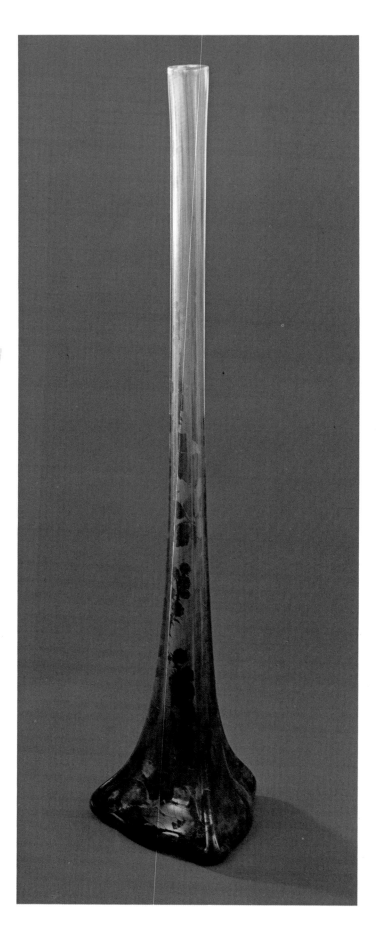

and the smoothly polished surface is always striking. The Daum factory was constantly making chemical experiments and developed many polishing techniques and different surface treatments in its experimental workshops. Indeed, laboratory work sometimes became more important than work on the polishing bench. The Ateliers d'Art à la Verrerie de Nancy saw the origin of countless special shapes, which attest the fantastic attitude of the time to hollow glass. The early Daum glasses of about 1890 combine symbolic ornament with almost abstruse vase shapes. About 1900 long-necked vases were

in favour. The ornamental vessel shown here (ill. 216) with a height of 90 cm, is formally extremely decorative, a kind of miniature Eiffel tower in glass. The slim neck of the vase is elongated above a roughly triangular base in such a way that the overlay of polychrome glass powder (*pâte de verre*), fused in and applied, is shown to advantage. The glass powder process, although used by other European and American manufacturers, was the brilliant invention of Daum Verrerie at Nancy and especially of its art glass workshops, which constantly created new forms. The

various kinds of glass powder had different consistencies: coarse or fine, light or dark, gleaming or matt. The glass-powder method had the advantage over the technique of applying pieces of glass to the hot surface, in that it made possible greater variety and faster work. Finally the glass powder was used as pure colour and painted between and over the flashed glass layers, which could be etched and tinted with fluoric acid.

105

220 Robert Oerley, armchair with saddle seat, *c.* 1899. Front legs curved, rear legs slightly "stilted". Back and arm-rests in one piece with projecting profile. Solid fumed oak. Height 74.5 cm, width 66 cm, depth 54 cm, height of seat 45.5 cm. J. Hummel, Vienna.

221 Adolf Loos, stool with round slightly concave seat, earlier than 1900. Three curved legs, thickening towards the feet, mortised into the solid wood of the seat. Cherry wood. Height 35.2 cm. The design by Loos was later made on a large scale by Liberty's of London. Executed by Josef Veilich. Private collection, Vienna.

222 Bernhard Pankok, bedside table, *c.* 1898. Short, slightly curved legs, square design, cube-like cupboard with door. Opening above it, supported on the right by a thin column. A cupboard with a small door occupies half the opening. Flat, slightly projecting top, carved matt oak. Metalwork by Firma Kirsch, Munich. Decoration: early Anglo-Saxon ornament. Height 100 cm, width 55 cm, depth 40 cm. Bavarian National Museum. Inventory no. SW 120.

223 August Endell, large four-legged table, with curved, irregularly indented top and similarly treated central shelf, 1899. Broad feet relate to the outlines of the top. Endell used animal skins and various branch forms as models, and so developed in his style what were virtually anthroposophical model forms, which had never been seen before. Lightly matted oak. Height 71 cm, length 115 cm, width 96 cm. Executed by Wenzel Till. Private collection, Munich.

Compare *(right)* Wilhelm Bölsche, *Entwicklungsgeschichte der Natur,* Berlin, 1896, p. 132. The outspread membranes of the flying vertebrates were described and illustrated many times by Ernst Haeckel and Wilhelm Bölsche. In the case of these animals, they were "sails" which prolonged their leaps into the air. The silhouettes of these animals in flight are bizarre and novel.

Plant and Floral Models and the Abstract Play of Line

224 *(Above)* Karl Blossfeldt, *Polystichum munitum,* shield fern, young curled-up frond magnified six times. Karl Blossfeldt's photographs are not dated. But based on comparisons, it can be assumed that the fern photos were taken soon after 1900, as were the slit-leaved teasel and fuller's teasel with leaves dried on the stem, magnified four times. These photographs of teasels are known to have been taken by Blossfeldt before 1904. *Cf.* Karl Blossfeldt, *Urformen der Kunst,* Berlin, 1929, p. 83.

225 Hermann Obrist, study of a curled-up fern. Much magnified, presumably copied from Blossfeldt. Marked below right in pencil "IV 8". Pencil on transparent paper, 27.2 x 11 cm. State Graphics Collection, Munich.

226 T.T. Heine, vignette, growing fern and ornamental thorn twig. *Pan* 1903, p. 177, supplement (private collection, Munich.) The curled-up fern was an art nouveau symbol because it was no longer a question merely of a floral pattern, but of representing the growing form of the plant under tension. Heine developed an ornamental vignette form from Blossfeldt's nature photographs.

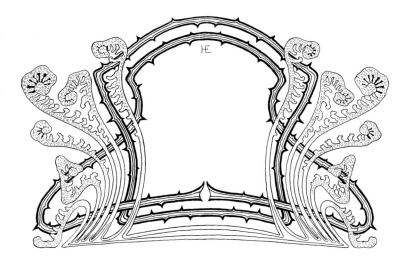

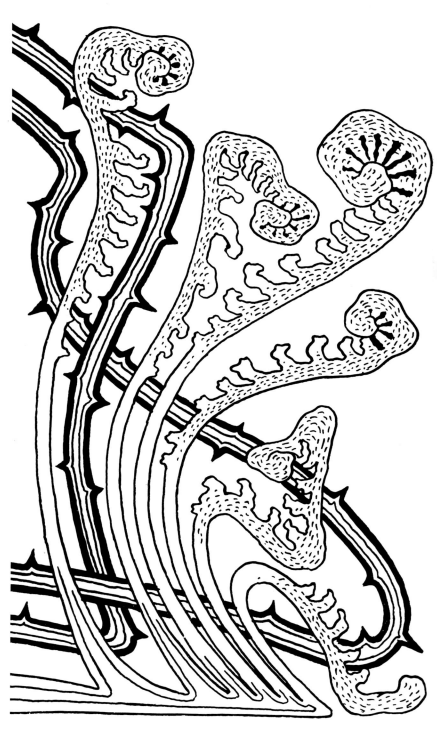

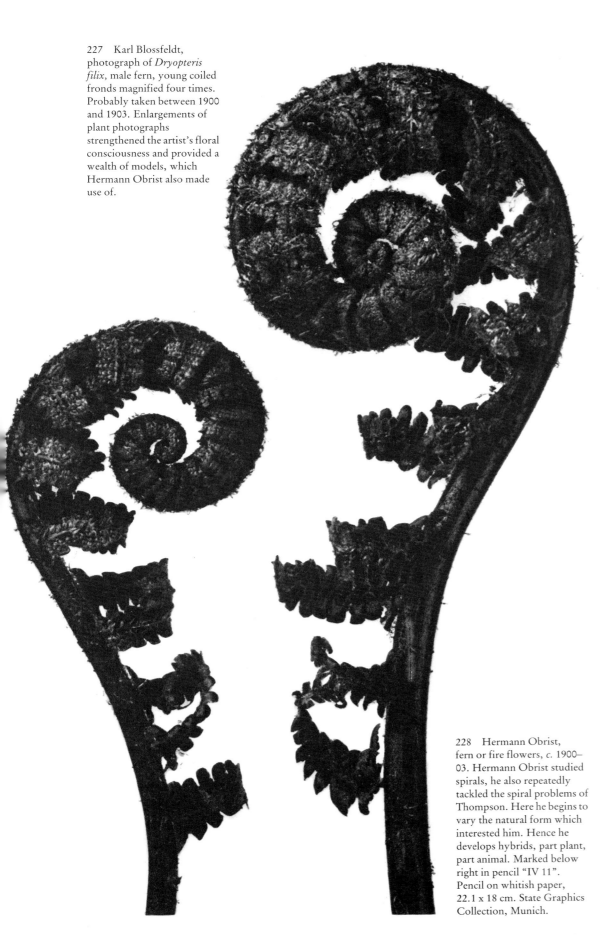

227 Karl Blossfeldt, photograph of *Dryopteris filix*, male fern, young coiled fronds magnified four times. Probably taken between 1900 and 1903. Enlargements of plant photographs strengthened the artist's floral consciousness and provided a wealth of models, which Hermann Obrist also made use of.

228 Hermann Obrist, fern or fire flowers, *c.* 1900–03. Hermann Obrist studied spirals, he also repeatedly tackled the spiral problems of Thompson. Here he begins to vary the natural form which interested him. Hence he develops hybrids, part plant, part animal. Marked below right in pencil "IV 11". Pencil on whitish paper, 22.1 x 18 cm. State Graphics Collection, Munich.

Around 1900-5 line, in its real formal value, was examined by artists. In Germany and Austria people had become more sensitive to the conception of line and tried to come to conclusions empirically, i.e. from the idea to direct outward appearances. In so doing the tendency to tauten the line is obvious. In his *Kunstformen der Natur*, Ernst Haeckel had represented plants and animals which exhibited clear-cut outlines and above all an abstract play of lines, the like of which had not been seen before. The everyday things of the environment, too, were now seen more strongly in their constructive value, without their inherent significant value

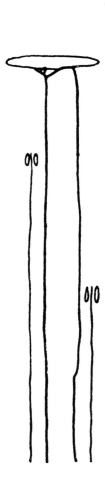

being encroached upon. The starting points of the motifs, especially in furniture design and receptacles, remained mainly floral, that is to say they were motivated by the form of growth.

D. Faber wrote in the *Wiener Abendpost* for 6 October 1903: "Line…, developing or returning to itself, and thus as the limitation of a form, contrives to be significant not only as decoration or organic structural necessity, but also as expression, as a graphic sign, as the realization of an idea or an emotion."

In the floral and post-floral art nouveau period, the line became the sign of a concentration which produced a completely new ornamentation. Van de Velde said: "Line is a force; it derives its force from the energy of those who drew it." Thus line won an influence on the content and the expression of the created object, and the characteristic value of the line allows the artistic expression to achieve a convincing intrinsic value. The works of August Endell and Hermann Obrist were close to the spirit of the Van de Velde quotation.

After Endell had become interested in Rudolf Steiner as a student of philosophy, he always found anthroposophical ideas an enrichment. Obrist, on the other hand, was more strongly attracted to Haeckel's theory of nature. He was constantly alternating between craftsman, sculptor, draughtsman, furniture designer, architect and theoretician. In 1898 he drew a non-objective figure which anticipated all modern artistic endeavours.

After 1886, Hermann Obrist had visions, which grew more frequent with the passage of the years. He not only saw cities appear in the air with an architecture surpassing anything ever seen before, he simultaneously experienced the deep-sea world as described and illustrated by Ernst Haeckel. Apparently he had fainting fits associated with waking dreams.

Obrist commented on these impressions in a later manuscript and added many drawings to it.[1] But nature remains his starting-point and it is always the primordial landscape, the creation story or the underwater world which inspires him to new

artistic statements. The intention and will of
Obrist to abstract the basic forms of nature
emerge clearly in his somnambulistic writings.
On the road from image to sign there is an ever-
increasing density and tautness in the pictures.
Ornamentalized linear tensions are referred to the
human psyche (ills. 99, 132). The element of
growth is seen from the viewpoint of a specific
"intensified curvature" which is also visible in his
furniture designs (ill. 146). The linear stenograms
in his somnambulistic writings are frightening
and sometimes bizarre. In Obrist's work, line
acquires a new strength; he demands "deepened
impression" instead of "quick impression".[2] In
the search for new content he chose new motifs,
discovered new forms and filled himself with new
rhythms. Things now appear as characters with
independent qualities, freed from the context.
Obrist found his ideas manifested in one basic
line. This was the spiral, by which in many cases,
he meant the line of the screw. He writes:
"Everything spirals, radiates, whirls, turns in a
circle."[3] In the spiral, the simultaneous double
movement, forwards and concentrically around
the axis, was important to him. He could only
represent this dynamic process by line.

In contrast to Obrist was the line *constructed*
by Richard Riemerschmid, its virtual antithesis.
To contemporaries, the obvious polarity of
the treatment of line could also combine into a
synthesis, as the cultural sociologist Friedrich
Naumann saw in his essay "Deutsche Gewerbekunst" ("German industrial art"): "The
formal language of the new German industrial art
is generally speaking more naturalistic than
geometric, but one has only to remember Van de
Velde and Behrens to say that the geometric or
linear forms also possess powerful supporters."
In our view, the most outspoken is the naturalism
of Riemerschmid and Pankok, but it is always
clearly separated from the mere reproduction of
chance impressions of nature. The peculiarity of
the development hitherto is that the naturalists
and the linear artists do not appear to us as
two separate groups, because so much drive to
stylization is present in naturalism and so great a

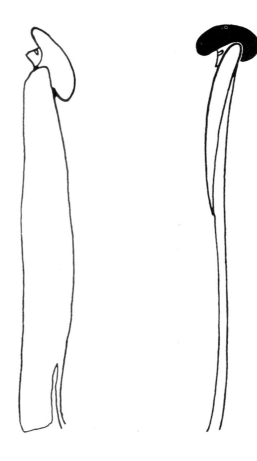

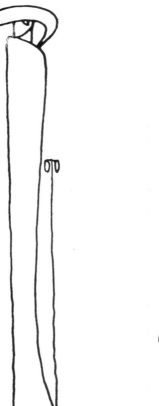

229 *(Opposite)* Hermann
Obrist,
two studies after a calyx, *c.*
1894. Marked below right in
pencil "III 5". Pencil on
transparent paper fixed to
cardboard, 26 x 17.3 cm.
These drawings clearly show
Obrist's aim of combining
vegetable forms with
representations of the human
body. In so doing he followed
a twofold path. He makes
female figures with a
suggestion of the Hellenistic
grow out of his calyx
representations. Then again
he uses the human
appearance, abstracts it and
transforms it into vegetable
images. Thus, to discover and
represent the statuary
element in the vegetable and
human spheres became one of
Obrist's constant
preoccupations. State
Graphics Collection,
Munich.

230 Josef Hoffmann,
engravings of grotesque
female figures developed
from a plant. *Ver Sacrum*, 4th
year, no. 328, pp. 121–35.
The attempt to derive the
human figure out of a plant
was a constant theme around
1900. It was solved in
different ways, on the one
hand as flat linear decoration
on the lines of the engraver's
art, and on the other by
attempting, as Kolo Moser
often did, a greater
morphological changeability
from flower to man.
Hermann Obrist also tackled
these problems.

231 The brothers Thonet, bentwood flower-stand (detail, opposite), c. 1890 (1888). The flower-stand is shown here as an example, for it combines the diversity of form characteristic of Germany in the 1870s with the vigorous swirling line of art nouveau. Height 82.4 cm, diameter 60 cm. Bavarian National Museum, Munich. Inventory no. SW 184.

tendency to fantastic multiplication of the line is found in linear art that both meet at many points. We are literally overwhelmed with new forms which have become indescribably richer in a few years. Before, we had no idea what wealth of creativity we carried slumbering inside us.

"The new art, then, has different directions which are followed simultaneously by different people: it is constructive on the one hand and sensitive on the other. It does not correspond to the head and heart of a single man and therefore has no king or dictator. Because of its diversity, it may dissolve and fall to pieces before it reaches full maturity, if the circle of creators in which people make friends with each other, is not closed."[4]

In the search for new contents for applied art at the turn of the century, Richard Riemerschmid concerned himself with new motifs. With him, the flowers and stems of plants become form without ornament. With the rhythmical repeated surface pattern which either limits or appears to be endlessly continued, he contributes to the modern foundations of a twentieth-century

system of ornament – thus there are rhythmic lozenge shapes, transverse rows of triangular trees and calyxes which are spiritually related to the Japanese *kakemono* system.

Structurally oriented art nouveau works with pictorial signs, whose unity and uniformity are achieved by line. As a result, a clearing of space in the sense of corporeal rounding can arise on the one hand and models in "ornamentalized nature" are chosen. On the other hand, the line, which now emerges more autonomously, can also be used as a structural element for furniture. "Signs" are also used for the structure of vessel shapes which are adopted from nature's repertoire. The vegetable quality of the fruit form, the centralizing, arranging principle of the plant stem is adopted in a constructive linear system which often exhibits the character of the plant and nothing more (ill. 146). The simplification of line in art nouveau made it adaptable. This applies to ornament insofar as it is no longer made up of small details as in the early art nouveau period, but the reduction of the linear effects an extension of, and in, the surface. From this, bentwood furniture draws an aesthetic effect. The silhouette-like form of the line, the "bentwood line", encloses a surface in which an inner surface, a negative ground as it were, simultaneously arises (ills. 318, 319). The linear surrounding shows the construction of bentwood furniture in the silhouette in which the originally natural form shows through. The stylized, springy tense elements of the bentwood are still subject to vegetative bending lines, but in a purified version – they are, without adornment, determined by the highest utility. This "purified version" can be observed even more strongly in cabinet-made furniture, especially in the designs of Richard Riemerschmid, Bruno Paul and Josef Hoffmann and his circle. All these artists go to work differently and they also design small works of art which sometimes correspond to this same idea. They show the increased precision of strongly expressive lines which often lead from the abstracting surface pattern to the cube (ills. 319, 359, 383, 389, 393 and 412).

European furniture of the art nouveau perod differs from country to country. England is considered to be the model for a rectilinear functional direction which increased in Scotland to a marked vertical and horizontal "plank" style see p. 121). This conception follows the Viennese Secession style which forms an international centre in the Wiener Werkstätte around 1900. Germany developed furniture constructions aimed at serial production. For art nouveau furniture, Germany is looked on as the meeting-point of national styles, in which the constructive elements from England, the formal details from France, symbolic tendencies of Spanish Gaudiana (works by Gaudi or in his style), block-like outlines from Scandinavia and modern-style analogies from Holland combine into a successful synthesis which contains independent elements and for years remained strong enough to introduce the early *Werkbund* ideas in 1907.

The reform of European art furniture in the 19th century came from England. Handicrafts are the creative base of art. William Morris helped to realize these ideas. He founded the firm of Morris, Marshall and Faulkner which encouraged and directed handicrafts in England from 1861. Equally active was the Arts and Crafts Exhibition Society. The items of furniture are mostly constructed of frames and upholstery which stand between angular corner rods. The rectilinear conclusion of the thin cornice is lightly profiled, large forged fittings characterize the silhouette of the chest furniture. The architects Mackmurdo and Baillie Scott (p. 121) designed very restrained but extremely practical furniture.

An individual note which had a great effect on Europe was struck by Scottish art nouveau furniture.

The Glasgow school was dominant, with the architect Charles Rennie Mackintosh (1868-1928, ills. 272, 274), Herbert McNair and the McDonald sisters. Later Talwin Morris and E.A. Taylor joined the circle. Mackintosh gave his furniture a clear articulation, the visible high side-rails emphasized, the rush seat inserted between them (ill. 274). The loadbearing parts find support

232 The brothers Thonet, wash-stands, detail from Thonet catalogue 10053. The photograph shows the branch-like construction of the supports, which correspond to specific natural models in the plant kingdom. Photograph after Giovanna Massobrio, *Casa Thonet,* Rome, 1980, p. 123 *et seq.*

233 Karl Blossfeldt, photograph, *c.* 1900–06, after the stem of the Indian balsam, *Impatiens glandulifera.* Stem and ramification lifesize.

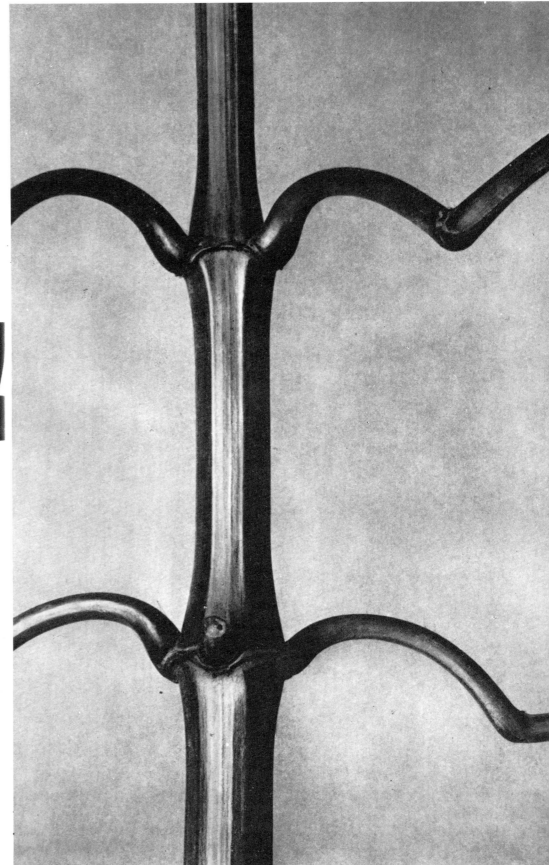

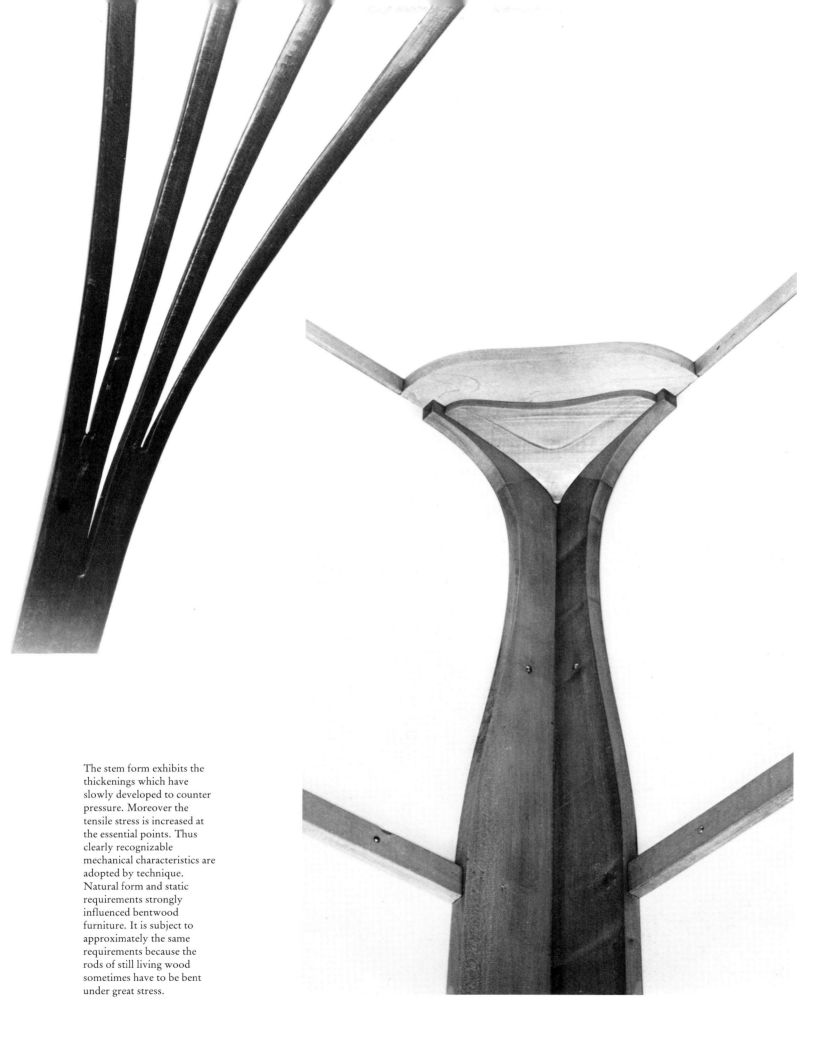

234 The brothers Thonet, detail of the back of the chair shown below. It consists of branch-like divisions which clearly show the clefts, the central one being deeper than the two side ones. This leads to a more marked curving of the outer branch-like elements. Through the clustering below and the spreading out above a permanent equilibrium arises, because the natural form is used to counter pressure and tension.

235 Henry van de Velde, corner bracket in a living-room, *c.* 1904, *Steinholz* (an artificial wood made of sawdust and chemicals) matted and polished. 325 x 35 cm. The swelling shape exhibits the upward striving vigour of the natural form. Supporting elements of props and stays are supplied by side-shoots and superimposed boards. Van de Velde had made a close study of the linear principle of plant growth. From a residence in Hamburg-Blankenese.

236 The brothers Thonet, beechwood chair, stained dark brown, matt. Height 93.2 cm, width 57 cm, height of seat 45 cm. Private collection, Vienna (see also detail).

The stem form exhibits the thickenings which have slowly developed to counter pressure. Moreover the tensile stress is increased at the essential points. Thus clearly recognizable mechanical characteristics are adopted by technique. Natural form and static requirements strongly influenced bentwood furniture. It is subject to approximately the same requirements because the rods of still living wood sometimes have to be bent under great stress.

in the vertical struts which connect the frame and the plate between. The harmony of the dimensions of the bearing struts in Mackintosh's furniture is striking. The colour varies between dead black and white. He won no recognition in Scotland with his fireside chairs developed on steep lines, but he was widely acclaimed in Europe. The covering material for the furniture, mostly woven by Margaret (1865-1933) and Frances (1874-1921) McDonald, who had carefully studied Japanese *kakemono* or emblem art and especially *katagami* (coloured patterns), were works of art in themselves. The weblike ornament, with its incisive individual forms, was asymmetrically or symmetrically embroidered, woven or painted. The colour constellation in which the wood was prepared, matt violet, cyclamen, lime green, some yellow and alabaster white, was important. In addition to these heraldic colours with their Far Eastern influence, the impressive high-backed throne-shaped chair (ill. 272) was obligatorily accompanied by a little pedestal table which was placed next to the chair. On it stood precious ornamental vases.

British art preferred less floral decoration on furniture than the French art nouveau movement. Arthur Heygate Mackmurdo (1851-1942) gave powerful impulses to the constructive stylistic phase, and in general in England the "Yachting Style" and "Liberty Style" were influenced by furniture designers. They include Charles F. Voysey (1857-1941), E.W. Godwin (1838-86), George Walton (1867-1933), M.H. Baillie Scott (1865-1945), Ambrose Heal (1872–1959), Ernest Gimson (1864-1920) and others. Riemerschmid's work is especially characteristic of the constructive linear structure of furniture. Hermann Obrist wrote about him: "Beside the impulse of pleasing force, the attractive harmony, the relations and lines... we find the following qualities in his works: clarity, constructive logical reason, a simplicity at times going to the limits of sobriety, yet never overstepping them, but in spite of that we also find a feeling for a certain enjoyable comfort."[5]

Richard Riemerschmid (1868-1957), a native of Munich, represented, among German art nouveau architects, a logical style in his development. His pieces of furniture between 1895 and 1905 point the way for the next generation of artists. They are characterized by a clear line, functional usefulness and well thought-out colour schemes, as well as personally designed textile coverings. The artist did not work solely as an interior decorator, he was also town planner, textile designer and painter. In 1897, together with Bruno Paul and Bernhard Pankok, he was a founding member of the *Vereinigten Werkstätten für Kunst im Handwerk* (United Artistic Handicraft Studios) in Munich. In 1900 he displayed a room at the Universal Exhibition in Paris. His design for the Munich Kammerspiele concert hall (1901) was exemplary. From 1912 to 1924 he was head of the School of Arts and Crafts in Munich and in 1926 Director of the Werkschule at Cologne.

Riemerschmid's furniture is mostly made of light-coloured woods. The original natural colour of oak, walnut and yew is important. The feeling for doing justice to the material grows with constructional experience. Graining as used by Riemerschmid was made an essential part of the decoration and the static starting-points in the area of the side-rails and in the rod-and-frame layouts are structurally emphasized. This is achieved both by struts and by strengthening the starting-points (ills. 258, 259). Riemerschmid understood how to lead the important elements of the piece of furniture, with the technically necessary factors, to an artistic statement.

The large mirror (ill. 256) shows that formal and technically successful bracing which is indispensable for containing the glass of the mirror. Table-like structure and plane mirror surface are harmonically combined in a forward and backward movement. Riemerschmid produced this piece as early as 1898; in the same year he achieved a solution that was unique for the period with his writing-desk group (p. 127), consisting of chair, desk and occasional table. The formation is distinct, the functionality advanced. In another direction, Charles Rennie Mackintosh

237 Japanese painting instruction book (block book), *c.* 1850. Design for kimono pattern, printed in seven colours. Published in Tokyo. 25 x 18.3 cm. Private collection. An example of the erupting, swirling Japanese line which was obligatory for art nouveau.

developed, for his rooms in Windyhill at Kilmacolm, a style which was a synthesis of Japanese wall articulation and western furnishing. This difficult undertaking consisted in fitting such items as chest, bench, table and chair in their volumes into the wall. Mackintosh achieves his goal not by building cupboards into the walls as the Japanese do, but by placing them parallel to and touching the walls – in other words, the pieces of furniture are fixed in position yet always referred to the background. The association is further supported by white wall surfaces and dark vertical and horizontal frieze-like divisions by posts and inlaid stripes.

Gustav Klimt also followed this experiment, in that he fashioned the anteroom to his studio in the "Japonisme" Secession style. A decisive point is the Japanese paintings which are composed into a large right-angle by their framing and hanging. Plank-like seats with bar divisions, designed by Josef Hoffmann, are geometrically displayed and are parallel to the wall in relation to the large cupboard.

There was a great deal of interest in Japanese domestic interiors. Nevertheless, the simplified geometric house style as developed by Adolf Loos (1870-1933) also required new furniture. Loos had got to know the architecture of Frank Lloyd Wright during his study trips to Chicago, Philadelphia and New York and he drew special conclusions from it, as the planning of the Dr Beer villa on Lac Leman makes clear. But mainly the Wiener Werkstätte arrived at a synthesis, which transferred the character and atmosphere of the Japanese house into a three-dimensional furniture programme. The exchangeability of single pieces of furniture and whole series or programmes was developed by standardization after a modular system, analogously to influences from Japanese wall division and its standardizations.

238 August Endell, two chairs, shield-shaped upholstered back, 1896. Elm, cover fabric designed by R. Riemerschmid. Height 94 cm, width 45 cm, depth 45 cm. Bavarian National Museum, Munich. Inventory no. SW 111.

239 Occasional table in matt elm, 1896. Three-legged with three-sided incurved top and intermediate shelf in the form of a stretched animal skin. Legs terminate in flammulate decoration. Height 67.5 cm, diameter 55.5 cm. Bavarian National Museum, Munich. Inventory no. SW 111.

The two chairs by Endell with upholstery by Richard Riemerschmid have square seats with rounded corners. The legs and seat correspond to a Chinese Ting of the Huai style (ill. 158). The ornamental carving at the end of the arm rests of the desk chair is reminiscent of spongy bone capsules, and the top rail thickenings have grown into cartilage. Endell and Obrist were both concerned with associations; the latter made detailed comments on the above-mentioned themes. Altogether, the middle 1890s were a fruitful period for August Endell the author, who reconciled the sectarian currents of the time, but did not, like Hermann Obrist, develop a practical programme.

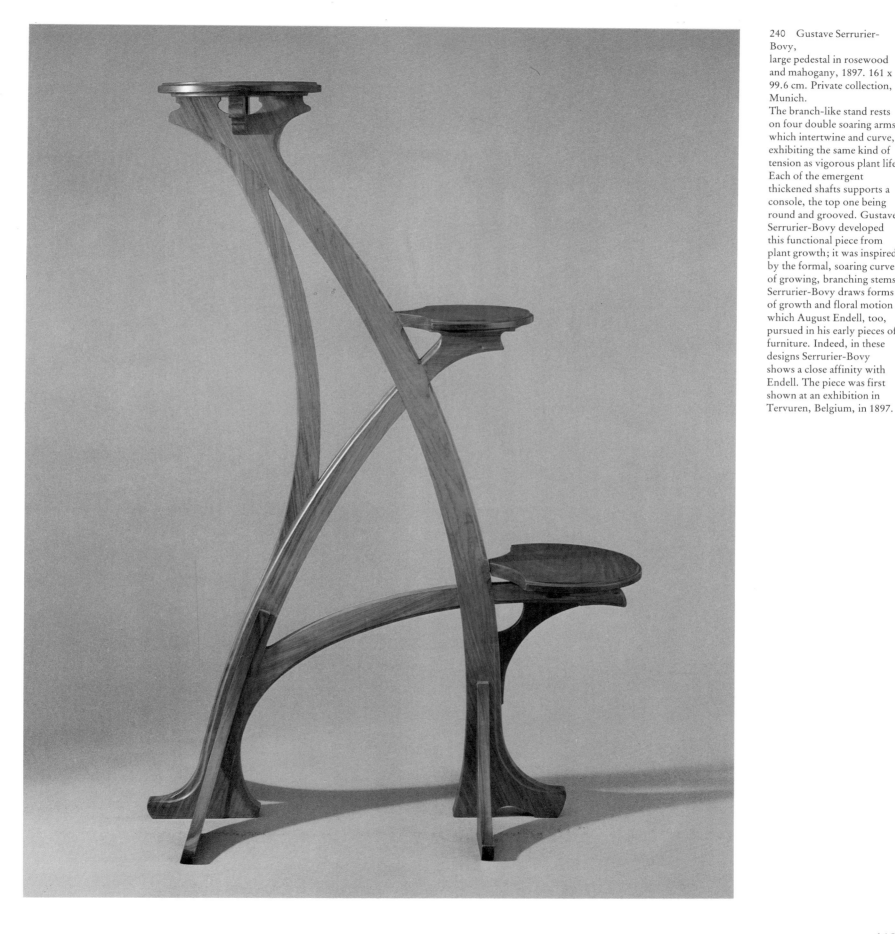

240 Gustave Serrurier-Bovy,
large pedestal in rosewood and mahogany, 1897. 161 x 99.6 cm. Private collection, Munich.

The branch-like stand rests on four double soaring arms which intertwine and curve, exhibiting the same kind of tension as vigorous plant life. Each of the emergent thickened shafts supports a console, the top one being round and grooved. Gustave Serrurier-Bovy developed this functional piece from plant growth; it was inspired by the formal, soaring curves of growing, branching stems. Serrurier-Bovy draws forms of growth and floral motion which August Endell, too, pursued in his early pieces of furniture. Indeed, in these designs Serrurier-Bovy shows a close affinity with Endell. The piece was first shown at an exhibition in Tervuren, Belgium, in 1897.

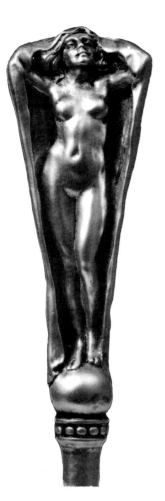

If art nouveau is to be designated as the "glassy period" and as an international style, because of the multiplicity of forms and methods of working, the existing tradition of their native lands takes the foreground in the work of silversmiths and designers. In England, the land of table silver, Christopher Dresser (1834–1904) was able to anticipate the constructional direction of art nouveau as early as 1880, because the Queen Anne period already preferred simple vessels going back to stereometric forms. The silver of Charles Louis Tiffany & Co., New York, committed itself to 16th-century European forms with Mannerist influence, and France favoured baroque variations. In Germany the most varied stylistic tendencies were cultivated. Every kind of variation is represented from medieval silver tankards to the Neo-Byzantinism of Ernst Riegel. Peter Behrens, Joseph Olbrich and Otto Eckmann followed new paths, which were raised to an impressive peak of construction by Henry van de Velde. The Wiener Werkstätte, with Adolf Loos, Josef Hoffmann and Koloman Moser, was a centre of Secession art in Vienna. It formed a close relationship with the Dutch school of Jan Eisenloeffel (1876–1957), and the Dutch in turn linked up with the English school.

246   Charles Robert Ashbee,
detail of ladle on opposite page.

247   Bowl (previously attributed to Kolo Moser), Vienna, c. 1900. Chased polished copper, tapering conically with flat, slightly convex rim. Height 7.5 cm, diameter 11.2 cm. Private collection, Vienna.

248   Charles Robert Ashbee,
hotplate with cover, c. 1900–06. Hammered, electroplated white metal, bell-shaped cover with amethyst knob, dish with double base and reservoir. Height 16.2 cm, diameter 24 cm. Guild of Handicraft, London. Private collection, Munich.

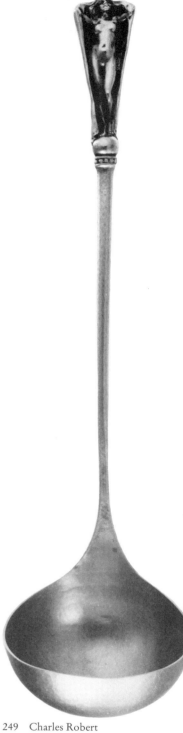

249 Charles Robert
Ashbee,
bowl with convex foot, wide
shaft in the form of openwork
flower stems and leaves, tall
cup projecting at the lip with
a floral frieze running round
it, convex lid with upstanding
knob inlaid with mother of
pearl. Accompanied by
massive ladle, the handle of
which terminates in a female
nude in plastically articulated
relief. Height 36.8 cm,
diameter of bowl 24 cm, of
base 22.3 cm. Ladle 36.5 cm.
Collection Frank Jaeger,
Munich.

Without the English Liberty style, even the art of the Wiener Werkstätte would have taken a different course. Arthur L. Liberty (born 13 August 1843 at Chesham, died 2 May 1917 at Great Missenden) was a textile merchant in London. Starting in 1875 he imported oriental, mainly Japanese, materials and set up his own textile firm. In 1901 W.R. Haseler and A.L. Liberty founded the firm of Liberty & Co. (Cymric) Ltd. As early as 1899 Arthur Liberty commissioned a series of designs which were sold under the name "Cymric" by jewellers and silversmiths. From 1894 the firm was included in the commercial register for the sale of silverware. The following firms and independent silversmiths worked for Liberty & Co.: W.R. Haseler, Oliver Baker, A.H. Jones, Bernard Cuzner, Reginald Rex, Arthur Gaskin (Birmingham School of Art) and Archibald Knox, Jessie M. King and Rex Silver (Glasgow School).

250 Charles Robert Ashbee,
butter knife, chased silver with green agate, c. 1901. Handle in the form of a silver basket containing a ball. Marked "Guild of Handicraft, London". 15.9 cm. Bavarian National Museum, Munich. Inventory no. SW 89.

251 Shallow chased silver bowl of English design, c. 1901–02, set with opals on the upper edge. Base: bluish-green champlevé enamel, 4.2 x 15 cm. Execution probably by the Guild of Handicraft. Collection Frank Jaeger, Munich.

One of the most important designers of church and table silver was the English architect Charles Robert Ashbee (1863–1942). He founded the Guild of Handicraft in London and designed silver vessels of graceful structure with the simplest of basic forms and widespread handles. The delicately composed semi-precious stone ornament is functionally adapted to the static points. The stones are the animating eyes, so to speak, of the silver body (ill. 253). The beautifully curved surfaces are fashioned with such subtlety that the hammer blows might merely have touched them. The same manner of working was adopted by Bernard Cuzner, who subjected his vessel forms to stereometric bodies, a conception which anticipates the ideas of the Werkbund.

252 (*Opposite*)
Bernard Cuzner, sugar bowl, *c.* 1898. Chased silver, gilded inside, two opals. Marked on base with hallmark and horseshoe. 8 x 12.5 cm. Milk jug, *c.* 1898. Chased silver, gilded inside, two opals. Marked on base with hallmark and horseshoe. 16.5 x 5.3 cm. Bavarian National Museum, Munich. Inventory nos. SW 85, 83.

253 (*Opposite, below*)
Charles Robert Ashbee, bowhl with two wide, looped handles, *c.* 1905. Chased silver with green agates. Marked on base "G. of H. London". Height 6.5 cm, diameter 11 cm, width 27.8 cm. Bavarian National Museum, Munich. Inventory no. SW 86.

254 Charles Robert Ashbee, ornamental goblet (*above, detail of lid and knob*), 1901. Chased silver, champlevé and yellowish moonstones. Decoration: swimming fish. Marked under foot, "G. of H. Ltd." 18.5 cm. Bavarian National Museum, Munich. Inventory no. SW 80.

255 Richard Riemerschmid or Ernst Riegel, ornamental goblet with conical shaft, cup flat mounting, bell-shaped foot, and four lateral handles under the cup. Lid with baluster holding a spherical agate. Decoration: spiral patterns. 19.8 x 12.5 cm. Collection Frank Jaeger, Munich.

256 Richard Riemerschmid, dressing-table with mirror, 1898, natural walnut. 192 x 69 cm. Bavarian National Museum., Inventory no. SW 123.

257 Richard Riemerschmid, brass table-lamp with three bulbs, c. 1900. Pointed, mushroom-shaped metal shade above thin incurved support. 35.5 cm. Executed by Dresden Handicraft Studios (Dresdner Werkstätten für Handwerk). Württenberg, Landesmuseum, Stuttgart.

258 W. Nerdinger, music-room chair with diagonal struts, c. 1898–9. Height 78.5 cm, width 49 cm, depth 48 cm. Executed by Vereinigte Werkstätten. Private collection, Munich.
The designs of Richard Riemerschmid clearly show that they favoured natural models, but the outwardly floral appearance is no longer dominant; instead we find clearly drawn contours and curved lines intruding into the surface, which favour an abstract pattern. The leading lines of the furniture silhouette often suggest a taut feather or the stem of a plant, which is intended to be more a sign than a decoration. The vegetable, curving line of the plant is constrained by its constructional element and from this the chair acquires its functional significance.

126

259 Richard
Riemerschmid,
desk and occasional table,
1898. Desk height 92 cm,
length 140 cm, depth 93 cm.
Natural walnut, brass handles
and key. Bavarian National
Museum, Munich. Inventory
nos. SW 109, 106, 108, 102.

260 Chair: height 77 cm,
seat width 43.5 cm, depth 48
cm. Elm; covering, blue and
white calyxes. Occasional
table natural walnut. Height
77 cm, top 48 x 48 cm. Table
lamp. L.C. Tiffany. Bavarian
National Museum, Munich.
Inventory nos. 109, 106, 108,
102.

261 Richard
Riemerschmid,
candlestick, c. 1898. Flat
stand, asymmetrically placed
socket with handle issuing
from it and merging with the
outer edge. Chased brass, 8.5
x 21.2 cm. Bavarian National
Museum, Munich. Inventory
no. SW 100.

262 Hermann Obrist, three-legged flower-stand internally braced, *c.* 1898. Below the upper edge, wrought-iron ornaments forged and riveted. Decoration: leaf and flower forms. 106 x 37.8 cm. Kenneth Barlow, Decorative Arts, Munich.

263 Josef Maria Olbrich (attributed), flower-stand, *c.* 1900. On a four-legged base with cross-struts and ring mounting rises a brass container which is also connected with a ring beneath by vertical supports. Iron and brass. 75.8 x 38 cm. Private collection, Vienna.

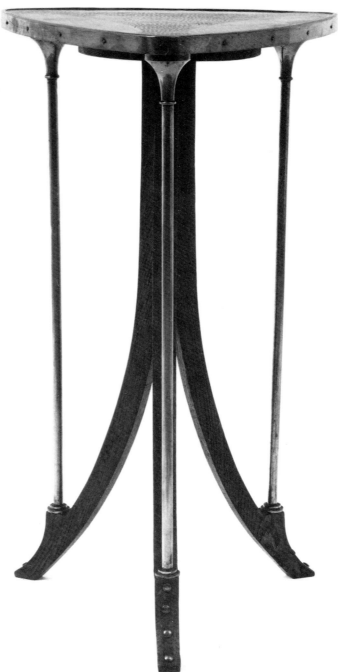

264 Hans Ofner (attributed), occasional table, *c.* 1905, with brass base on six double brass supports decorated with spheres. The outward-bent silver-plated brass rods hold a hexagonal top with a glass inlay and brass surround. 79 cm. Mark on foot "ARGENTOR CX"; this is the Argentorwerke of Vienna, founded in 1887. Information from Dr G. Woertel, Munich. Private collection, Munich.

265 Richard Riemerschmid, small brass-topped table, *c.* 1900, with three legs and brass struts. Stained walnut. Made for Liberty & Co., London. 78.3 x 41.5 cm. Brass nails near the bottom of the wooden feet. Bavarian National Museum. Inventory no. SW 116.

266 Richard
Riemerschmid,
decorative fabrics, *c.* 1900,
linen and cotton or artificial
silk. Decoration: triangular
shrubs in transverse rows in
yellow and olive on white;
triangular shrubs in
transverse rows in blue and
olive on white; tendrils and
flowers in transverse rows in
black and yellow on
brownish blue; calyxes on
slender candelabra stems in
red on blue; lozenge pattern
in blue on white, framed in
olive; pattern of up-turned
squares on blue, framed in
olive. Made for the Dresdner
Werkstätten für
Handwerkskunst (later
Deutsche Werkstätten).
Bavarian National Museum,
Munich. Inventory nos. SW
186 a-f.

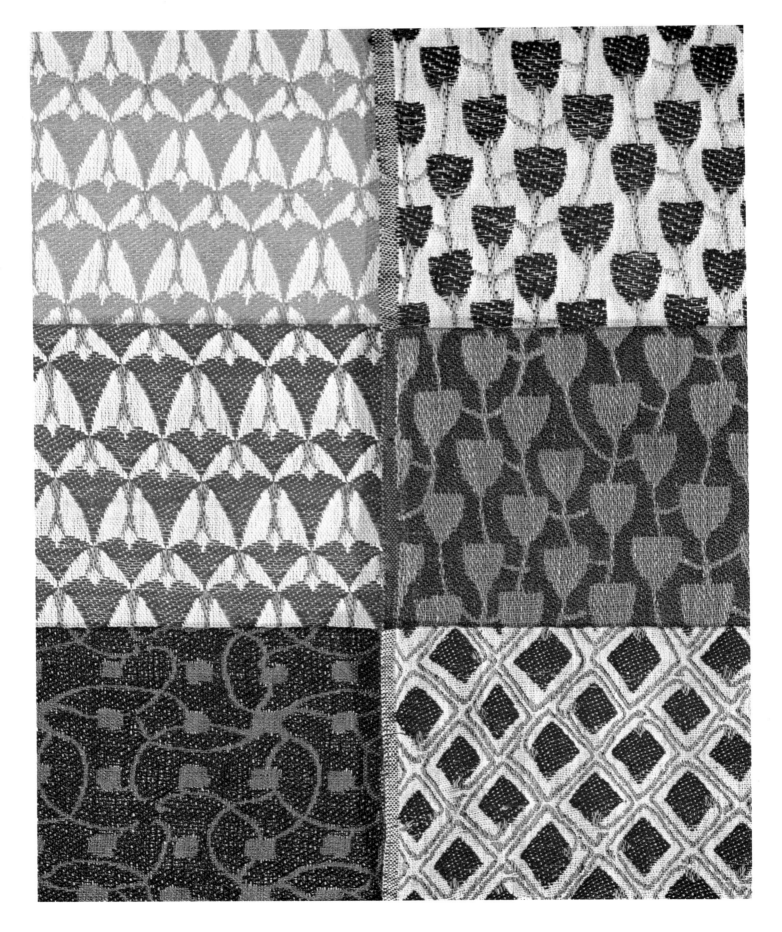

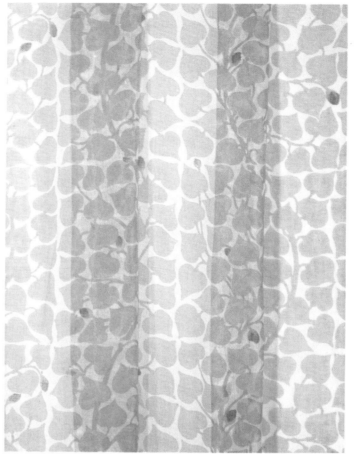

267 Josef Hoffmann, decorative fabric for the Wiener Werkstätte (detail of a remnant). Abstract mushroom pattern with decorative division into squares. Silk rep and cotton. 36.5 x 72.2 cm. Private collection, Vienna.

268 Richard Riemerschmid, curtain material. Linden leaves on branches in golden-yellow, violet and white. Cotton voile. 130 x 215 cm. Bavarian National Museum, Munich. Inventory no. 186.

269 Otto Eckmann (design), 1897, cotton and linen. Decoration: stylized water-lilies above bands of waves in orange, green and yellow. 175 x 130 cm. Bavarian National Museum, Munich. Inventory no. SW 185.

270 Otto Eckmann (design), curtain material (detail), with decoration of water-lilies, 1902–04. Voile, matt orange, green, yellow. Bavarian National Museum, Munich. Inventory no. SW 188.

131

271 I.S. Henry,
English armchair, *c.* 1895.
Massive polished mahogany,
red leather, ornamental studs.
Highly developed back in the
manner of the Scottish
fireside chair with decoration
of stylized lilies in shallow
relief. Rear legs curved, front
legs tapering below with
slightly swollen extremities.
Height 122 cm, width 57 cm,
depth of seat 56.2
cm. Austrian Museum of
Applied Art. Inventory no.
H. 1260.

272 Charles Rennie
Mackintosh, chair with high
back, *c.* 1900. Oval cross-
piece at head height. Stained
oak. Height 137.6 cm, width
49.6 cm, depth of seat 43.6
cm. Private collection,
Munich.

273 Josef Maria Olbrich,
armchair, matt-finished
sycamore wood. High back
divided by slender uprights,
head rest slightly curved, as
are the arm rests; trapezoidal
seat broadening out towards
the front and covered with the
original material; swelling at
bottom of legs. From the
house of the Viennese actress
Maria Wölzl. Execution:
Josef Niedermoser. Height
110 cm, width 58 cm, depth
of seat 53.2 cm. Austrian
Museum of Applied Art,
Vienna.
The chair forms all show the
high backs taken from Anglo-
American furniture. The
fireside chair was the model.
The back was protected from
cold by an overhanging
cover. The predominant
feature is the homogeneity of
the chair seen from the front,
the constructive formation by
austere right-angled
articulation of top rails and
supporting elements. The
constructive treatment is
visible, because the struts in
the top rail area are always
right-angled or square.

That offered considerable advantages when it came to mortise and tenon joints. The foot rods or struts were used structurally by Mackintosh. Stability, usefulness and practicality were significant features of nineteenth-century colonial furniture in New England, which particularly stimulated Mackintosh.

274   Charles Rennie Mackintosh, ladder-back chair, c. 1899–1901. Legs with cross-struts, slightly trapezoid seat. High vertical back with seven cross-bars. Oak, stained black. Height 104.5 cm, width 45 cm, depth 42.5 cm. Private collection, Munich.

275 Archibald Knox,
Liberty vase with three stems
formed into handles.
Decoration in low relief,
alpine violets on the upper
edge, lower part stamped.
Cast polished pewter, in
shape like a winged projectile.
Bavarian National Museum,
Munich. Inventory no. SW
141.

276 School of Arts and
Crafts, Vienna, vase on
circular base with recessed
foot, c. 1905. Body also
recessed, with four vertical
divisions. Glazed stoneware.
19.2 x 24 cm. Private
collection, Vienna.

277 Johann Julius
Scharvogel, vase with three
twisted handles, c. 1902.
Stoneware with two layers of
glaze, whitish-yellow on
black (under-glaze after
Japanese model). Under the
base: distinctive coat of arms,
workshop shield, and "J.J.
Scharvogel, München". 19.3
x 9.2 cm (diameter of base).
Bavarian National Museum,
Munich. Inventory no SW
61.

influenced the shapes of artistic products. Constructional methods which were mainly adopted from the engineering world develop out of the floral elements. This industrial form was to have an alienating effect on all materials, although the technical object was partly connected with floral models. The floral element led to technical usefulness. The stereometric bodies in cylindrical form show the clarity that was aimed at. There are also forms resembling projectiles, as manufactured by the firm of Kaiserzinn, around 1902. Emphasis on constructive functional means began. Side struts are still planted against the vessel wall. Angular handles extend root-like from the base, to merge comparatively deep below the edge of the vessel. Slanting struts convey – despite vestigial hints of plant origin – the spiral motion of a screw thread. The same kind of element is repeatedly demonstrable in creative art at the turn of the century. The silver lamps of Henry van de Velde and Karl Koepping's glasses owe their formal effect to the same assumptions which acquire intensity depending on the material. Further development is exemplified by a terracotta vessel by Julius Scharvogel (1854–1938). Here all the vegetable conceptions are excluded. Clear construction with concise handles twisting from the shoulder to the edge suggest a technical apparatus rather than a flower vase. Also the finely sprinkled hard gloss glazes contribute to the conception of a screwhead or a threaded nut. Through the screw-like handles the vessel acquires a dynamic force which the original spiral movement round the middle makes symbolically clear.

278 Archibald Knox, tobacco jar, *c.* 1904. Cast polished pewter. Decoration: encircling flower and leaf motif. Stamp on the bottom "Tudric 0194". 11.5 x 10.8 cm. Bavarian National Museum, Munich. Inventory no. SW 87.

279 Peter Behrens, crystal jar in pewter mounting in the form of a bonbonnière. Silver-plated pewter, the lower edge running inwards on three rods which join the upper metal edge. The three-part handle consists of stem structures which arch over the flat surface of the lid. 13.2 x 14.6 cm. Private collection, Munich.
It is striking how technical and industrial models

280 Henry Clemens van de Velde, oval tray with projecting ivory handles and an oval opening, *c.* 1904. Edge sloping inwards. Silver and ivory. 64.5 x 42.8 cm. Execution: Theodor Müller, Weimar. Punched with half-moon and crown and Van de Velde sign. Kenneth Barlow, Decorative Arts, Munich.

281 Henry Clemens van de Velde, plate with four irregular interruptions, curved edge, edge sloping inwards, *c.* 1905–06. Silver 800. 56 x 32 cm. Punched with "Theodor Müller" and Van de Velde sign and no. 1074. Execution: Theodor Müller, Weimar. Kenneth Barlow, Decorative Arts, Munich.

282 Henry Clemens van de Velde, jardinière rising in a boat shape from an oval vase, bellied wall, curved rim turning into two lateral lugs, silver 875. 15 x 44 cm. Punched with "Theodor Müller", half-moon and Van de Velde sign. Execution: Theodor Müller, Weimar. Kenneth Barlow, Decorative Arts, Munich.

283 Henry Clemens van de Velde, round plate on circular base. Edge curving slightly outwards, as handles four internal curves with edge sloping inwards. Centre engraved with monogram. Silver 925. 30.5 cm. Punched "Theodor Müller", half-moon and crown and Van de Velde sign. Execution: Theodor Müller, Weimar. Kenneth Barlow, Decorative Arts, Munich.

284 Porcelain with under-glaze painting, *c.* 1905. Execution by the Royal Porcelain Manufactory, Meissen. Bavarian National Museum, Munich. Inventory nos. SW 45–51.

137

285 Henry Clemens van de Velde, upholstered mahogany chair, fan-shaped back, slightly curved legs, *c.* 1895. Height 74.5 cm, width 60 cm, depth 43 cm. Bavarian National Museum. Inventory no. SW 1212.

286 Henry Clemens van de Velde, press with five drawers and shelf, two side-pieces and top, in white lacquered beech. Height 134 cm, width 59.2 cm, depth 38.5 cm. Knut Günther, Frankfurt, London and New York.
The supporting legs in their significant arching together with the casing show the constructive stresses which give the piece its lightness. The simple, clear articulation has a cleanly functional line which gives expression to the idea of usefulness.

287 Henry Clemens van de Velde, occasional table, from the Hohe Pappeln villa, Weimar, 1907. White lacquered beech. Height 60.5 cm, width 69.2 cm, depth 60.4 cm. Knut Günther, Frankfurt, London and New York.
The essential and static points of departure are emphasized. The three legs carry over into a light supporting structure, so that the triangular top, together with the struts that are deliberately left visible, emphasizes the functional and structural elements.

288 Henry Clemens van de Velde, oak chair, c. 1903. 96.2 x 46 cm. Model from the Nietzsche archives. Kenneth Barlow, Decorative Arts, Munich.

289 Deutsche Silberwerkstätte (Berlin). Fruit bowl on four feet with zigzag ornament, c. 1904. Double bowl, the upper one held by four pilasters. The circular bowl has floral cloisonné ornamentation on the outer wall. Punched on foot: claw, 800 and distinctive sign. Silver, 18.3 x 23 cm. Collection Frank Jaeger, Munich.

290 Jan Eisenloeffel, teapot, c. 1910. Flat base, bellied body, projecting spout and flattish lid, handle with tubular wrapping, circular ornamentation in white opaque enamel below the knob on the lid. Rim of lid with bead moulding; polished silver. Execution: Cornelius Begeer Co., Utrecht. Sign of designer and master stamp "CB" on five-pointed star. Height 10.7 cm, width with spout 18.2 cm. Collection Frank Jaeger, Munich.

291 Jan Eisenloeffel, cream jug in rather similar form, with bead moulding on the lip, and handle at the side, c. 1910. Height 4.4 cm, diameter 7.6 cm, diameter with handle and spout 12.2 cm. Collection Frank Jaeger, Munich.

The bodies of Jan Eisenloeffel's pieces acquired an austerity which Christopher Dresser had already begun in England in 1877. Clear oval and spherical forms were now the points of departure for the "restrained" form. The vessel types of the Chinese Sung and Persian Nishapur periods provided the necessary stimuli. The newly created vessels, the most significant of which were the work of silversmiths, no longer needed ornamental accessories or even pictorial decoration. Admittedly, Eisenloeffel still emphasizes the central motif with opaque enamel inlays, but they are of a purely constructional nature. He generally supplies the centralizing point under the knob with an ornamental motif. He renounces ornamental accessories on the actual body of the vessel, which has now achieved that surface tension which gave new significance to the slogan "Form without ornament". Consequently, Eisenloeffel's forms with their stereometric effect no longer need any decoration. Eisenloeffel uses the expression of the volume of the vessel in a tactile surface which determines the genuine utility of the object.

the highest degree. The artist has almost found the abstract material form of expression which manifests itself formally and ceremonially and appears unusual and individual. This reality may mean the greatest victory of the modern artistic discipline and forms the fourth phase in his ascending line of development which brings him to Berlin to concern himself with the problems of modern industry. The artist is attached to AEG in Berlin to give modern electrical appliances, light fittings, architectural elements and other degenerate functional forms devoid of any artistic impulse, the sound typical form which they require as an objective artistic conception. This appointment is a sign that the development of the modern movement stands at a turning-point after the past decade, and collaborates in the real task of the century in industry which essentially determines the cultural image of our day."

292   Peter Behrens, electric kettle on insulating base, octagonal body, bead moulding slanting inward on the shoulder, round lid and black knob, tubular handle with wickerwork, angular with rounded edges, polished white metal. Height (with handle) 23 cm, width 20,5 cm. Distinctive coat of arms on base. Execution: AEG, Berlin. Private collection, Munich.

293   Peter Behrens, brass teapot with tubular wickerwork handle, wooden knob and hammered striped decoration, c. 1907–10. The flat base supports a strongly curved body with a short spout adapted to the curvature of the body. On one side the electric plug. The lid, adapted to the curvature, has a black wooden knob. The handle is held by powerful hinges which emphasize the functional system. Execution: AEG, Berlin. Marked under the base with a distinctive coat of arms and "3602, 27". Height 23 cm. with handle. Private collection, Munich.

Joseph August Lux wrote in *Das Neue Kunstgewerbe,* 1908, p. 171: "On the way to abstraction, Peter Behrens has reached a refined regularity after his confused beginnings. This artist, who is strong, logical and consistent in his thinking, has made tremendous progress in the course of the last ten years. Now he leaves even the Viennese behind, after receiving from them what was needed to continue in his prescribed path. He himself must have had a good idea of the goal which his skill achieved, by which I do not mean his technical, empirical and practical skill, but his ability as an artistic intellect. The powerful rhythm of the simplest spatial elements which can be firmly placed in a geometric equation, which distinguishes the Mackintosh group in Glasgow and returns individually and freshly minted in the Viennese circle, is a perception now also possessed by Behrens, who consciously strives for visual harmony; by the refinement of simplicity it produces a more impressive effect than by overloading with ornamental elements, baroque notions and decorative whimsy. Again and again it is a beginning and a point of departure, like everything simple, as it can simultaneously be a sign of maturity, a clarification, being cured of ornamental confusion, a revelation of new unusual beauty and a final goal. Extremes come into contact; what was history and the zenith of past art appears again as the most modern criterion of production struggling to achieve symmetry. The artist spiritualizes his individualistic manner until it becomes a kind of generally accepted form of expression, like that classical one which is simultaneously material in

294   Jan Eisenloeffel, coffee-pot, cream jug and sugar basin in chased brass, *c.* 1902. Coffee-pot 22.5 cm. Private collection, Munich.

295   Jan Eisenloeffel, teapot with four-legged spirit heater, *c.* 1902. Conical body with long projecting spout, lid with black wooden knob. 30.5 x 36 cm. Private collection, Munich.

143

296   Otto Wagner,
lamp from the waiting-room
of a railway station in Vienna,
c. 1896–7. Cast white metal
and pressed glass. Pear-
shaped body with traditional
classical ornament; simplified
shape in accordance with the
technical objective. 70.2 x 30
cm. Private collection,
Vienna.

297   Josef Hoffmann,
coal scuttle with shovel, *c.*
1905. Blackened tin-plate
with bronze handle and
knob, iron shovel with
wooden handle. Height 55.2
cm, width 36.5 cm, depth
45.5 cm. Private collection,
Vienna.

298 Adolf Loos, table lamp, *c.* 1900. Brass and copper with glass hangings, hammered metal shade. Execution J. Helg (?). 50.2 x 32 cm. Private collection, Vienna.

Everyday appliances developed rapidly between 1896 and 1905. The Wagner lamp is still reminiscent of the gas lantern with all its technical conditioning factors, though Wagner reduced the ornament in favour of utilizable form. In his table lamp Adolf Loos chooses such forms as hemispheres, multiple shafts and a square base which became standardized later. Josef Hoffmann tackles a commonplace object like the coal scuttle and develops from its practical purpose an unornamented form.

299 Josef Hoffmann, table lamp in the form of a Japanese lantern, *c.* 1907 or later. Spherical shade divided into sections, foot roughly hemispherical, with fruit-like rib divisions. Brass, white silk with black braiding. Signed "J.H. Wiener Werkstätte". 31.2 x 14 cm. Museum of Arts and Crafts, Cologne.

300 Otto Prutscher, stem glass, *c.* 1907. Flashed blue cut crystal, cylindrical cup. Decoration: stem with openwork. 20.8 cm. Sold by E. Bakalowits & Sons, Vienna (probable manufacturer: Adolfshütte, Winterberg). Private collection, Munich.

301 Peter Behrens, two glasses with broad gold rim (white wine and champagne), *c.* 1903. Slightly raised foot, straight slender shaft, shallow wide cup (for champagne) or tall cup with slightly projecting lip. Execution: Benedikt von Poschinger, Oberzwiesel, Bayerischer Wald. 19 cm. (white wine), 12.5 cm. (champagne). Private collection, Munich.

302 Vienna, after 1900. So-called "Art for all", here illustrated as an example of "technicalized" objects with no ornament. Six coloured liqueur glasses on a glass tray with metal mounting. 13 x 34.2 cm. Private collection, Vienna.

303 Adelbert Niemeyer, three glasses, two for champagne and one for white wine, *c.* 1904. Crystal with golden lily decoration. 19.6 x 9.9 cm. (champagne glasses), 19.7 x 9.3 cm. (white wine glass). Private collection, Munich.

304 Cologne-Ehrenfeldt (Rheinische Glashütte AG), four stem glasses, *c.* 1902. Decoration: leaves in coloured overlay, cut and polished greenish glass, stem coloured in the melt. 14.5 cm. Private collection, Munich.

305 Gustav Siegel
(presumably designed by),
armchair, *c.* 1900. Front legs
and arm rests made from one
piece of bentwood, as are the
rear legs and back.
Beechwood with brownish
stain. Height 89 cm, width
50.2 cm, depth 53.3 cm.
Dismantled for illustration.
Private collection, Munich.

306 Joseph Hoffmann
(attributed), chair, *Die
Fledermaus*
cabaret model, barrel-shaped
above horseshoe base,
vertical round wooden legs,
the rear ones rising to form
the back. Terminating in
semicircular arm rests and
back. Beechwood, painted
black and white, height 74.3
cm, width 58 cm, depth 46.3
cm. Execution: Jacob and
Joseph Kohn. Dismantled for
illustration. Private
collection, Munich.

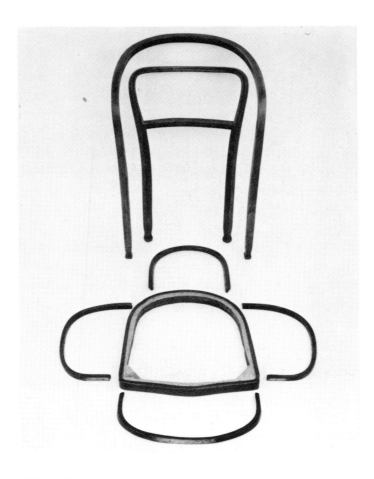

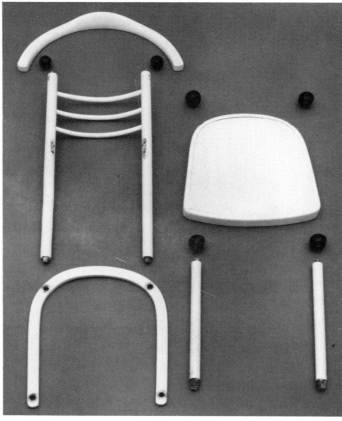

Bentwood Furniture: Form and Function

The spiral of bentwood furniture begins from a specific point and develops from there "along the radius vector with a speed increasing as its distance from the pole", in other words the equiangular spiral as defined by d'Arcy Thompson, *On Growth and Form*, p. 176; this, with its broad sweeping line, had always influenced the artistic imagination. As a decorative principle, it offers greater possibilities than the spiral of Archimedes, which is comparable to a coiled rope and was certainly the tensest ornament in furniture design in the second half of the 19th century. Michael Thonet used the equiangular spiral as the basic form for his bentwood furniture, from which, multiplied in symmetrical assembly, originated the diversity of the Thonet programme. Later, S-bends, double curves and circles were added as secondary forms. This form of the equiangular spiral which often occurs in nature (see ills. 95, 308, 312) points to the forces which work on it and are effective inside it. With Thonet, it was achieved by clamping beechwood rods in circular iron presses and then subjecting them to treatment with steam and glycerine. The furniture produced in this way exhibits simultaneously the most decorative and the most useful form, the floral and the functional impulse.

The primary requirement of wooden furniture is that it does not break, in other words that it can withstand and compensate for stress and pressure tensions. D'Arcy Thompson quoted the example of the Forth Bridge to show how nature could solve such problems and modifications of nature's processes could lead to technical solutions: "The Forth Bridge, from which the anatomist may learn many a lesson, is built of tubes, which correspond even in detail to the structure of a cylindrical branch or stem. The main diagonal struts are tubes twelve feet in diameter, and within the wall of each of these lie six T-shaped 'stiffeners', corresponding to the fibro-vascular

307 Bentwood chair (so-called Moser chair), in stained beechwood with brownish matt. Like Gustav Siegel's chair of 1900, the chair represented a decisive technical variation in bentwood production with the front legs and arm rests in one piece joining on to the back. Also important is the slightly rectangular section of the bentwood. The chair legs are held by a horsehoe-shaped element which once again is slightly raised above the floor by small swollen feet. The rear legs are slightly splayed, to counter which the front legs are drawn inward a little. These elements are important stabilizing processes on the horseshoe piece which holds pressure and tension together. Emphasis is given to the spheres underneath the narrow seat-rails, which represent another stabilizing element. In its construction and lightness this piece of furniture is one of the most important pieces of the bentwood generation, around 1905–10. Height 83.3 cm, width 56 cm, depth 56.5 cm, seat height 45.8 cm. Private collection, Munich.

149

308 Karl Blossfeldt, young coiled fronds of the maidenhair fern, *Adiantum pedatum* (photograph, x 8) – natural forms which the equi-angular spirals impressively demonstrate. Karl Blossfeldt, *Urformen der Natur*, Berlin, 1929, no. 8.

309 D'Arcy Thompson, *On Growth and Form*, 1917, p. 220 (the published preliminary studies of his research began soon after 1900). Thompson observes about the equi-angular spiral: "In mechanical structures curvature is essentially a mechanical phenomenon. It is found in mechanical structures as the result of bending, or it may be introduced into the construction for the purpose of resisting such a bending moment. But neither shell nor tooth nor claw are flexible structures; they have not been bent into their peculiar curvature, they grow into it."

310 Profile of bent form by the Thonet firm. The parts aI, aII, aIII and aIV were built up following various production processes. The bar *h* was introduced and bent at aI until it stopped at aIV. The bending technique corresponds to many natural processes inasmuch as quick-motion processes, so to speak, work through the system. The rod, made flexible by hot air and glycerine, is gradually adapted to the bent shape, which in the free world of nature is effected over a period of time.

150

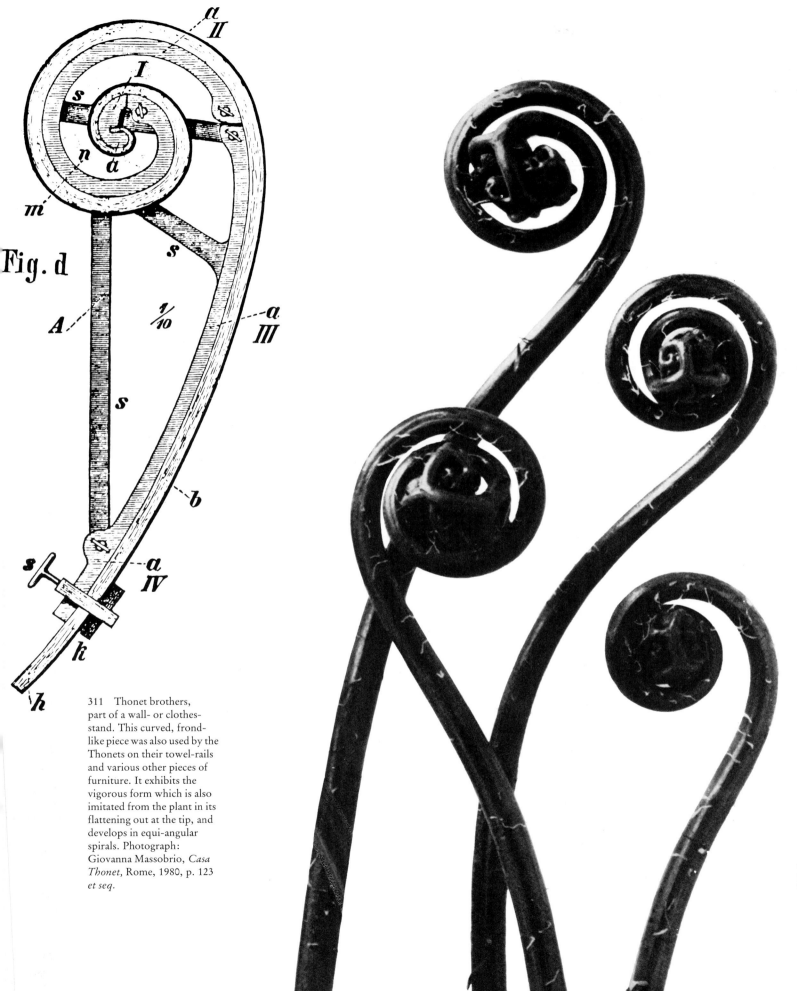

Fig. d

312 Karl Blossfeldt,
photograph of maidenhair
fern, *Adiantum pedatum,*
young coiled fronds
magnified eight and twelve
times. Almost certainly
before 1904. (Detail from
Karl Blossfeldt, *Urformen
der Natur,* Berlin, 1929).

313 D'Arcy Thompson,
the Spiral of Archimedes (*On
Growth and Form,*
Cambridge University Press,
1942, p. 752 *et seq.*). *Cf.* ill.
310.
Thompson explains this spiral
form when he says that it can
be approximately compared
to a rope rolled up by a sailor
on the deck.
The spiral of Archimedes is
closer to the circle and does
not exhibit the same tension
as the equi-angular spiral.
That mainly concerns the
aesthetic effect, although it is
visually more illustrative than
the equi-angular spiral.
Nevertheless it was chosen by
Hermann Obrist in order to
bring active movement into
his representations and to
indicate the tempo of the
spirals.

311 Thonet brothers,
part of a wall- or clothes-
stand. This curved, frond-
like piece was also used by the
Thonets on their towel-rails
and various other pieces of
furniture. It exhibits the
vigorous form which is also
imitated from the plant in its
flattening out at the tip, and
develops in equi-angular
spirals. Photograph:
Giovanna Massobrio, *Casa
Thonet,* Rome, 1980, p. 123
et seq.

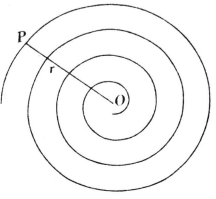

bundles [of plants]. In the same great tubular struts the tendency to 'buckle' is resisted, just as in the jointed stem of a bamboo, by stiffening rings or perforated diaphragms set twenty feet apart within the tube. We may draw one more curious, albeit parenthetic, comparison. An engineering construction, no less than the skeleton of a plant or animal, has to *grow*; but the living thing is in a sense complete during every phase of its existence, while the engineer is often hard put to it to ensure sufficient strength in his unfinished and imperfect structure. The young twig stands more upright than the old, and between winter and summer the weight of leafage affects all the curving outlines of the tree. A slight upward curvature, a matter of a few inches, was deliberately given to the great diagonal tubes of the bridge during their piecemeal construction; and it was a triumph of engineering foresight to see how, like the twig, they at last came straight and true."[1]

The experiments carried out by Michael Thonet in the 1840s and 1850s, based on the accurate observation of static data in plants, showed him the mathematically calculable curves which can arise by exerting a vertical pressure on the horizontal. In this connection, he first developed a process for using layers of wood glued together, which was very complicated and expensive. Mature solid wood constantly proved to be the right material. Through its natural advantages, the technical and mechanical problem could be solved by transformation into the "floralistic basic form", but in its "secondary plant-like quality" it also offered the prerequisites for adapting style pluralism to fulfilling functional purposes.

In the history of European furniture the Thonet chair is the most flexible object and the easiest to move and it met the needs of many spheres of life. Even in those days, furniture could be stacked. It was hygienic, very stable, fitted the body and did not cause sweating. Bentwood furniture suited every room and every kind of living situation. It was cheap to produce and sell. The flexibility of the wood was preserved; through all the technical treatment it was always a natural material.

However, the force during the bending process under steam could not be too strong, for "Bend or break" (the motto of the Thonet family) also had its limits. The elasticity and breaking-point of bentwood was shown by nature. If breaking was to be avoided from the outset, the radius of the curve had to correspond to at least 30 to 35 times the thickness of the material.[2]

Care had to be taken that in the bending process the grain ran lengthwise through the wood, in other words the tree's age rings had to be at right angles to the direction of bending. Under the effect of steam and glycerine the wood can be bent, but snapping inside the zone of tension could not be excluded. Here Michael Thonet developed a simple process. On the exterior of the curve he backed the steam-heated rod with a steel strip which matched its form (ill. 311).[3] The strip was extremely resistant, and it was kept taut by metal struts and clamps. Pressed in the strip, the fibres of the wood were brought to their functional form during heating and fixed in it after cooling. The rod bent into an ornament had become a resilient part of the supporting framework because the wood had not become rigid in the strip through complete hardening.[4]

In Thonet furniture a slight flattening was observable at the curving point of the wooden rods.[5] On the outside of the curve the wood fibres were stretched, on the inside they were compressed. Hence the transition to the use of bent flat rods, which were important for the designs of Hoffmann and Moser.[6]

In the production of bentwood furniture, the integration of cube and square, i.e. of the right-angle, was a hindrance. To deal with the problem of including cubic rectilinearity in a bent supporting system the firms of Thonet and Felix Kohn called in Josef Hoffmann as an adviser (ill. 315). The result was a synthesis of the Viennese "plank style" for the rich, also called "Kistenwohnstil" or "Kasterl-variationen", with the "Thonet scrollwork" and the "solidified bending" of a long wooden rod (ill. 201).

Around 1900, tension and the existence of considerable pressures had become popular

152

scientific material, mostly through the enlargements of plant stems which illustrated Gerlach's books.[7] Wilhelm Bölsche, who based himself on Ernst Haeckel's general scientific writings, repeatedly referred to this problem.[8]

Karl Blossfeldt made convincing contributions shortly after 1900 with his photographs of plant stems. The thickenings on plant stems often had an ornamental and decorative role in floral art nouveau. Riemerschmid deprived them of this function. During constructive art nouveau, bentwood furniture adopted the thickenings in the form of stereometric stabilizers such as spheres and ovoids (ills. 315, 327), which had the task of balancing tension and pressure and so lessening or neutralizing the "compression pressure".[9]

Riemerschmid, who kept his distance from bentwood furniture, shaped the side-rails on his furniture in accordance with the lines of tension – actually it is a refined "floralism" which draws its inspiration from the growth and form of plants and leads to the "three-dimensional arabesque", which requires the pressure lines to take creative shapes (ills. 256, 257).

Bentwood furniture, compared with, say, a chair by Van de Velde or Riemerschmid, often consists solely of a visible supporting frame and the internal stiffenings (for example a bentwood half-hoop between armrests and side-rails as in ills. 320, 462), whereas Van de Velde introduces "vigorous" linear side-rail silhouettes and springy curved legs to the whole body of the chair and so makes it correspond to the seating posture of the occupant (ill. 285).

Riemerschmid forms his music-room chair with a short body-hugging back with low arm rests, so as to give the performer complete freedom of arm movement during practice (ill. 258). Bentwood furniture was not fundamentally suited to such individualistic uses. This group of items of furniture was generally needed for large-scale use and sometimes that even resulted in pieces that were unusable or could only be used briefly (ills. 319, 320, 327).

For example, the small chairs for the Fledermaus Café were actually only intended for short stays, because the rods bent into a cross exerted painful pressure on the upper lumbar region after a very few minutes.

314 Thonet brothers, chair, demonstration model bent out of one rod. Before 1870. Beechwood. Museum of Trade and Industry, Vienna.

153

315 Josef Hoffmann, the "Sitting Machine", *c.* 1905. Removable components and structural elements point to functional models. Beechwood and stained mahogany. 111.5 cm. Execution: Jacob and Josef Kohn, Vienna. Collection Frank Jaeger, Munich. *Cf.* ill. 462.

The Viennese furniture designers had established that there was a direct connection between form and stability. Nature also supplied them with models, for the bending load of a branch or a plant stem was a constant stimulus and attracted the attention of constructors. In natural structures, the thinness of cross-sections resisting bending stresses was particularly important from the constructional viewpoint. The stronger the load, the flatter they became before they curved. Moreover, it was established that thickenings appeared on the compressed sides of the bending. These load zones were also instinctively perceived in furniture-making. Just like a plant stem, the early chair legs of the Thonet Co. and the Kohn firm had a thickening which can be clearly studied in the pictures opposite.

316 Detail of chair by Thonet brothers, *c.* 1855. Beechwood, stained brown. Height 92.5 cm, width 41 cm, depth 51 cm. The photograph is taken from the book *Gebogenes Holz*, Vienna, 1979.

317 *Opposite, below:* Karl Blossfeldt, detail from illustration in *Urformen der Natur* (Berlin, 1929), p. 103. Photograph taken *c.* 1905. Karl Blossfeldt was born at Schilo (Harz) in 1865. In 1898 he was an assistant at the Royal School of Arts and Crafts in Berlin, and produced his first photographs of nature as early as 1899. About 1900 he developed a particularly individual way of seeing cross-sections, the main effect of which was to make the constructions of plant stems visible. In a series of photographs which show the growing development of the plants studied, the viewer and, above all, the artist of the time are made aware of the changes which take place under specific stresses. The books of S. Schwendener, *Das mechanische Princip in anatomischen Bau der Monocotyleen* (Leipzig, 1874) and *Zur Lehre von der Festigkeit der Gewächse* (Berlin, 1884, pp. 1045–70),

made natural scientific premises visible to architects and artists. Both these books explained the processes which go on inside plant stems, but they also dealt with the problem of stability with regard to form and mechanical efficiency, which was later discussed at length in the press. This investigation had an indirect effect on the artists of that time. Wood was a growing material and hence furniture-making, by its constructional nature, was essentially a matter of form, and mechanical means of achieving it.

318 Otto Wagner,
storage shelves for the
Austrian Post Office Savings
Bank, 1902. Bent
beechwood, stained brown.
Aluminium rivets. Height
138 cm, width 120 cm, depth
36 cm. Execution: Jacob and
Josef Kohn. Private
collection, Vienna.

Thonet furniture was the furniture commonly used by Viennese architects and artists. The simplified form, the insight into constructional methods, the simple transposable system, the silhouette-like form, which when required could be adapted to cabinet-maker's work, the functional practical form (the furniture was extraordinarily light to move) were the prerequisites which resulted in furniture for the people. Furniture-buyers were deluged with propaganda about its practicality, and this had a great influence on public taste and the general attitude to home-making. Thonet furniture enouraged an individual approach to furnishing one's home, which Adolf Loos also advocated when he claimed: "And anyone who wants to make a home, must specify everything. Otherwise he will never learn. It will probably be full of mistakes. But they

are his own mistakes. Through self-discipline and a serious approach he will soon recognize these mistakes. He will make changes and improve."
What is a home, asks Adolf Loos and answers sarcastically: "Only one image stands out: the young girl who has committed suicide. She lies full length on the floor. One hand still clutches a smoking revolver. On the table a letter, the farewell letter. Is the room where the drama unfolded tasteful? Who's going to ask that question? Who's going to worry about it? It's a room, and that's enough! But supposing the room is furnished by Van de Velde? It isn't just a room. Then it's –. All right, so what is it really?" (Adolf Loos, *Trotzdem*, 1900–30, Vienna, 1982, pp. 42–3).

319   Kolo Moser (attributed), stool with bentwood rods at the sides, beechwood, stained mahogany and polished. Seat covered in leather, with brass discs and rivets. Height 65 cm, width 52 cm, depth 35 cm, seat height 39 cm. Execution: Jacob and Josef Kohn. Private collection, Vienna.

320   Otto Wagner, stool for the Austrian Post Office Savings Bank in Vienna, *c.* 1904. Made of four bentwood squares with rounded corners, and seat of perforated plywood. Beechwood, stained olive-brown, aluminium rivets. Height 47 cm, width 42 cm, depth 42 cm. Execution: Thonet brothers. Private collection, Vienna.

157

321 Josef Hoffmann, Jacob and Josef Kohn, display cabinet, 1904, with three shelves and a double glass door to the upper compartment. Beechwood, semicircular with four struts extended upwards, and moulding over the ball decoration. Illustrated in the catalogue of Jacob and Josef Kohn, *Österreichische Aktiengesellschaft zur Erzeugung von Möbeln aus gebogenem Holz* (Austrian Bentwood Furniture Construction Company). Height 180 cm, width 92.3 cm, depth 44.5 cm. Kunsthandlung A. Ritthaler, Diessen.

322 Toilet-glass and drawer, *c.* 1903. Polished walnut, brass fittings. Imprint in intarsia "After Josef Hoffmann". Height 51 cm, width 42.5 cm, depth 42.5 cm. Private collection, Vienna.

323 Joseph Hoffmann (presumably designed by), treatment couch, before 1910. Bent polished beechwood, wickerwork surface and head rest. Length 165 cm, width 65.4 cm, height 46.2 cm. Private collection, Vienna.

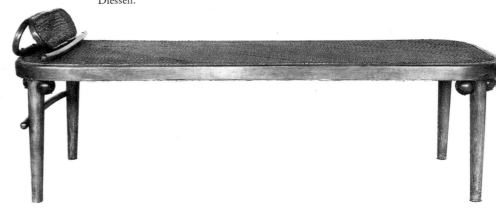

324 Kolo Moser (presumably designed by), display cabinet, 1904. Polished bentwood, stained mahogany, original brass fittings; collector's compartments of beechwood with greenish internal surface. Heigth 184.2 cm, width 114.4 cm, depth 41.5 cm. This is what is known as a Moser cabinet. Illustrated in the catalogue of Jacob and Josef Kohn. Collection Frank Jaeger, Munich.

325 Josef Hoffmann, occasional table, *c.* 1904. Rectangular top with bevelled corners, round rods for legs, spheres as stabilizing elements. Beechwood, stained black, spheres painted white. Height 70 cm, width 68.2 cm, depth 43.3 cm. Execution: J. and J. Kohn. Private collection, Vienna. In 1905 the Viennese art critic Berta Zuckerkandl wrote in her book *Zeitkunst*, p. 27 *et seq.*:

"One cannot see enough of these pieces of furniture which support and carry in such a logical proportion, bend to fit the body so ideally and yet rely so strictly on their good style. There are small silver baskets, teapots, salt cellars of such a practical shape, there are clock-cases, mother-of-pearl boxes, ivory chests ornamented with severe and sharply engraved bronzes, there are glasses, which magnificently epitomize the restriction imposed by their material. There are candelabra and lamps which ideally serve the needs of illumination in place of the then dominant wax candle. All this primarily served its purpose. All this was inter-connected by its unified perception of structure, by an identical ideal form. The poetry of the everyday shuns the show-off pose of society. The artists who try to give the machine-

326 Vienna, 1905–07, occasional table, slightly oval, projecting top with surround below it into which four slender round rods are fitted. They enclose a shelf with four spheres below it as stabilizing elements. Beechwood painted black and white. Height 73 cm, width 43.4 cm, depth 36.2 cm. Execution: J. and J. Kohn. Private collection, Vienna.

made existence of our outward life the most intimate relaxation inside the home have felt that strongly. They achieve this by spiritualizing created functional art with the finest differentiations of purpose as well as of feeling. Almost any stimulus can correspond to an interpretation of form, for the artist as interior decorator has infinitely enriched his range of vision. Because he has become a man of the workshop. Because he has created complete clarity in every material via the organic."

327   Joseph Hoffmann (attributed), chair with horseshoe-shaped base, 1905–7. Round wooden legs screwed into the seat rails, slightly concave seat area, back slightly flattened off and limited by outcurving round rod. Three cross-bars, balls as stabilizers. Bent beechwood, stained black, contemporary upholstery. Height 74.5 cm, depth 53 cm, width 45.2 cm, seat height 44.8 cm. Execution: J. and J. Kohn. Private collection, Vienna.

328   Josef Hoffmann (attributed), coffee-house table, *Die Fledermaus* cabaret model, *c.* 1905–7. Rectangular, slightly bevelled base, above it a compartment, and symmetrically placed rectangular legs fitting directly into the top. Brass ball decoration on the lower drawers. Height 75.3 cm, width 46.7 cm, depth 39.5 cm. Private collection, Vienna.

161

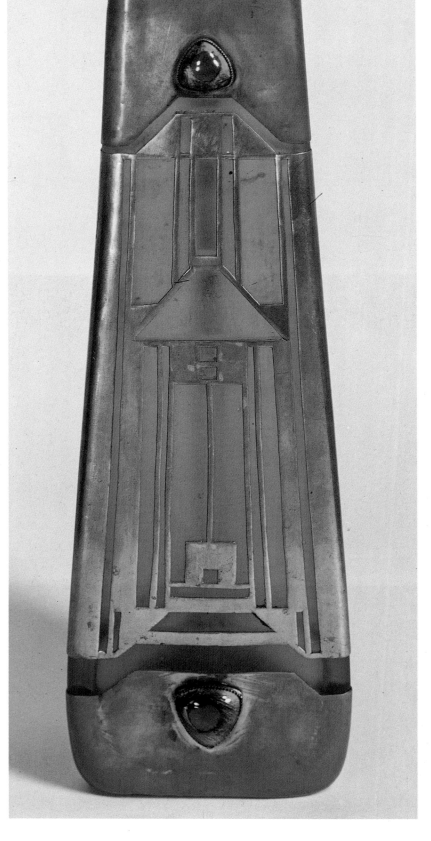

329 Franz Messner (attributed), tulip-shaped receptacle in metal mounting, *c.* 1902. Calyx glass by the firm of Johann Lötz Witwe, Klostermühle Glassworks (near Reichenstein in Bohemia). Vertically ribbed surface, with yellowish-green, gold, pink and violet lustre. 27 x 9.8 cm. Mounting of white metal rising conically from the foot and forming four rolled-up leaves around the calyx. J. Hummel, Vienna.

330 Josef Hoffmann, vase with outspread foot and lip, the latter supported by four glass stems; iridescent green glass. Execution: E. Bakalowits & Sons. 18 x 8.7 cm. J. Hummel, Vienna.

331 Kolo Moser (attributed), glass vase with mounting and inlaid stones, *c.* 1900. Matt pink glass, coloured in the melt. Mounting of gilded and silver-plated sheet copper. 30x2 x 9.4 cm. Private collection, Vienna.

332 Adolf Loos, liqueur glass, *c.* 1902. Stereometric body of massive crystal, tapering from the base. 17.4 x 5.2 cm. Execution: E. Bakalowits & Sons. Private collection, Vienna.

333 Tall vase in metal mounting, *c.* 1902. Execution: Johann Lötz Witwe, Klostermühle Glassworks (near Reichenstein in Bohemia). Decoration of metal mounting, geometric pattern. J. Hummel, Vienna.

334 Kolo Moser (presumably designed by), vase in metal mounting, *c.* 1901. Green glass with narrow foot, bellied body, slender neck with flat outspread lip, greenish glass. 30.2 x 10.2 cm. Private collection, Vienna.

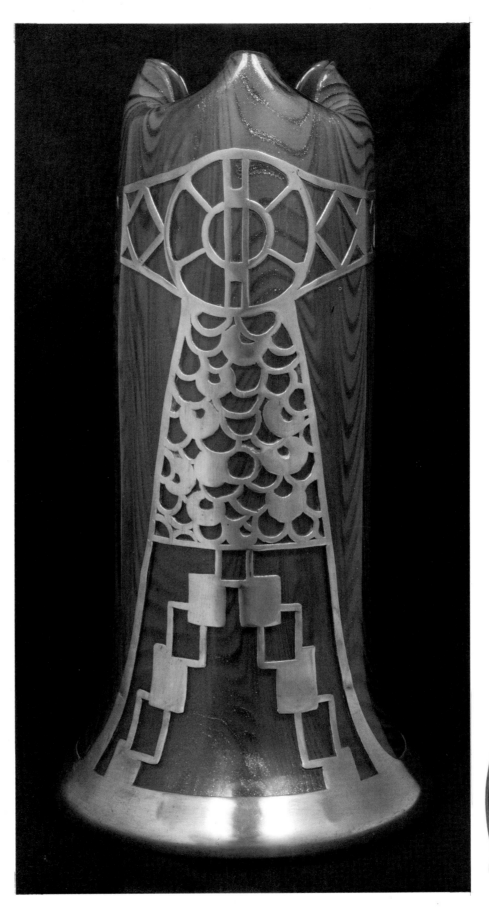

336 Josef Hoffmann (attributed), coffee-house table, later than 1905. Round stepped foot, double leg with decoration of balls, round top with wide edge. Stained black oak, foot of hammered brass. Height 73 cm, diameter of top 56 cm. Private collection, Vienna.

335 Josef Hoffmann, the "White Chair", *c.* 1903. Armchair with high back, trapezoid front and rear legs on two base struts facing inwards towards the rear and joined by a cross-strut. Tall back narrowing slightly towards the top, two black balls at the front of the arm rests. Painted black and white beechwood, new blue leatherwork, wooden components restored. From the living room of M. Biach, Vienna. Illustrated in *Innendekoration,* 1905, p. 48. Height 123 cm, width 56 cm, depth 54.5 cm. J. Hummel, Vienna.

337 Josef Hoffmann, chair, round wooden legs, the rear legs tapering and forming the back. Back in two parts with ball decoration in the middle. Mahogany-stained and polished beechwood, saddle seat of pressed plywood. Height 110 cm, width 44 cm, depth 42 cm. Execution: Jacob and Josef Kohn, *Österreichische Aktiengesellchaft zur Erzeugung von Möbeln aus gebogenen Holz* (Austrian Bentwood Furniture Production Company), exhibited at the Wiener Kunstschau 1908 in the small country house of J. and J. Kohn, Vienna. Wolfgang Richter, Galerie Alt-Wien, Munich.

338 Josef Hoffmann's so-called 'Purkersdorfer chair', *c.* 1904. Round wooden legs, rear legs rising and bent to form the back; central part a bent flat-sided oval with perforated plywood inset; seat upholstered, with ornamental studs on the sides, and balls as stabilizers on the front legs. Natural polished beechwood, seat covered with leather. Height 100 cm, width 45 cm, depth 43 cm. Execution: Jacob and Josef Kohn, Vienna. Private collection, Munich.

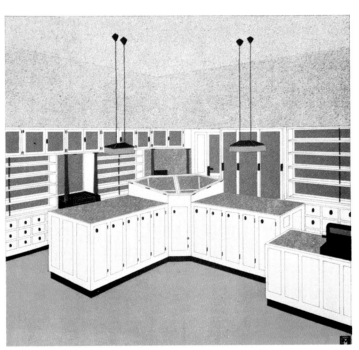

The art critic Felix Poppenberg described Viennese *Ensemblekunst* as follows: "Thus a refined reciprocity was achieved. The room served the objects, and the objects, quite apart from the charm of the individual pieces, gave the room a decorative atmosphere through their overall setting. The Viennese *Ensemblekunst* is brilliantly preserved here. Even when one completely abstained from looking at individual pieces, when one left the material aspect and only absorbed the impression of the room with its division and gradations of colour, one experienced a feeling of sophisticated taste. And that is the specifically Viennese feature, namely that in spite of the fact that this layout was executed according to strictly functional principles without any auxiliary constructions to create an atmosphere and that all factors served the whole as necessary organic components, an imaginative atmosphere still imposed itself, overcoming all the sobriety."

339 Karl Bräuer, design for a schoolroom, chromolithograph, *c.* 1902. 15 x 20.7 cm. Private collection, Vienna.

340 Max Benirschke, design for a government office, *c.* 1901–2. Black ink, mixed technique, chalk and tempera. 19.5 x 30.3 cm. Private collection, Vienna.

341 Hans Stubner, design for a glove shop, chromolithograph, 15 x 20.7 cm. Reproduced in *Das Interieur* (Anton Schroll, Vienna, 1903). *Cf.* ill. 363. Private collection.

342 Maurice Herrgesell, design for a shop. Chromolithograph (colour print), *c.* 1903. Signed "MH", 16 x 16 cm. Private collection, Vienna.

343 Rudolph Tropsch, design for a working corner, 1901. Supplementary page to *Das Interieur*. Chromolithograph, signed below right "Tropsch 1901". 30 x 19.5 cm. Private collection, Vienna.

Josef Hoffmann had a strong enough influence on his contemporaries to form a school. It was mainly Hoffmann's writings that influenced his circle. He writes, "I believe that a house should stand there like a casting, and that its exterior must also betray its interior to us.
Of course I do intensify the medium but I plead for the mutual unity of the rooms." (In his *Sämtliche Schriften*, vol. 1, Vienna and Munich, 1962, p. 393.)

"The ultra-modern interiors in the most delicate shades possible between green and grey, we owe to the inventive taste of Josef Hoffmann, the admirable colleague of Olbrich. From him too stem all kinds of special household furniture in the showrooms, e.g. the famous cart-shaped chairs and the dark-blue chest in the *pointilliste* room that fits so remarkably well into this world of colour. The newly invented tall Spaun glasses from Klostermühl, that 'Austrian Tiffany' as we should like to call it, are naturally iridescent. They look exquisite and obviously have a future. All in all the new Secession exhibition is probably more serious and more artistically worthwhile than anything similar held in Vienna before." (L. Hevesi, *Acht Jahre Secession,* Vienna, 1906, p. 102.)
The material beauty described here, which emerges more clearly through the simplifying structure, has enough power and possibilities for development to overcome the false stylistic imitation of the *Gründerzeit*.

345 Adolf Loos, armchair *c.* 1898–9, with slightly outspread front legs of tapering wooden rods, supporting cross-struts high up, rear legs curving in towards the saddle seat. Walnut-coloured stain on beechwood, leather seat, foot casings of nickel-plated brass. Height 73.2 cm, width 50 cm, depth 54 cm, seat height 47.3 cm. Execution: J. Kohn. Private collection, Vienna.

344 "Elephant's trunk table", *c.* 1900, previously attributed to Adolf Loos in the relevant literature. After Vera J. Behal in *Alte und Moderne Kunst*, no. 52, p. 50. Workshop: F.O. Schmidt after details by Max Schmidt. Execution and details: overseer Berka. Obviously a team who needed guidance. Eight-legged table with top in a series of curves. Walnut, top with inlaid polished amethyst druse, shoes and table edge of polished copper. 63 x 87 cm. Private collection, Vienna.

346 Adolf Loos (attributed), rectangular window with diagonal struts, brass and crystal, *c.* 1900. Height 47 cm. Private collection, Vienna.

In this "elephant's trunk" form the table shows the ludicrous additions after floral models which also drag in historical models. The exaggeration is "built out" in the chair form. Nevertheless the struts of the back are still related to swelling plant stems. The insert shows the ornamental value of a constructed and composed object without ornament under the restraint of geometric models.

Adolf Loos, who described so clearly how he drew his later furniture designs, observes:

"Modern man, the man with modern nerves, does not *use* ornament; on the contrary, he shuns it. None of the objects we call modern have any ornament." (Adolf Loos, "Ornament und Erziehung", in his *Sämtliche Schriften*, vol. 1, Vienna and Munich, 1962, p. 392.)

Loos knew the publications of Hermann Muthesius, such as *Stilarchitektur und Baukunst,* and especially the lectures he gave between 1896 and 1899. The horizontal and the vertical were now for Loos the line for "constructional furniture form". He observes, "To seek beauty in form and not to make it dependent on ornament is the goal towards which all humanity strives." (Adolf Loos: *Ins Leere gesprochen*, 1897–1900, Vienna, 1981.)

347 Adolf Loos, shelves with compartment, or room divider, *c.* 1900. Clear repetitive rectangular articulation with unemphatic plank base. Small drop compartment beside the shelves, mahogany veneer, brass fitting. Height 121 cm, width 90 cm, depth 30 cm. Private collection, Vienna.

348 Karl Adolf Franz (Wallern Technical College), casket, c. 1912 or earlier. Oval plan, clearly articulated body with flat top. Decoration: four ornamental bands of upright ovals in black rectangles alternating with striped decoration. Matt dark-brown pearwood, with mother-of-pearl inlays in ebony veneer. Height 17 cm, width 31.5 cm, depth 17.5 cm. Austrian Museum of Applied Art, Vienna. Inventory no. WI 1177. In comparison with the small chest opposite, it becomes clear that in the period from 1904 to about 1912 a change took place in the Wiener Werkstätte style. The tendency to the simplified cube, the more strongly emphasized, flat, almost geometric ornament predominates from 1910. A marked to-and-fro movement of the spatial conception is avoided, as exemplified in the 1905 chest. The extremely precise work of the basic oval shape is reflected again in the oval decoration. After 1910, abstract clarity of line leads at first to a increased use of clear-cut linear surfaces, but after World War I this in turn leads to a materialistic cult stressing the prestigious and the fashionable.

349 Johanna Maria Hollmann, small chest-cum-table with enamel decoration and rectangular plan, *c.* 1905. The small chest is supported by two extended cubes which are included in an overall rectangular system, leaving two openings on either side of the chest, with a slightly profiled top and square openings at the sides. The chest has two doors, and enamelled paintings of two girls in the Japanese *kakemono* manner (cloisonné enamel on sheet-brass). Wooden components, macassar-ebony veneer, inlaid framing of light sycamore veneer, drawers with ivory knobs. Austrian Museum of Applied Art, Vienna. Inventory no. WI 600.

350 Hans Christiansen, six-legged armchair with bronze feet, c. 1910. Back and side struts are independently inserted elements. Execution: Ludwig Schäfer Co., Mainz. Height 100 cm, width 60.5 cm, depth 53.5 cm. Museum of Arts and Crafts, Cologne. Inventory no. A. i553c.

351 Bruno Paul (attributed), chair with curved front legs, c. 1906. Four struts under the seat sides; the back is developed from the rear legs with three cross-bars and slightly curved termination. Wickerwork seat. Matt stained mountain-ash. Height 85.3 cm, width 47 cm, depth 49.2 cm, seat height 46.3 cm. Private collection, Vienna.

172

354 Bruno Paul, chair, c. 1901. Slightly curved front and rear legs, and curved back which continues so as to form the arm rests and front legs. Curved vertical and horizontal cross-struts which suit the ornamental verve. Upholstered seat of mountain-elm. Height 78.5 cm, width 40.8 cm, depth 44.3 cm. Execution: Vereinigte Werkstätten für Kunst im Handwerk, Munich. Kenneth Barlow, Decorative Arts, Munich.

355 Anton Pospischil, armchair, c. 1901. Three squared rods form the front legs, and slightly curved rear legs issue into the back supports, both with slits. Flat saddle seat. Y-shaped struts near the feet lead to the rear legs. Matt polished oak. Height 75.2 cm, depth 49 cm, width 66.5 cm, seat height 46 cm. Private collection, Vienna.

352 Armchair in the style of Gustav Siegel, c. 1900. Both front legs are from one piece of bentwood, as are the rear legs and back; the seat is held in the centre by two squared bentwood elements, and bentwood arches are fitted below the seat edges for stabilization. Bronze shoes with three engraved bands. Signed "J. und J. Kohn, Wien" (the firm's label on the inner seat frame under the upholstery). Solid beechwood, polished and stained. The chair represents a decisive technical innovation in bentwood production. Front legs and arm rests run up behind the back in one piece. At the Exhibition of the Viennese School of Arts and Crafts, Spring 1901, in the Austrian Museum of Art and Industry, this type of chair was given special prominence in the press as an avant-garde innovation. Height 89 cm, width 50 cm, depth 53.2 cm. Austrian Museum of Applied Art, Vienna. Inventory no. WI 4.

353 Franz Messner, toilet chair. Diagonal piece without arm rests, stool shape. Back with two sides of equal height. Square seat, squared wood foot struts between the rear legs to give increased freedom for the feet. Solid matt and polished sycamore. Veronese green cotton damask with pattern. Height 76.3 cm, seat 43 x 43 cm. Austrian Museum of Applied Art, Vienna. Inventory no. H 2076.

356 Bruno Paul, chair. Rectangular seat with rounded corners, shield-shaped back raised in the centre and merging with the arm rests. Upholstered seat and back. Solid stained and matt walnut. Height 85.2 cm, depth 57 cm, seat height 45 cm. Kenneth Barlow, Decorative Arts, Munich.

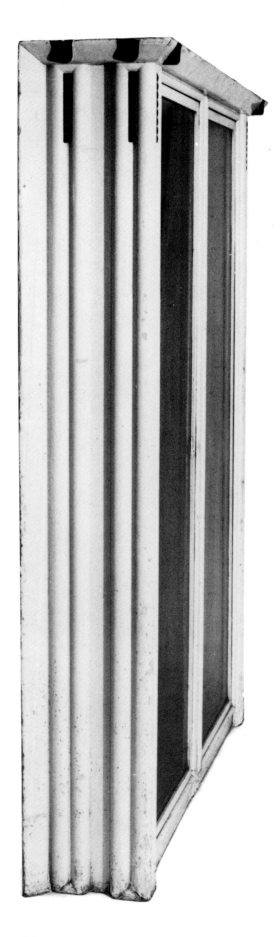

357 Wiener Werkstätte, shallow showcase with two doors, highly profiled side areas and short protruding cornice, c. 1903. At the corners and sides of the cornice, triglyph-like attachments. At the sides of the doors and on the sides, below the cornice, eight vertically placed squares, treated in relief. Beechwood, painted blue and white. Height 205 cm, width 115 cm, depth 35 cm. This showcase formed part of the interior decoration of the Wiener Werkstätte and the Wittgenstein-Stonborough home. J. Hummel, Vienna. *Above:* detail of the cornice area.

358 Kolo Moser, chair for the Purkersdorf Sanatorium and the Viennese Secession. Chest-shaped chair on square plan, sides and back of rods arranged vertically above square base supports. Webbed seat. Beechwood painted white. Height 71.3 cm, width 66.3 cm, depth 65.3 cm, seat height 43 cm. The illustration shows the room prepared for the Viennese Secession. Private collection, Vienna.

359 Josef Hoffmann (attributed), small cupboard, c. 1905, above square, slightly recessed black base. The cupboard is divided by two doors. The upper part has five drawers behind the door. Beechwood, painted black and white, polished interior. The fittings have the rose hallmark of the Wiener Werkstätte. Key fitting identical to the forms in the Wittgenstein home. Height 114 cm, depth 64 cm, width 41 cm. J. Hummel, Vienna.

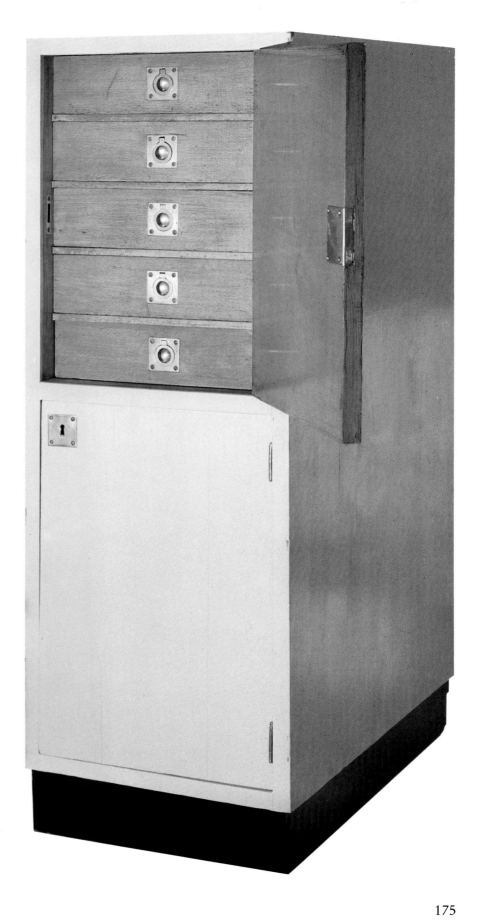

175

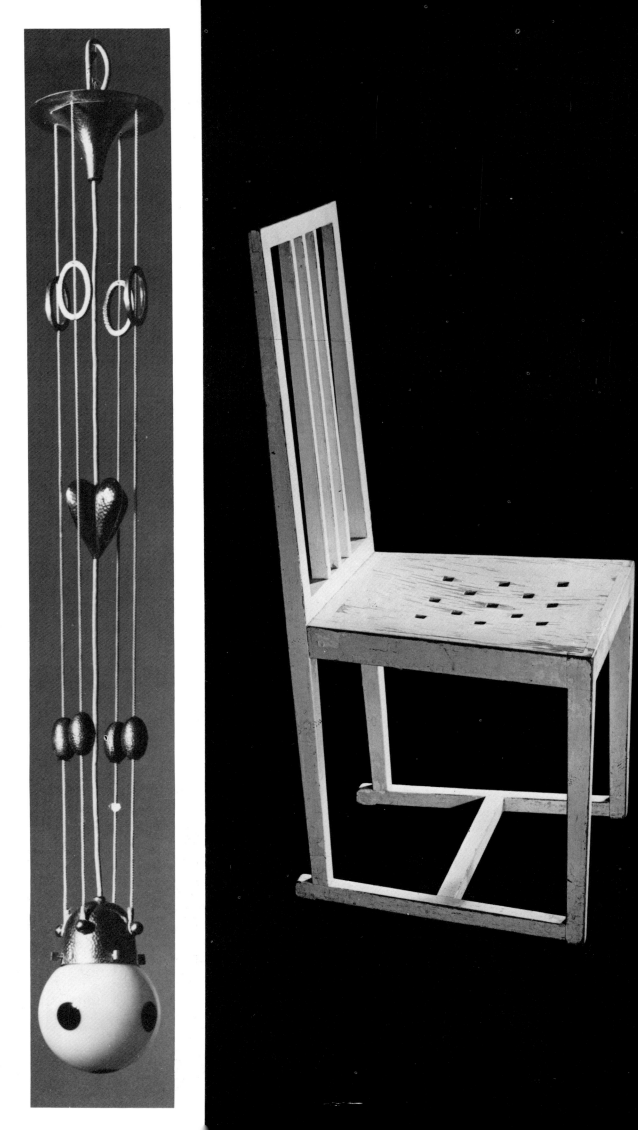

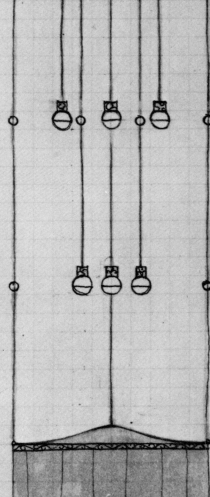

SPEISZIMMER –
LUSTER
MESSING VERGOLDET

1 : 10

362 Eduard Josef Wimmer, candelabra design for the Koller house with the superscription "dining-room candelabra, gilded brass", followed by the monogram of E.J. Wimmer (information kindly supplied by Dr Pichelkastner). Pencil, Indian ink and colour on squared paper, c. 1907. 24.1 x 18.2 cm. Private collection, Vienna.

363 Johann Stubner, design for a glove shop illustrated in *Das Interieur III* (Vienna, 1902), p. 416. Private collection.

364 Karl Witzmann, kitchen with sideboard, checkerwork pattern on floor and ceiling, influenced by Josef Hoffmann. Illustrated in *Das Interieur III* (Vienna, 1902). Private collection.

365 Josef Hoffmann, chair with closed-in back, 1901-2. Mahogany-shaded matt beechwood. Back sloping towards the front and enclosed in squared bentwood. Aluminium rivets, aluminium fittings at ground level in front and at the sides. Height 79.5 cm, width 60 cm, depth 63.5 cm. Execution: Jacob and Josef Kohn, Vienna. Private collection, Vienna.

360 Josef Hoffmann (presumably designed by), hanging lamp from the Biach residence in Vienna, c. 1903, consisting of round hemispherical bell-jar, four suspension cords with a central cord for the electric current, suspension rods decorated with egg-shaped elements and rings. Bell-jar with coloured circular glass applications. Plated German silver, glass sphere coloured a whitish shade in the melt. Length 118 cm, diameter of glass sphere 33.5 cm. Private collection, Vienna.

361 Josef Hoffmann (attributed), chair, c. 1903. Back with three struts, plywood seat with ornament of squares, side and central braces at foot, protruding slightly at the rear. Beechwood painted white and polished. Height 100.5 cm, width 42.2 cm, depth 44.3 cm. Private collection, Vienna.

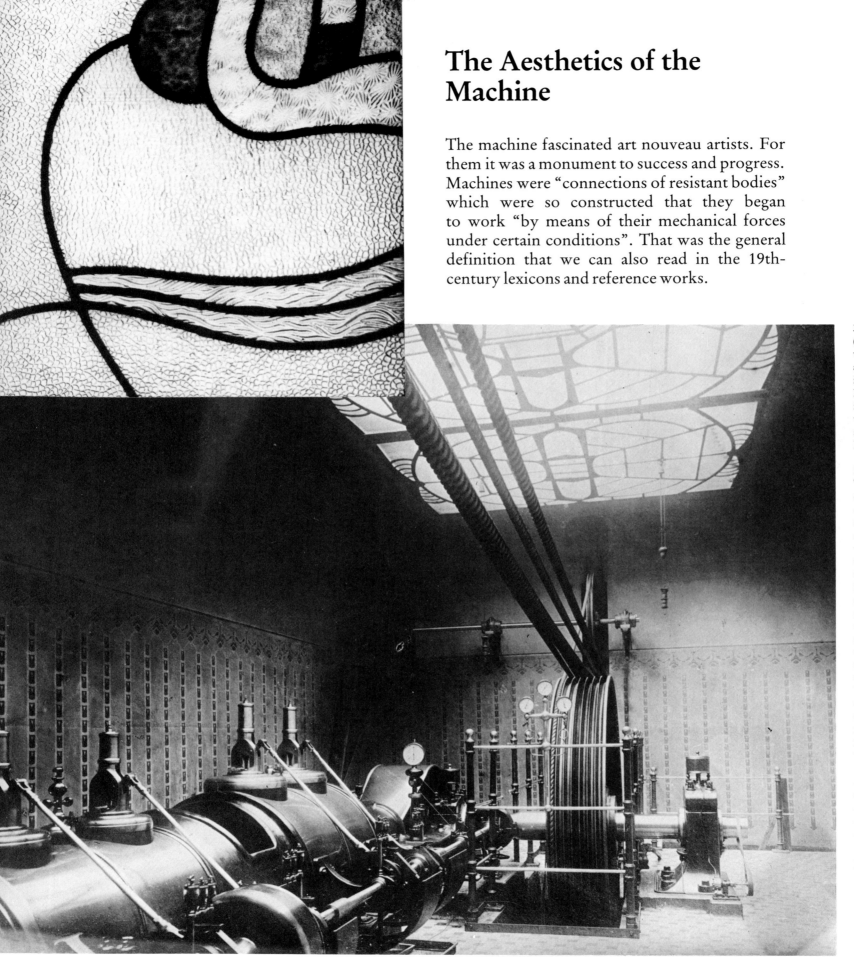

The Aesthetics of the Machine

The machine fascinated art nouveau artists. For them it was a monument to success and progress. Machines were "connections of resistant bodies" which were so constructed that they began to work "by means of their mechanical forces under certain conditions". That was the general definition that we can also read in the 19th-century lexicons and reference works.

366 Josef Maria Olbrich (attributed), stained-glass window, c. 1900. Coloured and variously structured glass in brass mounting. Decoration: climbing flowers indicated by abstract lines which are inlaid in the glass square as stays. 32 x 32 cm. J. Hummel, Vienna.

367 Henry van de Velde. The engine room of the firm of K.H. Vorster, after a design by Van de Velde. A striking feature of the engine room is the wall decoration which separates the wall from the ceiling area by an abstract floral frieze. The tapestry-like floor, which is also achieved by tiles, gives the room a personal note so that the machines animate it like aesthetic objects. The overhead lights, which illuminate the room brightly, are shaped in typical Van de Velde ornamentation based on models from nature. They are abstract calyxes which indicate that technology and nature are to be seen as a unity.

368 Vienna, c. 1900, vase (detail). Pewter support, four rods on flat square base, holding cut glass receptacle by Loetz Glassworks. c. 1902. 36 x 11.5 cm. Private collection, Vienna.

The connection of individual mechanical components to a machine does not exclude all movement; it merely hinders those movements which are unnecessary and disturbing for the machine's purpose. About 1900, artists recorded some of their observations of floral function. They saw in the plant a mechanism of motion in which movement took precedence over morphology.

Recognition of the machine and mechanical efficiency had not always prevailed. Nikolaus Pevsner writes in his *Pioneers of Modern Design:*[1]

"Morris's attitude of hatred towards modern

369 Peter Behrens,
AEG turbine hall, Berlin.
Construction period *c.* 1907.
For further discussion, see p. 182, margin.

370 *Right:* August Endell, trotting-racecourse, Berlin-Mariendorf, frontal view of the first grandstand. Karl Scheffler, editor of the periodical *Kunst und Künstler,* wrote the following appreciation of this building in 1913: "To the best of my knowledge, Endell is the first man to have overcome the 'interim' character of racecourse architecture and created something which is not only pleasing in itself, but also exhibits new possibilities of development. He has brought the basic forms which come automatically to mind into a rhythmic arrangement and grouped them in such a way that one can talk about a specific racecourse architecture for the first time." With this commission, August Endell demonstrates that from then on the functional and constructive shaping of architecture which Muthesius and Poelzig, among others, had also foreshadowed becomes possible. However, the essential thing is that the functional and constructional formative elements are brought out by an artist who started from nature and was one of the principal creators of the floral style in German art nouveau. The trotting-racecourse at Berlin-Mariendorf is consequently important evidence of the thematic elaboration of new ideas and the permeation of the creative process in Germany by constructional possibilities about 1910 to 1915.

In the decor of the variety theatre for Ernst von Wolzogen, Endell draws exclusively on the starfish forms which he had seen in Ernst Haeckel's books. The countless photographs taken by Karl Blossfeldt had shown him the way. Endell thus advanced beyond the accepted art forms of nature into the underwater world, a step towards a structural possibility which went further than the traditional Renaissance-like floral themes.

371 Plate 41 in Ernst Haeckel, *Kunstformen der Natur* (Leipzig and Vienna, 1904). Endell copied in stucco the strong latticed spiny shells of *Acanthophaeta*.

372 *Left:* August Endell, variety theatre for Ernst von Wolzogen in Köpenickerstraße, Berlin, 1901. Colours: brown, grey, red, violet, light green, blue, silver. Decoration: acanthus, palms and panicles. Destroyed in 1943.

373 *Below:* August Endell, ceiling ornament for a house on the Steinplatz (Uhlandstraße), Berlin, 1906-7. Painted white stucco, carved and partly polished.

D'Arcy Thompson had this to say about form and mechanical efficiency in his book *On Growth and Form* (Cambridge University Press, 1942), pp. 970-1: "When the engineer constructs an iron or steel girder to take the place of the primitive wooden beam, we know that he takes advantage of the elementary principle we have spoken of, and saves weight and economizes material by leaving out, as far as possible, all the middle portion, all the parts in the neighbourhood of the 'neutral zone'; and in so doing he reduces his girder to an upper and lower 'flange', connected together by a 'web', the whole resembling in cross-section an I or an H. But it is obvious that if the strains in the two flanges are to be equal as well as opposite, and if the material be such as cast-iron or wrought-iron, one or other flange must be made much thicker than the other in order that they may be equally strong … The I or H girder or rail is designed to resist bending in one particular direction, but if, as in a tall pillar, it be necessary to resist bending in all directions alike, it is obvious that the tubular or cylindrical construction best meets the case … The quill of the bird's feather, the hollow shaft of a reed, the thin tube of the wheat-straw bearing its heavy burden in the ear, are all illustrations which Galileo used in his account of this mechanical principle; and the working of his practical mind is exemplified by this catalogue of varied instances which one demonstration suffices to explain." So the bending load was reconstructed from plants and the experiments, stimulated by plant structures, were carried over in practice into high technology. At all events, efficiency of buildings and the art of glass-making was always guaranteed by natural scientific observations.

methods of production remained unchanged with most of his followers. The Arts and Crafts Movement brought a revival of artistic craftmanship not of industrial art. Walter Crane (1845 – 1915) and C. R. Ashbee (1863 – 1942) may be taken as representatives of this. Walter Crane, the most popular of the disciples of Morris, did not go one step beyond the doctrine of his master. To him, as to Morris, 'the true root and basis of all Art lies in the handicrafts'. His aim, therefore, just like Morris's, was 'to turn our artists into craftsmen and our craftsmen into artists'. Moreover, he agreed with Morris in the conviction that 'genuine and spontaneous art … is a pleasurable exercise', and was led by such premises to a romantic Socialism identical with that of Morris. The same conflict which was pointed out in Morris's doctrine is to be found in Crane. He too was compelled to admit that 'cheapness in art and handicraft is wellnigh impossible', because 'cheapness as a rule … can only be obtained at the cost of the … cheapening of human life and labour'. Crane's attitude towards machine production also corresponds to Morris's. His dislike of 'the monsters of our time clad in plate-glass [and] cast-iron' – Ruskin had been the first to inveigh against railway stations and the Crystal Palace – is tempered only by the consideration that machinery may be necessary and useful as 'the servant and labour-saver of man' for a 'real saving of labour, heavy and exhausting labour'… The first architects to admire the

machine and to understand its essential character and its consequences in the relation of architecture and design to ornamentation were two Austrians, two Americans, and a Belgian: Otto Wagner (1841 – 1918), Adolf Loos (1870 – 1933), Louis Sullivan (1856 – 1924), Frank Lloyd Wright (1869 – 1959), and Henri van de Velde (1863 – 1957). To these five, one Englishman should be added, Oscar Wilde (1856–1900)."

Ernst Haeckel regarded scientific and technical progress, of which the machine is a valid symbol, from another standpoint:[2]

"If we rightly label our century the age of the sciences, if we regard with pride the immeasurable significant progress in all its branches, we are accustomed to think less about the extension of our general knowledge of nature and rather more about the directly practical successes of that progress… But however highly you may value this development of the new science for our practical living, from a more general point of view it must be less important than the influence which the advances of science will gain over the total knowledge of man, and over his whole outlook and ways of thought… Nevertheless, amidst all this admirable theoretical progress, there can be no doubt that the theory formulated by Darwin easily takes first place."

Yet even in 1852 Gottfrid Semper had written, in *Science, Industry and Art:* "With its methods borrowed from science, the machine makes child's play of the most laborious and difficult tasks: it cuts the hardest porphyry and granite like chalk and polishes them like wax. Ivory becomes malleable. The machine sews, knits, sticks, cuts, paints, digs deep into the sphere of human art and puts every kind of human skill to shame."[3]

In 1884 Huysmans wrote, of machines: "By the mighty play of their iron arms they will produce the beautiful as soon as beauty directs them."

The machine was the spur; to overcome the resistances imposed by use was the prevalent question of the period.

In his design for a machine-shop, Henry van de Velde brought resistances dictated by the use of cables and driving machinery into an aesthetic

183

unity with the surrounding space (ill. 367). The midline is formed by the cable. To the left of it are the machine housings with vents which are treated as if they were the tops of artistically formed vessels. The back wall of the shop is decorated with a typical Van de Velde pattern, and the skylights are large geometrically ornamented panes of glass. The line of lights guarantees a lucid arrangement by means of the bright skylight, the coloured glass of which also suggests a museum by the transfiguration of what is displayed (objects, machines).

In 1901 Henry van de Velde observed in his *The Renaissance in Modern Arts and Handicrafts:* "Any thought other than that of usefulness or function becomes dangerous."[4]

And Peter Behrens noted in a lecture delivered in 1910: "Just as the regularity of nature does not imply culture, construction does not necessarily imply art."[5]

In 1912 Peter Behrens built the assembly hall in Berlin's Hussitenstraße (ills. 369, 375). The AEG had commissioned him and he was allowed plenty of time for constructing the hall. Behrens made numerous sketches to solve the relations of space and machine that would make sense in form. His idea was not simply to create a covering roof for the machine room; he intended the actual construction of the hall to be indicative of machine production. In the case of the Raupert house in Hagen, Westphalia, he treated the side facing the street with a combination of technical detail and historical tradition, in which the uncluttered façade strives for a basic norm. When building the Hagen crematorium he applied the same principles: a hall partitioned by geometric ornaments, reflecting the Renaissance and the machine at the same time indicates the coolness of a mechanized burial process.

Peter Behrens, who started from the floral tendency in art nouveau, has in this way created a combination of traditional geometric ornament and the modern need for elimination that emphasizes as the purpose of form the machine-like and also, partly, anonymity.

Heinrich Tessenow observed, in *House Construction and So On:*[6]

"Technology always looks for the smallest form and the greatest force, accepting form only as unavoidable." What industry produced became, about 1905, more interesting for the aesthetes and even purely technical implements were put up as models. The cultural critic Felix Poppenberg speaks of the effect of a "precise machine or a resilient railway bridge with its criss-crossings and giant filigree webs… on which nothing happens for the sake of decoration, on which function is everything, but which moves us aesthetically through the language of successful achievement."

He continues: "Thus there is something appealing about the mighty crystal lens of a porthole-eye with its powerful brass rim round it, in the pure mixture of glass and metal, combining transparency and sturdy strength, that may help to satisfy those needs for perfection that are so often disappointed, and give us the rare feeling of security raised above doubt.

"Ships' lanterns, with their sunken, thick-walled glass coverings and solid metal screen-work protecting and defendng them, have a similar effect.

"Racing boats, with their long, arrow-like form, are also 'beautiful' in themselves and for their purposefulness."[7]

Adolf Loos wrote his first articles for newspapers and journals in 1897-8. In his criticism of Viennese art nouveau, known as the style of the Secession, which at that time had just reached its zenith, he noted:

"The deeper a people stands, the more extravagant it is with its jewellery, with its ornament. To look for beauty only in the form and not to make it dependent upon the ornament is the goal towards which all mankind strives."[8]

For Loos, pure beauty in an individual work of art means "to bring the highest degree of its use value into harmony with the other parts". Thus he views the engineers as our Hellenes: from them we get our culture. And he goes so far as to name the plumber as the one who builds a house for culture, that is, the authoritative culture of today. Hermann Muthesius, too, calls for new beginnings of an ordered architecture with a goal in view, in which the objects of life are included.

He says: "These are demands that arose from new economic and transport conditions. As for the latter, the 19th century brought us new building materials: iron and glass."[9]

"The principle of construction behind the exhibition palace of iron and glass soon invaded other spheres. The railway station, the market hall, the museum with the glass-covered court-yard, all forms of large building roofed with a vault of glass, and finally the office building in the city, with large glass surfaces overlooking the street – all are children of the same mode of thinking. The development of the office building, the upper-middle-class house, took place mostly in the rapidly expanding city of Berlin. Berlin was the embodiment of a true cultural achievement, which could point to Messel's Wertheim department store as an example that could right-fully be called classical.

"The centre of gravitation around which the pendulum oscillates (and which alone in change is lasting and mathematically comprehensible) is decisive in the tectonic arts where unchanging requirements dictate materials, practicability and construction methods."[10]

Besides setting goals for construction, the "beautiful machine" merits exhibition in the museum as something worth seeing. Josef Hoffmann writes: "We have the museums to thank for showing you everything but this. What have they not shown us? With the exception of the ethnographical section, which strangely, in spite of its highly artistic contents, they have hidden away in the natural history collections, they seem today to have completely forgotten their duty. Or have you seen a beautiful machine in an arts and crafts museum?"[11]

377 Catalogue of the International Exhibition, Paris, 1900. Graphic design: Bernhard Pankok. Allgemeine Elektrizitäts-Gesellschaft, Berlin, advertising section, p.l. 24 x 19.5 cm. Private collection, Munich.

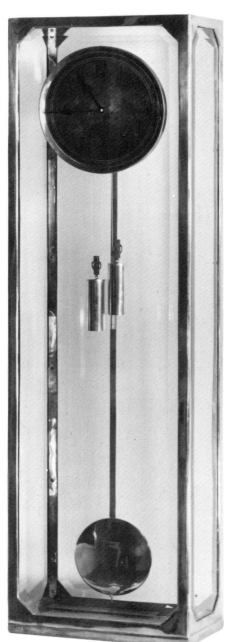

378   Otto Wagner, wall clock from the boardroom of the Austrian Post Office Savings Bank, *c.* 1904. Stained brown oak, cut crystal. Works of clock: A. Baronek, Vienna. Height 135 cm, width 41 cm, depth 19 cm. Private collection, Vienna.

379   Adolf Loos, wall or standing clock, cut glass mounted in copper, *c.* 1906-7. Height 143 cm, width 42 cm, depth 24 cm. Private collection, Vienna.

380   Josef Hoffmann, table clock, *c.* 1902. Square basic form with projecting moulding, beech painted black and white. Height 36.5 cm, depth 29 cm, width 52 cm. Private collection, Vienna.

381   Adolf Loos,
table clock, copper and cut
crystal, *c.* 1904. Works by
Mann & Co., execution by J.
Heeg. Height 42 cm, width
36 cm, depth 25 cm. Private
collection, Vienna.
The clock combined technical
apparatus with new artistic
functional form. The
mechanical problem alone,
which is always inherent in
the clock, is now made visible
again in its structure. This had
concerned the precision
clock-makers of past ages.
Nevertheless, form without
ornament in combination
with technical construction
and functional use led Adolf
Loos to this judgment:
"Absence of ornament is not
absence of attraction, but
works as a new attraction, it
animates. The mill that does
not clatter wakes the miller
up."
Adolf Loos: "Ornament und
Erziehung", in *Sämtliche
Schriften* (Vienna and
Munich, 1962), vol. l p. 393.

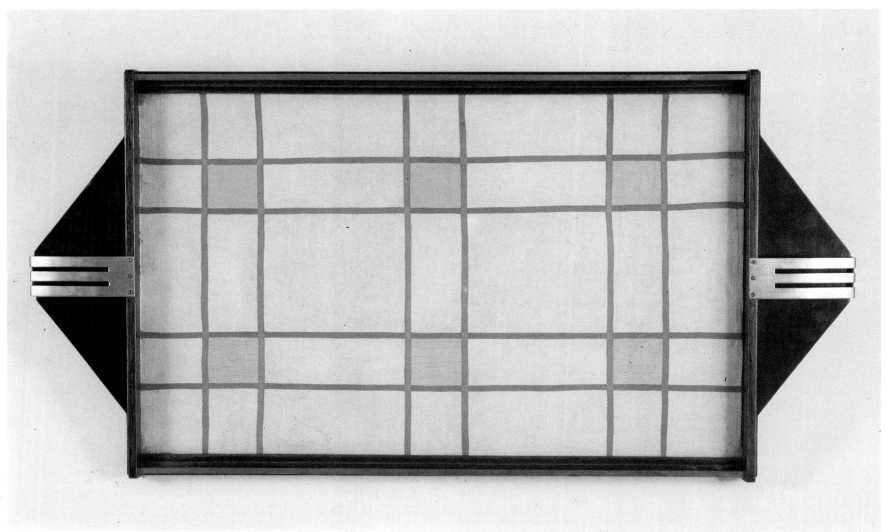

382 Adolf Loos,
hanging lamp after a Spanish model, 1899-1900. From the Turnowsky residence, Wohllebengasse 19, Vienna IV; brass and glass, 30 x 20 cm. Execution: Johann Heeg. Private collection.

383 Gustave Serrurier-Bovy,
serving case with tray, *c.* 1902-3. Upper part glassed in, walnut with brass fittings. Screws on the brass parts as structural decoration. Base of tray with appliqué embroidery in rust-ochre and light yellow on fine linen. Height 103 cm with tray, width without tray 60 cm, width with base moulding 45 cm, width of tray 39.5 cm, length 77.4 cm. Private collection, Munich.

Serrurier-Bovy laid particular emphasis on constructional fashioning in his second creative phase of functional structural development. As an artist, Serrurier-Bovy shows that in the west, too, the same forms are used that led to a new stylistic development in Vienna. Straight lines, a feeling for geometric arrangement and ornamental restraint are decisive pre-requisites for Serrurier-Bovy. Nevertheless, he does not choose the pluralistic standard pattern, but develops each single object out of its unique structural functionalism.
Basic forms were crying out ever louder for simplification,

and this applies to all kinds of objects, such as glass windows or furniture, but a simplification of apparatus, based on specific cubic norms, also made itself felt. The period from 1902 to 1903 was consistent evidence of this in Vienna. Cabinet-made furniture was emphasized uncompromisingly in its separate structural parts. A striking feature is that corners and edges were specially stressed in order to differentiate it from bentwood furniture. In contrast to the blurring roundness of bentwood pieces, cabinet-made furniture adopted the tectonic sharp edges which particularly characterized Viennese work of the period. Again and again it is the square as a basic norm which determines the overall surface. The intensification of black and white, light and dark, is drawn into the combination of constructive exteriors. Bentwood furniture acquires metal ornamentation with head and disc forms. Ornamental values and constructive indications are creatively combined.

384   Josef Hoffmann and A. Messner,
stained-glass window, 1903. Geometric ornamentation and various kinds of glass for the different surfaces and colours. Designed for the Biach residence, Vienna. Pressed glass in lead frame. 47 x 47 cm. J. Hummel, Vienna.

385   Kolo Moser (attributed), beechwood chair, c. 1903. Painted white, with upholstered back and seat, and aluminium shoes on the legs. Emphasized cross and lengthwise struts in the lower part of the chair, producing squares at the sides; central cross bar moved back to allow more room for the feet. Height 95 cm, depth 45 cm, width 45 cm, seat height 46 cm. Private collection, Vienna.

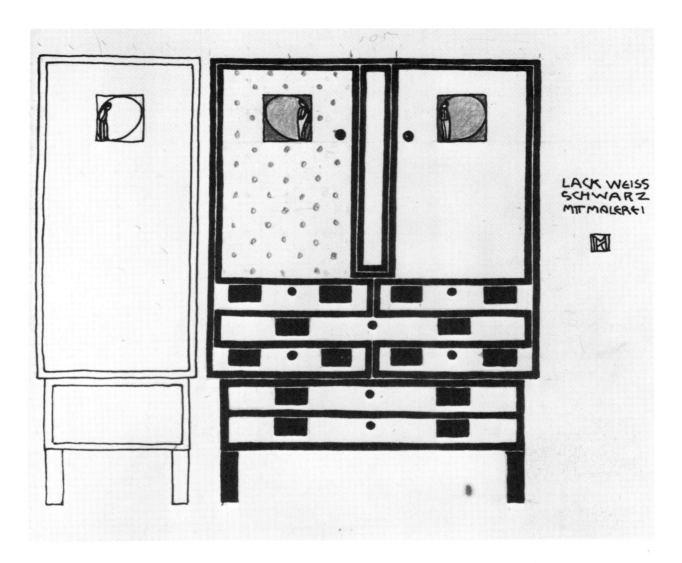

LACK WEISS SCHWARZ MIT MALEREI

386 Kolo Moser, design for a collector's cabinet, *c.* 1903. Black and white lacquer with painting, signed by Kolo Moser on the right "Lack weiss schwarz mit Malerei" with his monogram below. Indian ink and crayon on squared paper. 23.7 x 21 cm. Private collection, Vienna.

387 Kolo Moser (attributed), painted white beechwood table for porcelain etc., *c.* 1902. Metal mounting and felt top, removable drawers, spherical metal feet. The table is of rhomboid shape with cut away bevelled sides to accentuate its functional character. Height 80 cm, width 161 cm, depth 75 cm. J. Hummel, Vienna.

388   Josef Hoffmann,
sauce boat, before 1907.
Elevated bowl on wide base
with curved handle leading
from lip to edge of base.
Polished white metal. Height
8.2 cm, diameter 17 cm.
Execution: Wiener
Werkstätte. Private
collection, Vienna.

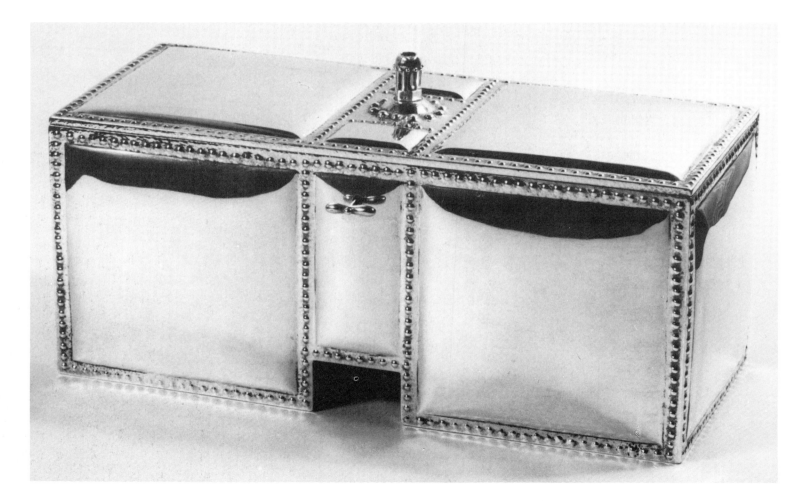

389   Josef Hoffmann,
cigar and cigarette box, 1905-
6. Two cube shapes joined by
a rectangle, bead-mould
surround, framing lightly
hammered, hinged lid.
Hexagonal dove-blue crystal
on the knob. Silver 800,
stamped with monogram
'WW', trademark 'JH', 'JW'
(Josef Wagner) and Viennese
hallmark (A 3). Execution:
Wiener Werkstätte. Height
14.7 cm, length 27 cm, width
12.4 cm. Private collection,
Vienna.

390 Josef Hoffmann, coffee-pot on irregular octagonal base, 1905. Straight sides with short pointed spout, flat lid level with the hinge, and tall wooden knob. Right-angled ebony handle. Geometric ornament. Silver stamped with monogram 'WW', rose mark 'JHAE' (Josef Hoffmann, Adolf Erbrich), and Viennese hallmark. Execution: Wiener Werkstätte. Height 24.8 cm, width 17.6 cm, depth 5.8 cm. Private collection, Vienna.

391 Josef Hoffmann, eggcup and spoon, 1905. Elongated shape on shallow saucer, broadening out above. Decoration: three square holes in the lower part of the recessed wall. Silver 800, stamped, alloyed monogram 'WW', rose mark 'JH', and Viennese hallmark (A3). Execution: Wiener Werkstätte. 6.8 x 11.3 cm. Private collection, Vienna.

193

392 Josef Hoffmann, inkwell, *c.* 1907-8. This is in the form of a building with a dome and cross-ribbed articulation of the hinged lid, which is taken from a desk fitting. Plated German silver, hammered surface. Height 9.3 cm, width 8.4 cm, depth 11.8 cm. Execution: Wiener Werkstätte. Private collection, Vienna.

393 Josef Hoffmann, flower vase, 1905. Rectangular bowl between two open-ended cubes, hammered silver-plated brass, stamped with monogram 'WW' and rose mark 'JH', in the circle 'JB' (Josef Berger). Height 11 cm, length 39.2 cm, depth 12.2 cm. Execution: Wiener Werkstätte. Private collection, Vienna.

394 Josef Hoffmann, cigar box with spherical knob, 1904. Rectangular basic form standing on short drums, flat top with hinge. Plated German silver. 10 x 16.5 cm. Private collection, Vienna.

395 Josef Hoffmann, flower vase with candlestick, 1904. Four tubes around a centre, four cylinders in the upper part, hammered silver-plated brass. Stamped, alloyed monogram 'WW' and rose mark 'JH', in the circle 'JB' (Josef Berger). Height 28.7 cm, width 10.5 cm, depth 11.2 cm. Execution: Wiener Werkstätte. Private collection, Vienna.

396 Josef Hoffmann, box with lid, 1904. Flat rhomboid-shaped base, straight sides, flat lid, with high three-stepped handle consisting of ovoids. Hammered surface, silver 800. Execution: Josef Holi, Wiener Werkstätte. Monogram 'W.W.' (alloyed) and rose mark 'J.H.' Height 14.2 cm, width 15.3 cm, depth 7.7 cm. Private collection, Vienna.

397 Josef Hoffmann, bowl with lid on spherical feet, c. 1904-6. Flat lid with pointed oval handle and set with stones, hammered silver. Monogram 'WW' and trademark 'JH JB' (Josef Berger). 9.2 x 20.3 cm. Execution: Wiener Werkstätte. Private collection, Vienna.

398 Josef Hoffmann, confectionery box, 1904-5. Lozenge-shaped silver (800) container with abstract floral decoration on four sides, and spherical feet at the corners. Hammered silver, set with lapis lazuli. Execution: Josef Holi, Wiener Werkstätte. Monogram 'WW' (alloyed) and rose mark 'J.H.' Height 5.5 cm, length 18.7 cm, width 14.7 cm. Private collection, Vienna.

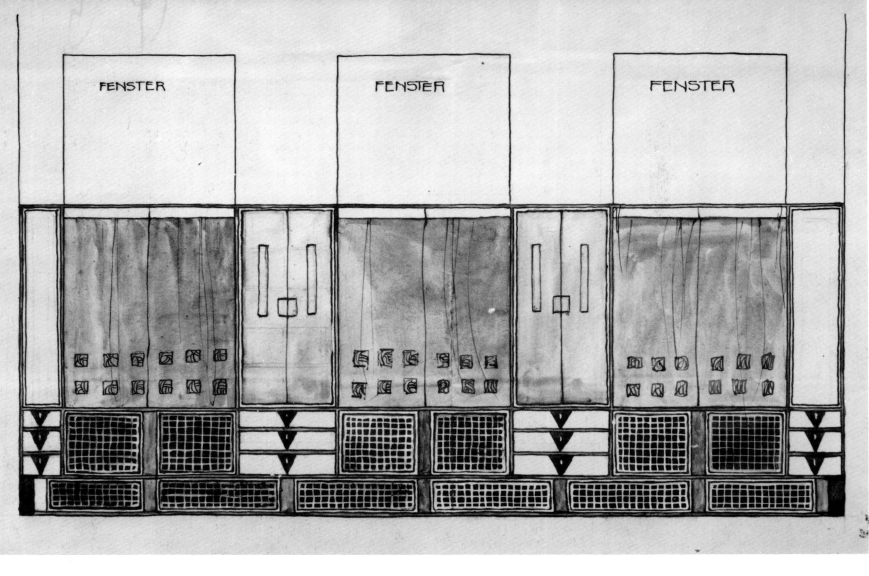

FENSTER FENSTER FENSTER

1 METER

KOLO MOSER

1:50

Cube and Square:
a Functional
Design Unit

The concept that Josef Hoffmann proposed in his representation of surface units in architecture or in handicrafts is that of a static equilibrium which he also achieves through surface decoration. Usually he employs the square with a dynamic black and white equation. Black and white appear as contrasts of light and dark material in a reciprocal relationship, emphasizing the constructive quality of the figurative. Hoffmann aims at an equilibrium of surface forms by producing a unity of light and dark effects and geometric surfaces. In Hoffmann's work a black surface becomes an indication for a black square, freed from customary forms and led by geometry away from the three-dimensionality of the Renaissance traditions. If Hoffmann derives the

399 *Opposite, above:*
Kolo Moser,
design for a room, *c.* 1902.
Articulation of a wall surface
in three window forms.
Below: a decoration of square
and rectangular forms,
which, transformed by the
modular system, emphasizes
the precise articulation.
Indian ink on paper, 34 x 23.2
cm. J. Hummel, Vienna. See
p. 198 for additional
comment.

400 *Page 196:*
Kolo Moser,
design for a room, before
1905. Wall with door, in the
middle a figure in a flowing
gown. Wall divided by a
pattern of squares around the
door. On the right, plan with
detailed square-patterned
ornament. Pencil and
tempera on paper. 40 x 25.2
cm. Private collection,
Vienna.
The Purkersdorf Sanatorium,
1904-8 (ill. on p. 197), was
Austria's first modern
functional structure. It
clearly shows reduction
influences even in the
modular relation of the
buildings's bodies to each
other. The overall structural
mass is mainly made up of
square and rectangular forms.
The window divisions make
the distribution of the inside
rooms perceptible. The
ornamental forms (squares
and rectangles) of the
windows give the whole
building its homogeneous
effect. The structure was
made of iron and concrete.
Here the functional
prerequisites for a sanatorium
are achieved by the external
form. Here modern
technique, medicine and the
pattern of existence are made
recognizable by an architect.
Hoffmann was in charge of
the equipment and fittings.
The Wiener Werkstätte also
played a predominant part in
the equipment. In the modern
way, there was a preference
for furniture which is easily
movable, and not condemned
to remain at a prescribed
point for ever. The firms of
Thonet and Kohn took over
the actual execution of the
installation.

401 *Page 197:*
Josef Hoffmann,
vase in the form of a metal
mast, *c.* 1905-6. Openwork
silver square pattern with
clear glass inlay. Rising from
a flat-arched foot, tall body
on hexagonal plan, with two
rectangular handles at the lip.
Silver 900. Hallmark 'W W'
(alloyed), rose mark 'JH',
head of Diana in hexagon (A
2). Execution: Wiener
Werkstätte. Kenneth Barlow,
Decorative Arts, Munich.

square from the cube in his constructions, he then transforms the surface into a cube and projects this into the rooms beyond the articulation of a façade. The scenography of the sequence of rooms is then always the image of the external architecture.

Epigrammatically it could be said that the surface forms in Hoffmann's artistic works are the bases of the representation; for he develops everything which bears the character of the objective from surface forms. Hoffmann the architect takes great pains to interconnect the affinity of forms by means of a modular system. The permeation of surfaces and planes occupies him in every sphere of his creativity. An astonishing feature is that his circle of disciples also adopts the multiplicity of surface forms. An attempt is made to see all these forms spatially, and especially to discover "a prototype of the object". The aesthetic of the Renaissance had raised perspective to an essentially scholarly scientific requirement. Hoffmann and his circle strive for a kind of return to surface architecture (*architecture plate et colorée*).

Around 1900, Viennese artists had no wish to be geometers, but geometry is, for them, as necessary as the spanner is for an automobile mechanic. The dimensions of the modular system which was influenced by Asia, especially Japan, was a general expression of the effort to test the use of geometry in the arts for the purpose of interpreting the imagination of the constructive as a new style. The pattern, it had been determined, achieves its purpose only if the decorated objects are used: "Further, the purposive aesthetic note is found in the iron filigree bowls and fruit baskets made by the Wiener Werkstätte. When in use, and only then, these screen bodies with their square perforations acquire their full decorative effect. The fruit bowls are so conceived that the colour effects of the apples, pears, and grapes play through the white enamelled openings of the wall, like the effect produced by the lattice porcelain of old Berlin. The dark patina of the napkin rings is designed so that their rectangles will complement the white damask linen.

"Especially delicate is a slender, upward-reaching, angular pillar with indented panels made of this lattice work. It has been designed for climbing flowers. Irregularly placed, easily detached and placed elsewhere on the lattice work are lattice boxes, like little balconies, from which twigs stretch out. Here too the true charm is only apparent when it is in use, when through the white espaliers green growth winds upwards and the airy, flower-clad tower rises with all the grace of a fountain. These objects, of little value in themselves, win laurels for art and ingenuity.

"Exemplary is a set of vinegar and oil cruets of Koloman Moser's famous, beautiful, silver table settings. The bottles are set in silver holders with a motif of small squared perforations.

"This pattern achieves its purpose only if the bottles are used, for the colours of the vinegar and oil shimmer through the rectangles, like enamel encrustations, of the silver surface.

"That is a decorative effect, free of any addition, produced by the inherent qualities of the object itself, effectuated, it goes without saying, by its own means, and thus so extraordinarily convincing."[1]

The flat, ornamental surface was the extreme contrast to the florally animated wall decoration. The relations with each other had again become visible in the living area.

"Rhythmic harmony of proportions, great simplicity of the forms, logical perception of the use to which it was to be put, these were the main characteristics of this Vienna style the technical perfection of which was distinguished by the exquisite use of materials which were always used as a flat surface."[2]

Constructive shaping of form often condenses media and objects in its floral rudimentary stages and develops from it an abstracting limitation by means of which buds and forms of fruits can be transformed in their function into stereometric bodies. Severity of form in the sense of abstract grid patterns, contrasts of black and white such as zebra decoration, geometric surface style, cylinder pluralisms and lattice and tube work

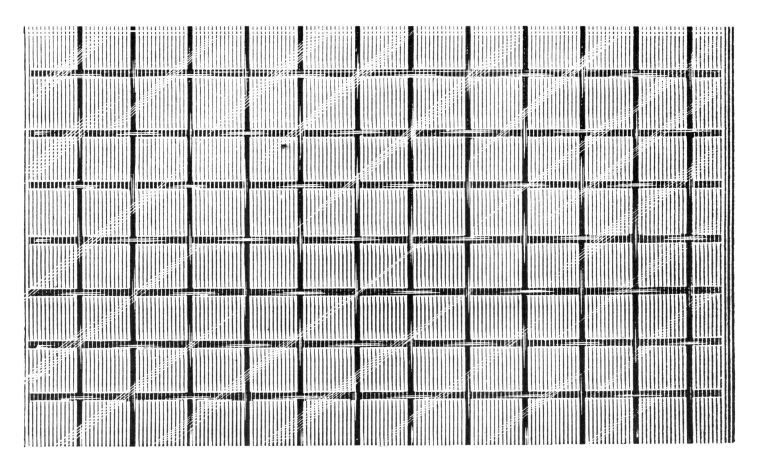

402 Reinforced glass, the best glazing material for overhead lighting, factory windows and floor constructions. By Friedrich Siemens, Dresden, in *Innendekoration* (Darmstadt, 1900), vol 11, p. 89. 37 x 28.3 cm. Private collection, Munich.

are prototypes that could, repeatedly and alternatingly, be inserted (ills., pp. 226-7). The formalist arbitrariness of art nouveau, for the Wiener Werkstätte, makes serial, but *not* mass, production possible in order to capture a wider market. In 1903 Josef Hoffmann and Kolo Moser conceived and established a production group for modern handicrafts which was close to the Vienna Secession.

Cubic rectilinearity, the feeling for geometric order and ornamental reserve were outward forms that gave precedence to the group-like series of objects over the individual single form; grid-patterned tin-plate, especially, in its cubic construction, introduced a new consciousness in regard to material (ills. 430-45).

The end result was a pluralistic unit pattern of squared sieve-like openings. The individuality of the surface pattern remained secondary; diaphanously, the sheathing resolved the object. The tin covering of the lamp (ill. 427), of the basket (ill. 428), or of the box was, of course, a limitation of the body of the receptacle but became "dematerialized" in form so that it allowed the artistic purpose behind it to become clearly visible. A conscious design had sprung up. The "co-operative" perforated style, never before seen in this form, based on the right-angle and tubular forms, transmitted that typical Viennese view that indicates a deliberate exaggeration of the Werkstätte ideas. Out of the constructive and floral dichotomy, a synthesis in favour of "the geometric space-surface body" was reached. Contrasting of functional rudiments makes the little baskets, flower stands, boxes, and lamps into objects, without acknowledging the penetrating purposiveness of the Van de Velde imitator. Everything that can be dispensed with is playfully left out. In a kind of paraphrase of the construction problem new forms arise that characterize the art of the Werkstätte. Swaying, hanging, adhering, and standing of suspension systems appear, predominantly in the right-angles.

403 Kolo Moser, flower vase, *c.* 1905. White lacquered sheet-iron. Decoration: openwork square pattern. 20.5 x 9.5 cm. Private collection, Vienna.

404 Cooling apparatus by
W. Schmidt Co., Bretten,
Baden, the largest factory
making cooling and distilling
apparatus. From p. 15 of the
advertising section, catalogue
of the International
Exhibition, Paris, 1900.
Graphic design by Bernhard
Pankok. 24 x 19.5 cm. Private
collection, Munich.

405 Coupling for a
tramway overhead system.
From p. 41 of the advertising
section, catalogue of the
International Exhibition,
Paris, 1900 (publicity by AG
Felten & Guilleaume
Carlswerk, Mülheim, Rhine;
graphic design by Bernhard
Pankok). 24 x 19.5 cm.

The connection of plants with scaffolding-like sheathing made of whitened tin-plate was exciting. The flower baskets, tables, stands, whatnots, pedestals, and cases with their architectonic effects led to an interconnection of objects. The plant and its holder are combined into a unity, in spite of the extreme differences in the consistency of the materials. However, presentation of the plant is the primary concern. Here decoration consisted of a perforated grid system that allowed light and air to reach the plants. It was a decoration that sufficed without the usual applied floral ornament. The proportioning of the perforated holder or pedestal became the most important concern. After the saturation of form of art nouveau, a limiting process of simplified construction began. Form leads not to a refined selection, but to the simple. The sober industrial form of the objects made under the influence of the Wiener Werkstätte represents an intensification of the basic form being sought for. By means of the sieve-like, punched perforation the simple tube can retain its pattern which leads to a pluralistic loosening of the walls of hollow objects. The communal theory of form or shape in the sense of the words of Christian von Ehrenfels renounces personal individuality because the perforated

whitened tin is to be understood as a collective design and is employed as such by Kolo Moser, Josef Hoffmann, Franz Messner, H. Ofner, and their disciples. Design as a group language and a co-operative sign in the consumption of art has been created here. Only the *Bauhaus* in Dessau in the 1920s adopted similar production ideas.

The simplified black and white decoration in glass and ceramic is to be viewed together with the whole limitation programme of the Wiener Werkstätte. New nuances of proportion were conceived and developed, while at the same time there was a stricter discipline of form. It connects vertical supports to the cube or the semicircle. Furniture exhibits slender posts, and with them lattice-like chairs, tables, and stools were designed. Doing justice to the material employed forces an acknowledgement of its nature. The stereometric basic forms allow the effect of the material and its usefulness to become a unity. This endeavour is clearly emphasized in hammered

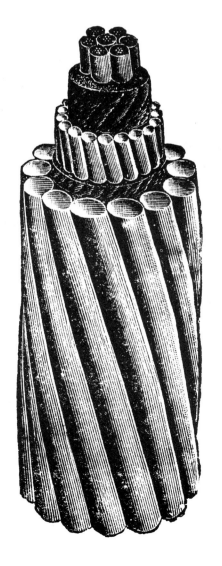

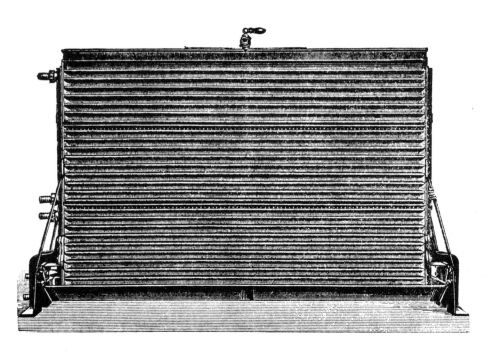

200

metal objects. Rods in the form of thin supporting props provide the objects with lightness and resolve the block by means of high "legs". Also the full curvature of the metal vessels (ills. 368, 431, 434) in connection with the perforated surfaces shows the constructive functional orientation which, together with the architecture, is to be seen as the total work of art.

The optimal use of space by means of built-in furniture and the wall parallelism so achieved, the clarity of construction, in plan and layout, and the honesty of natural materials occupied the Viennese architects. By means of light lattice-like surfaces and vertically striped articulation in the modular system, analogous arrangements were tried out, in theory and in practice, in international constructive art nouveau architecture.

Equally, Peter Behrens, Charles R. Mackintosh, and Louis Sullivan had decided to let the wall have the effect of a diaphanous surface. Its appearance is structurally analogous to Far Eastern models.

Frank Lloyd Wright and Bruno Taut and, finally, Adolf Loos gave concrete form to the perceptions in their practical and theoretical work. The careful construction of the supporting skeleton of all the furniture forms of these designers, the articulation of surfaces, the subtle holders, which in spite of their transition function retained their

individual quality, reveal the highest degree of economic planning. Again and again the furniture maintains a "floating" quality which is achieved by a delicately constructed arrangement of supports. Hoffmann, especially at the beginning of his Purkersdorf period, provides this effect with his stabilization spheres which give visual expression to new static data.

It is mainly in his furniture design that Hoffmann draws attention by the clear articulation of the constituent areas. In bentwood furniture this leads to the "transparency" of the forms of the article of furniture that, owing to its lightness, contains within it no static premises as does the furniture of cabinet-makers. Very often the composition of the design is dependent only upon the vertical order of the posts and the accompanying horizontal order of the frames. The individual supports thus become more meaningful; for example, the vertical carriers. If Hoffmann designs closed forms of furniture, then, however, the thin props receive, by means of the floating cover form which encases them, that peculiar significance which in spite of its compositonal grouping indicates certain sculptural effects.

406 Steel cable. From p. 40 of the advertising section, catalogue of the International Exhibition, Paris, 1900 (publicity by AG Felten & Guilleaume Carlswerk, Mülheim, Rhine; graphic design by Bernhard Pankok). 24 x 19.5 cm. Private collection, Munich.

407 Cross-section of a telegraph cable. From p. 41 of the advertising section, catalogue of the International Exhibition, Paris, 1900 (publicity by AG Felten & Guilleaume Carlswerk, Mülheim, Rhine; graphic design by Bernhard Pankok). 24 x 19.5 cm. Private collection, Munich.

408 Melchior Lechter, vignette for a section from Stefan George's *Teppich des Lebens* (detail), 1899. Chromolithograph, 32 x 28 cm. Private collection, Munich.

1901

HEFT 18

VER SACRUM

409 School of Kolo Moser, square pot, *c.* 1908. White body with white glaze; square openings in pairs on the sides as decorative ornament. Execution: Max Roesler AG, Rodach. Height 10 cm, width 10.2 cm, depth 10 cm. Private collection, Vienna.

410 Decorative ornamentation of square patterns. A page from the periodical *Ver Sacrum*, no. 18, 1901. Private collection.

411 School of Kolo Moser, pottery vase, 1905. Blue and white rectangular decoration arranged in bands. 19.2 x 9.3 cm. Execution: Langenzersdorf. Private collection, Vienna.

412 Kolo Moser (attributed), flower-stands between vertical struts, 1903–4. The top receptacle is full width. Sides decorated in black and white chessboard pattern. Base area of rectangular frame with cross-struts on which the vertical struts rest. Beechwood and sheet-iron painted white, with black and white chessboard pattern painted on. Height 85 cm, length 45 cm, width 45 cm. J. Hummel, Vienna.

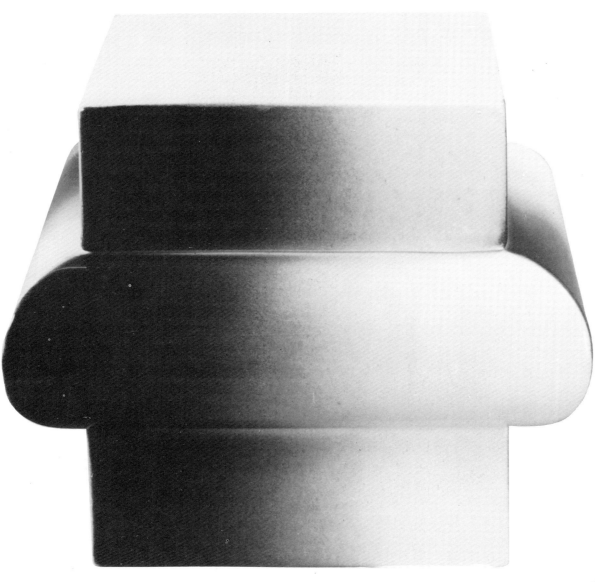

413 Dagobert Peche,
vase on rectangular plan with
central circular swelling, *c.*
1913–14. Neck with the same
dimensions as the base, rising
above the shoulder. Black and
white glazed stoneware.
Execution: Vereinigte Wiener
und Gmundener Keramik.
Height 20 cm. Private
collection, Vienna.

414 Cooling apparatus by
W. Schmidt Co., Bretten,
Baden, the largest factory
making cooling and distilling
apparatus. From p. 15 of the
advertising section, catalogue
of the International
Exhibition, Paris, 1900.
Graphic design by Bernhard
Pankok. 24 x 19.5 cm. Private
collection, Munich.

415 Josef Hoffmann
(attributed), coloured glass
flask, *c.* 1905. Recessed neck,
flat top above the lip with
spherical knob. Cylindrical
ribbed body with ground-in
stopper. Height 25 cm.
Private collection, Vienna.

416 Kolo Moser (attributed), vase, *c.* 1900. Flat foot ring, upright body, recessed neck, opal glass with applied black circles. Height 17.5 cm, width 18.1 cm, diameter of base 15.8 cm. Private collection, Vienna.

417 Berthold Löffler, green glazed pottery candlestick, *c.* 1905. Plate-like base, cylindrical form in centre, connected at the side with the base edge by a sail-like triangle with a hole for the handle. Stamped with monogram 'Lö', Viennese pottery mark. 14 cm. Private collection, Vienna.

418 Michael Powolny, flower bowl, 1906. White glazed bowl, white pottery, with base enclosed laterally by three blue glazed cylindrical forms. Execution: Wiener Keramik. 12 x 30 cm. Private collection, Vienna. Glass and ceramic forms show that between 1906 and 1914 artists were looking for a type which was liberated from so-called Renaissance models. Floral art nouveau no longer represents the vigorous plant form; instead, glassblowers and potters work from architectural forms and use individual stereometric forms such as the cube, cylinder, sphere or hemisphere. These "stuck together forms" are often reminiscent of machine parts, objects for the "living machine".

419   Joseph Hoffmann, table, 1903–4. Four legs broadening towards the bottom, which are held by a four-sided lattice motif, on the model of a Japanese Shinto temple gateway. Projecting top. Solid black fumed oak, treated with lime, with sycamore inlays and white metal foot covers. The type was produced as a sewing table. Height 79 cm, width 69.5 cm, depth 69.5 cm. Execution: Wiener Werkstätte. Private collection, Vienna.

420   Josef Hoffmann, stool of squared wood in shape of a die, with base struts. Solid sycamore stained black, webbing woven in chessboard pattern. Execution: Wiener Werkstätte. Height 35 cm, width 35 cm, depth 35 cm. Private collection, Vienna.

421 Josef Hoffmann, occasional table, *c.* 1905. Double frame with base struts and intermediate shelf; pine, painted black. Execution: Haus B. Koller, Vienna. Height 68 cm, width 50 cm, depth 50 cm. Private collection, Vienna.

422 Lady's writing-desk and stool in the style of Josef Hoffmann, *c.* 1903. Desk with three-sided lattice motif, high side rails, top unemphatic. Beech painted blue, upholstered stool. Height 75 cm, width 83 cm, depth 50.2 cm. Stool: height 46 cm, width 37.2 cm. Private collection, Vienna. Cabinet-made furniture directly following architects' designs clearly shows the relation to the room cube, at any rate much more strongly than bentwood furniture. Hoffmann's table is based on the Japanese *torii* or temple gateway. The widening cross-section of the feet indicates this clearly. The lattice motif is also adopted from the Japanese cultural world, because the bamboo lattice inside the living rooms of the teahouse exercises a space-dividing function. After 1904–6 Josef Hoffmann made further use of the Japanese modular system, in which he also included his furniture designs and architectural plans. Viennese cabinet-made furniture of the period, which was designed by architects and artists, is therefore more directly displayed against the room volumes than bentwood furniture which was more casual both in structure and in use. Because of their character, bentwood pieces were sometimes used as occasional furniture, intended to achieve the greatest usefulness in the smallest space. Bentwood coffee-house furniture is a good example. The representative form of the furniture cube, which preserves its architectonic severity through its square lattice-like decoration, is an important feature in the composition of the Viennese room.

424 Table on a cross-shaped base with flat underlays. Twin squared rods painted black support the round top above a square cross. Beech, painted black and white. Vienna, *c.* 1900. Height 78.5 cm, width 81 cm, depth 59 cm. Private collection, Vienna.

423 Josef Hoffmann (attributed), armchair, 1904–6. U-shaped base with cross-struts; four rods painted black which between them enclose the seat, the arm rests and the back. Contrasting white rods are arranged like a grille. Soft wood painted black and white. Height 85 cm, width 58 cm, depth 53 cm, seat height 45 cm. Private collection, Vienna.

426 Occasional or serving table after Scottish-Irish models, c. 1903. Narrow rectangular top with four legs and struts, double struts on the semicircular flaps, which can be opened out to enlarge the table. Beech, stained red and veneered. Probably of Viennese design. Height 75 cm, width 80 cm, depth 54 cm. Private collection, Vienna.

425 Josef Hoffmann (presumably designed by), chair, c. 1903. Runner-like base with central cross-strut. High seat side-rails, webbing seat, low back with slightly curved top bar. Stained oak. Height 77.5 cm, width 40 cm, depth 47.7 cm. Private collection, Vienna.

427 Josef Hoffmann, storm lantern with matt glass shade, *c.* 1904. Vase on circular base, holder with perforated edge, central cylinder holding the glass shade, curved lateral handle uniting cylinder and edge. Decoration: openwork square patterning. Stamped 'Wiener Werkstätte', silver hallmark, rose mark 'JH'. 19.5 x 17 cm. Private collection, Vienna.

The formalistic predilection of art nouveau within the Wiener Werkstätte was directed by clear-thinking basic research towards serial production in order to achieve wider consumption, but by no means mass production. The Wiener Werkstätte, one of the societies close to the Viennese Secession for the production of modern artistic craft work, was conceived and put into practice in 1903 by Kolo Moser and Josef Hoffmann. It began work at Neustiftgasse 13 in the VII district of Vienna. The rectilinearity of cubism, the feeling for geometric arrangement and ornamental restraint were decisive outward forms which encouraged serial production rather than individual pieces. In addition, tin-plate and silver-plate, with their cubic construction and grid patterns, contributed to a new consciousness of the materials employed. This resulted in a pluralistic standard pattern of square, sieve-like openings. Surface patterning became secondary but the surrounding casing made the wall, as it were, transparent. The tin-plate casing or the silver-plate of the lamp, basket or box was admittedly a limitation of the body of the object, but was dematerialized by the

428 Kolo Moser,
oil and vinegar cruets on
rectangular base, *c.* 1905.
Basket-like holder with
central handle, to right and
left oil and vinegar cruets.
Openwork square pattern,
silver and glass. Stamped with
monogram 'WW', trademark
'K M, A M', and Viennese
hallmark. Execution: Wiener
Werkstätte, Alfred Mayer.
17.2 cm. Private collection,
Vienna.

429 Josef Hoffmann,
flower holder on octagonal
plan with spherical feet, *c.*
1905. Small silver basket.
Stamped: monogram 'W W'
and trademark 'J H',
Viennese silver hallmark.
Decoration: openwork
square pattern. Execution:
Wiener Werkstätte. 9.3 cm.
Private collection, Vienna.

kind of paraphrase of the
constructive problem new
forms arise, which signalize
the art of the Werkstätte. The
floating, hanging, holding
and standing of the
supporting systems,
predominantly in a right-
angle, emerges.
The combination of plants
with scaffolding-like
surrounds of sheet-iron
painted white was
stimulating. The
architectonic effect of flower
baskets, tables, stands,
shelves, bases and boxes led
to a mutual combination of
objects. Plants and their
casing are brought into a
unity, although extreme
contrasts in the physical
make-up of the materials are
present. Nevertheless, object
and design remain secondary;
presentation of the plant is the
primary concern.

opening of the square holes.
The grid-patterned objects
clearly mark the conclusion
of a sublimating learning
process that produced results.
A conscious design had come
into being.
Simplicity, artistically
acquired and boldly
interpreted, was desired in
order to eradicate any

possible analogies. The "co-
operative" lattice-work style,
previously unrepresented in
this form, with the
rectangular base and the tube
shapes, transmits that
typically Viennese
conception – which indicates
a deliberate over-emphasis by
the Werkstätte. Out of the
dichotomy of the structural

and the floral came a synthesis
in favour of "the body with a
geometric surface". The
contrasting of functional
adjuncts makes the basket,
flower stand, box or lamp
into an apparatus without the
insistent functionality which
Van de Velde's imitators
acknowledge. Everything
superfluous is left out. In a

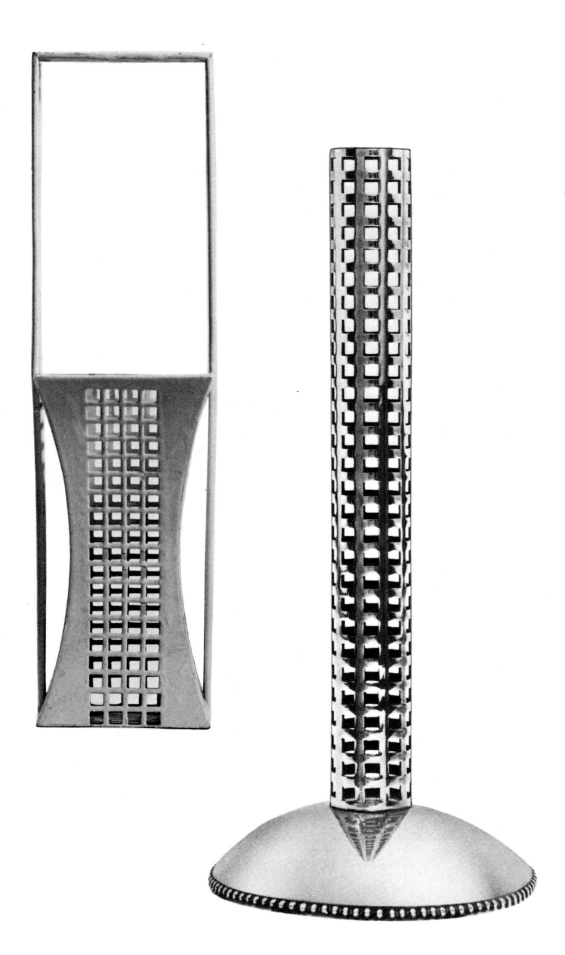

437 Josef Hoffmann, flower basket, *c.* 1905. Square plan, recessed towards the middle, high handle, incurving rectangle with square pattern, painted white tin-plate. Decoration: openwork square pattern. Height 26.9 cm, width 7.2 cm, depth 6.8 cm. Private collection, Vienna.

438 Kolo Moser, flower vase, *c.* 1905–6. Round base with bead-moulding, and hexagonal shaft with openwork square pattern. Execution: Wiener Werkstäte. 21.6 cm. Private collection, Vienna.

436 Josef Hoffmann, small flower basket, sheet-iron painted white. Decoration: openwork square pattern, pointed oval plan, oval handle, *c.* 1905. Height 25.5 cm, width 10.2 cm, depth 12.5 cm. Private collection, Vienna.

439 Kolo Moser, inkwell *c.* 1903. Sheet-iron painted white. Decoration: openwork square pattern. Lid slightly raised above recessed shoulder. 12.8 x 10.5 cm. Private collection, Vienna.

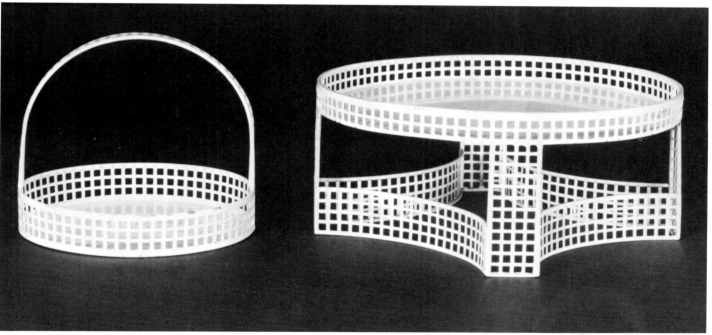

440 Flower basket, c. 1905. Circular base with right-angled handle continuing to the base. Decoration: openwork square pattern. 17.5 x 8.6 cm. Private collection, Vienna.

441 Table accessory for flowers and fruit on a pointed oval plan with straight sides, stilted on a pointed oval strip and two lateral supports of sixteen square holes. Height 8.5 cm, length 16.5 cm, depth 7.8 cm. Private collection, Vienna.

442 Vase with handle on square plan, handle protruding high above the straight sides. Tin-plate, painted white. Decoration: openwork square pattern. Height 16.5 cm, width 7.2 cm, depth 4.5 cm. Private collection, Vienna.

443 Basket, c. 1905, on octagonal plan with straight sides and high right-angled handle. Tin-plate, painted white. Decoration: openwork square pattern. 19.5 x 11. 2 cm. Private collection, Vienna.

444 Confectionery bowl with curved handle on oval plan. Tin-plate, painted white. Decoration: openwork square pattern. 16 x 14.2 cm. Private collection, Vienna.

445 Table accessory on oval plan held by four upright tin-plate elements. At ground level four concave connecting stays. Painted white tin-plate. 9.8 x 24 cm. Private collection, Vienna.

215

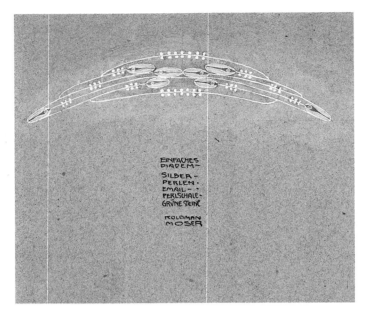

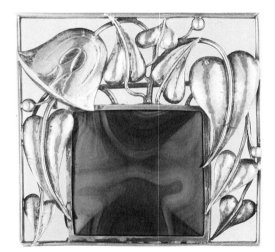

450 Kolo Moser, design for a tiara. Pencil, white and colour on brownish-red Ingres paper. 13.6 x 10.2 cm. Inscribed (in German): "simple tiara, silver, pearls, enamel, pearl shell, green stones, Koloman Moser". Private collection, Vienna.

451 Josef Hoffmann, brooch, c. 1910. Large, square, cloudy, greenish-blue malachite between silver leaves and harebells. Monogram of the Wiener Werkstätte 'W W' (alloyed), 'J H', head of Diana. Execution: Wiener Werkstätte. 5 x 5 cm. Private collection, Vienna.

452 Georg Klimt, bracelet, c. 1904. Arched granulated silver-gilt surface, set with amethyst and pearl shell. Diameter 8 cm. Private collection, Vienna.

453 Otto Prutscher, necklace and earrings, 1908. Platinum, pearl shell and platinum granulation. Stamped with monogram of Wiener Werkstätte, 'W W' (alloyed) and trademark. Execution: Wiener Werkstätte. Length 23 cm. Private collection, Vienna.

454 Powder-box by a Viennese silversmith, after 1912. Silver, champlevé and cloisonné enamel. Decoration: flowers and twigs. 3.2 x 5 cm. Private collection, Vienna.

455 Dagobert Peche, brooch, after 1915. Silver and champlevé enamel. Decoration: full-face portrait of a youth. Monogram of the Wiener Werkstätte, 'W W' (alloyed). Execution: Wiener Werkstätte. 2.5 x 4.5 cm. Private collection, Vienna.

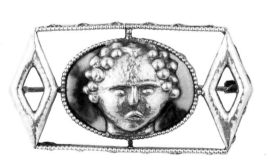

458　Necklace, silver-gilt, pearl shells, *c.* 1908. Marked with hallmark 'W W' (alloyed), rose mark 'J H, S T' (Stanislaus Teyc), head of Diana in pentagon (A). Execution: Wiener Werkstätte, Stanislaus Teyc. 10 x 2.8 cm. Private collection, Vienna.

459　Bracelet in gold, ivory and diamonds, *c.* 1913–14. Marked with hallmark 'W W' (alloyed) and rose mark 'J H'. Execution: Wiener Werkstätte for Mäda Primavesi. 4.8 x 21.2 cm. Private collection, Vienna.

456　Brooch, *c.* 1910, silver (900), partly gilt, slightly hammered surface, coral and chrysoprase. Marked with hallmark 'W W' (alloyed), rose mark 'J H', head of Diana in hexagon (A 2). Execution: Wiener Werkstätte. 4 x 5.3 cm. Private collection, Vienna.

457　Belt fastening, *c.* 1907. Gilded copper and champlevé enamel. Marked with stamp 'Wiener/Werk/stätte'. 6.9 x 6.5 cm. Private collection, Vienna.

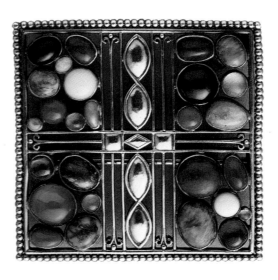

460　Pendant-brooch, *c.* 1910. Silver (900) partly gilded, lapis lazuli, corals, opals, amaldine, turquoise, chrysoprase, agate, moonstones, cornelian. Marked with hallmark 'W W' (alloyed), and head of Diana in pentagon (A 2), A. Execution: Wiener Werkstätte. 5.5 x 5.5 cm. Private collection, Vienna.

461　Brooch in gold (750) and coral, *c.* 1908. Marked with hallmark 'W W' (alloyed), and head of chamois (A 3), A. Execution: Wiener Werkstätte. 1.1 x 8.5 cm. Private collection, Vienna.

In 1907, Adolf Loos remarked in *Die Potemkin'sche Stadt* (in *Verschollene Schriften* 1897–1933, Vienna, 1983, P. 110):

"I mainly count on those people taking part in the migration whose job it is to make dwellings for us. That means our carpenters, upholsterers and decorators. But one professional class is excluded: the architects! Please do not think that I'm afraid of the copyists among them. On the contrary, I would be glad if every architect would create according to my way of thinking. But they won't. They will only misunderstand me. As they misunderstood me over the Museum Café. Since the opening of this coffee-house, every house looks as bare as a coffee-house. Earlier – it was the time of woods stained green, red, violet and grey, the time when every piece of furniture was pressed into a circle, or large rings of laths occupied the rooms (I shall only remind you that Josef Hoffmann's Apollo candle establishment at the Hof and the Museum Café originated around the same time) – there was at least a trace of what for my part could be called 'applied art'. But since then our sewer gratings must suffer in order to supply the decoration for flower vases and fruit bowls. That was not the idea. If the Museum Café had not come into being at that time, the whole decorative direction taken by Olbrich, Van de Velde and Hoffmann would have collapsed in ornamentalism. The coffee-house showed them new but wrong roads. I do not want to put them on the wrong road again. Culture has a right to be left finally in peace by the experimenters. But I hope a great many people may be convinced of what I intended."

462   Josef Hoffmann, armchair (sitting machine), *c.* 1905. Two flat rods (rectangular in section) are bent to form the sides and arm rests. Between them the seat is mounted between lateral boards with grilles. The hinged back has an inlaid board with an openwork square pattern inserted in a rectangular bentwood frame. The slope of the back is adjusted by a movable brass rod fitting between hemispherical knobs on the side-pieces. Balls as stabilizing elements at various points. Beech, stained mahogany. Height 111.5 cm, width 69.2 cm, depth 82.8 cm. Signed with the label of Jacob and Josef Kohn, Vienna. Frank Jaeger Collection, Munich.

463 Berthold Löffler, wooden jewel-case with chessboard pattern, *c.* 1902. Square plan on pointed angular feet. Soft wood painted black, white and yellow. Height 20 cm, width 35.2 cm, depth 15.3 cm. Private collection, Vienna.

In the series of illustrations it should be recognized that Loos abandons the restless "baroque" form of the elephant table and changes over to functional usefulness in his objects. See Adolf Loos, *Ornament und Erziehung* in his *Sämtliche Schriften*, vol 1 (Vienna and Munich, 1962), p. 392 *et seq.*

464 Cube-shaped pot *c.* 1902, with pattern of square holes in the vertical sides. White pottery, with white glaze. Possibly school of Kolo Moser, but see p. 202, no. 409. Height 102 cm, width and depth 10 cm. Private collection, Vienna.

465 Table chest,
c. 1904, hitherto attributed to
Kolo Moser. Cubical base
with chessboard pattern and
cubical top of tin-plate
painted white and decorated
with square holes in a lattice
pattern. Height 20.3 cm,
width 10.2 cm, depth 10.1
cm. J. Hummel, Vienna.

466 Occasional table after
Josef Hoffmann, c. 1903.
Square base with round top,
vertical side-struts with
chessboard ornament and a
shelf between them. Beech,
painted white, with black and
white chessboard pattern.
Height 78.5 cm, diameter 50
cm. Private collection,
Vienna.

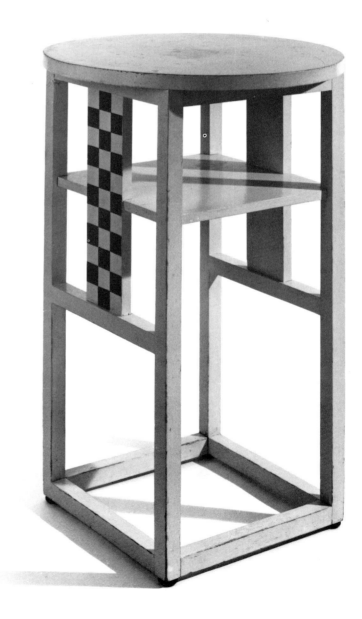

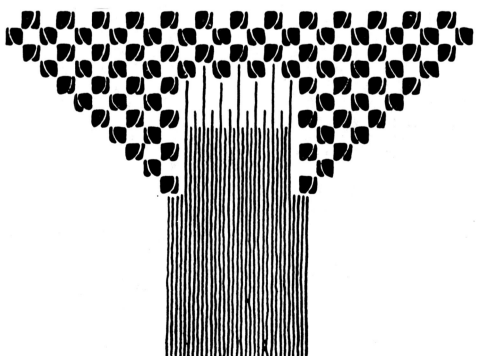

467 Kolo Moser,
textile design. Abstract
pattern, inspired by floral leaf
patterns which are
ornamentally transformed.
Illustrated in *Ver Sacrum*,
1900. Drawing-ink on paper,
16 x 16 cm. Private collection,
Vienna.

468 Kolo Moser,
abstract book ornament for
an article about George
Minne in *Ver Sacrum* IV,
1901. Page size, 25.5 x 24 cm.
Private collection, Vienna.

469 Wiener Werkstätte,
design for an endpaper, *c.*
1903. Rectangular forms
alternating with blank areas.
Decoration: flower stems
developed from the square
standing on end, as well as
from stem and leaf forms.
Indian ink with colour wash.
Private collection, Vienna.

470 Wiener Werkstätte,
textile design, before 1910.
Alternating abstract pattern
developed from the calyx of
the harebell. Four calyxes
contained in a square and
arranged in an alternately
negative and positive rhythm.
Indian ink on white paper.
28.6 x 22 cm. Private
collection, Vienna.

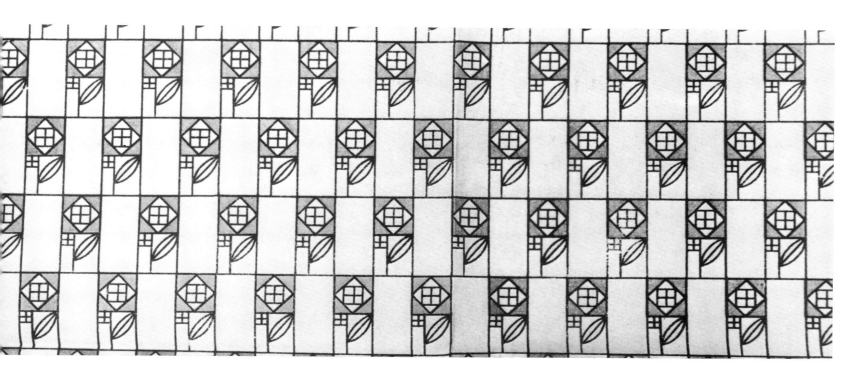

471 Berthold Löffler
and Michael Powolny,
cylindrical vase on flat base, *c.*
1908. White pottery with
black and white glaze.
Decoration: black vertical
stripes in the form of a grille.
Square pattern below the lip
under a horizontal ring. 22.4
x 10.2 cm. Private collection,
Vienna.

472 Berthold Löffler
and Michael Powolny,
cylindrical vase on flat base, *c.*
1908. White pottery with
black and white glaze.
Decoration: black lines on
white background. 22.8 x
10.3 cm. Private collection,
Vienna.

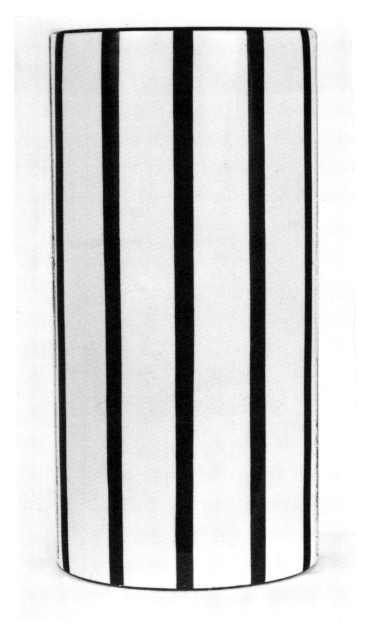

473 Josef Hoffmann,
design sketch and division of
a square, *c.* 1930. Pencil and
washed Indian ink on squared
paper, signed in blue ink 'J H'
in a circle. Height 31.5 cm,
width 21 cm, backing 42 x
29.6 cm. Private collection,
Vienna.
Black and white pattern
arranged with variations of
the logical lines. Attempt at a
modification of the regular
development. The late
designs are shown here to
prove that Josef Hoffmann
still clung to the square
composition in the works of
his old age and illustrated the
most subtle differentiations in
sketches.

474 Berthold Löffler
(attributed), round box with
lid, *c.* 1906. Decoration:
chessboard pattern.
Stoneware, glazed black and
white geometric decoration,
unsigned. 8.3 cm. Private
collection, Vienna.

475 Josef Hoffmann, design for a square composition, *c.* 1930. Pencil and Indian ink on squared paper, signed in blue ink 'J H' in a circle.
In this even freer design Hoffmann illustrates the irregularity in the rule. Each square differs from the others, and yet the experiment confirms the regularity and above all the calibrations of square-pluralism.

476 Michael Powolny, ceramic vase with geometric black and white decoration, glazed. Body rising from flat circular base and markedly recessed in the centre. Base and mouth are identical in size. Stamped with Viennese pottery mark. 14.3 x 8.1 cm. Execution: Wiener Keramik. Private collection, Vienna.

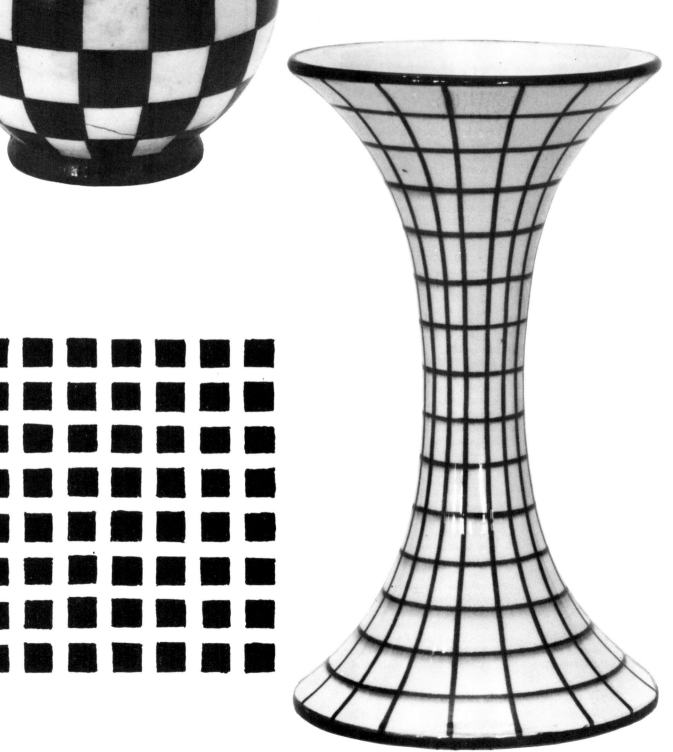

Munich, 1969.

Catalogue of the exhibition "Weltkulturen und moderne Kunst. Die Begegnung der europäischen Kunst und Musik im 19. und 20. Jahrhundert mit Asien, Afrika, Ozeanien, Afro- und Indo-Amerika." Munich, 1972.

Catalogue of the exhibition "Symbolismus." Munich, 1973.

"Begegnungen ostasiatischer und europäischer Kunsttraditionen in der Malerei und Graphik des 19. Jahrhunderts" in *Alte und moderne Kunst,* Vienna, 1974.

"Ostasiatische Gefäße aus Halbedelstein und ihre Sockelung als analoger Prozess in der Glaskunst um 1900" in *Extrait des Annales du 6 Congrès de L'Association Internationale pour L'Histoire du Verre.* Liège, 1975.

Zuckerkandl, B.: *Zeitkunst, Wien 1901-1907.* Vienna, 1908.

"Koloman Moser" in *Dekorative Kunst,* 7, 1904.

Periodicals, exhibition catalogues etc.

Alte und moderne Kunst. Österreichische Zeitschrift für Antiquitäten, Bilder und Kunstgegenstände. Vienna, 1966*ff.*

Art Nouveau, Textil-Dekor um 1900. Catalogue of an exhibition at the Württembergisches Landesmuseum. Stuttgart, 1980.

Catalogue of the Hamburg Museum of Arts and Crafts. Hamburg, 1972.

Das Interieur. Viennese monthly review of applied art. Vienna, 1900*ff.*

Dekorative Kunst. An illustrated periodical for applied art. Munich, 1897/98-1928/29.

Deutsche Kunst und Dekoration. Illustrated monthly for modern painting, sculpture, architecture, interior decoration and artistic work by women. Darmstadt, 1897-1934.

Die verborgene Vernunft, Funktionale Gestaltung im 20. Jahrhundert. Museum of Arts and Crafts, Zurich, 1971.

Die Wiener Werkstätte. Austrian Museum of Applied Art, Vienna, 1967.

Ein Dokument Deutscher Kunst. vol. 2, "Kunst und Dekoration 1851-1914." Exhibition catalogue, Hessisches Landesmuseum, Darmstadt, 1976.

Festschrift Josef Hoffmann zum 60. Geburtstag. Vienna, 1930.

Frühes Industriedesign, Wien 1900-1908. Galerie nächst St. Stephan, Vienna, 1977.

Gebogenes Holz, Konstruktive Entwürfe Wien 1840-1910. Vienna and Munich, 1979.

Glas aus Wien, J. & L. Lobmeyr. Von Biedermeier bis zur Gegenwart. Catalogue of an exhibition at the Bellerive Museum. Zurich, 1979.

Hohe Warte. Fortnightly periodical for the cultivation of artistic training and urban culture. Vienna, 1904-8.

Illustrierte kunstgewerbliche Zeitschrift für Innendekoration, Ausschmückung und Einrichtung der Wohnräume. Darmstadt, 1890*ff.*

Josef Hoffmann, Architect and Designer, 1870-1956. Exhibition catalogue, Fischer Fine Art Gallery, London, 1977.

Jugendstil, der Weg ins zwanzigste Jahrhundert. Heidelberg and Munich, 1972.

Jugendstil. Eine Auswahl aus der Schausammlung. Badisches Landesmuseum, Karlsruhe, 1978.

Jugendstil – 20er Jahre. Exhibition commentary. Künstlerhaus Galerie, Vienna, 1969.

Kunst und Kunsthandwerk. Monthly review of Architecture. Stuttgart, 1902*ff.*

Moderne Vergangenheit, Wien 1800-1900. Catalogue of an exhibition at the Künstlerhaus, Vienna, 1981.

Modern Vienna 1898-1918. Catalogue of an exhibition at the Cooper-Hewitt Museum, New York, the Sarah Campbell Blaffer Gallery, University of Houston, the Portland Art Museum and the Art Institute of Chicago. New York, 1978-9.

Objekte des Jugendstils. Catalogue of the collection at the Bellerive Museum, Zurich, 1975.

Schmuck – Tischgerät aus Österreich 1904/08-1973/77. Catalogue of an exhibition at the Galerie am Graben, Vienna, 1978.

The Studio. An illustrated magazine of fine and applied art. London, 1893*ff.*

Ver Sacrum: Mitteilungen der Vereinigung bildender Künstler Österreichs, I-IV. Vienna, 1898-1903.

Vienna, Birthplace of 20th-century Design. Part I: 1900-1905, Purism and Functionalism. Fischer Fine Art Gallery, London, 1981.

"Vienna 1900-1918". Special number of the cultural monthly *Du,* 23rd year, No. 4, Zurich, 1963.

Vienna, Turn of the Century: Art and Design. Fischer Fine Art Gallery, London, 1980.

The Whistler Peacock Room. Freer Gallery of Art, Washington, D.C., 1951.

Wiener Möbel des Jugendstils. Austrian Museum of Applied Art, Vienna, 1971.

Die Wiener Werkstätte. Modernes Kunsthandwerk von 1903 bis 1932. Catalogue of an exhibition at the Austrian Museum of Applied Art, Vienna, 1967.

Wien um 1900. Catalogue. Vienna, 1964.

Index of Artists

Almaric, Walter (1859 Sèvres – 1960 Nancy)
Worked in glass and ceramics, graduated of the National School of Manufacturing at Sèvres. In 1902 begins production of the so-called *pâte de verre*. From 1908 to 1914 employed by the firm of Daum, Nancy. Opened his own studio in 1919 to produce *pâte de verre*. Around 1925 had about 10 employees.

Ashbee, Charles Robert (1863, Isleworth, London – 1924 Kent)
Architect, designer of arts and crafts, writer and printer. Read Greek and Latin at Cambridge. Studied architecture with G.F. Bodley in London; there he established in 1886/87 the School of Handicraft, a studio where he taught architecture and design. He affiliated this studio with a like-minded group of artists, the Guild of Handicraft (re-established in 1902 in Chipping Campden, Glos.; closed down in 1907). Works (decoration, furniture, jewellery, and silver) were exhibited in London, Düsseldorf, Munich and Vienna. Appointed Professor of English Literature at the University of Cairo in 1915, civilian adviser to the British administration in Palestine, 1919 to 1923.

Bakalowits, E., & Sons
Purveyor to the Imperial and Royal Household, Vienna, retailer of art glass objects. Sold, among others, Koloman Moser's designs.

Beardsley, Aubrey Vincent (1872 Brighton – 1898 Mentone)
Self-taught; inspired by the Pre-Raphaelites and by Japanese woodcuts, he developed his own style which exerted a strong influence on the development of the art of book illustration and art nouveau. Illustrated *Volpone, Lysistrata,* and Wilde's *Salome.*

Behrens, Peter (1868 Hamburg – 1940 Berlin)
Architect, designer of arts and crafts, and painter. Pupil at Karlsruhe and Düsseldorf art schools. One of the founders of the Munich Secession; he designed new type faces for Klingspor in Offenbach. 1900 called to the *Künstlerkolonie* (Artists' Colony) in Darmstadt. From 1907 artistic adviser to the AEG in Berlin. 1922 appointed Professor of Architecture at the Viennese Academy. He designed and furnished his houses in Darmstadt (1900/1) and Neubabelsberg near Potsdam (1907/8). He constructed important industrial buildings: the turbine plant of the AEG in Berlin 1909, buildings for Mannesmann Tube and Pipe works in Düsseldorf, and the workers' housing project in Hennigsdorf. He also designed exhibition stalls, furniture, lamps, and knot carpets. His commercial art work comprises large-format woodcuts in colour, book illustrations, book jackets and posters. He also painted the portraits of the family of the Archduke of Hesse.

Berlepsch-Valendas, Hans Eduard von (31.12.1849 St. Gallen – 17.8.1921 Planegg, near Munich)
Started out studying architecture with Semper at the Polytechnic in Zurich. In 1872 in Frankfurt am Main at Stadel's Art Institute, studying under Sommer and Linnemann. From 1875 at the Munich Academy with Lindenschmidt. Visited England where, under the influence of the work of Morris and Crane, he changed his style. In 1897 represented in the Applied Art Section of the Annual Munich Exhibition.

Blossfeldt, Karl (1865 Schielo, Harz – 1932 Berlin)
Attended elementary and secondary schools in Harzgerode from 1871 to 1881; middle school certificate. 1881, three-year apprenticeship as sculptor and model maker in the Mägdesprung Forge and Art Foundry, Harz. Owing to his extraordinary gifts as a model maker the Marktwald Foundation awarded him a grant to begin study at the Royal Industrial Museum on 1 October 1884. Studied geometric and anatomic drawing, theory of projection, history of style, theory of style, composition and modelling. At the same time he received a practical musical education.
In 1891 he travelled to Rome to study with Prof. M. Meurer. Then visited Greece, Egypt, North Africa, and the rest of Italy. With Prof. Meurer Blossfeldt collected plants and parts of plants as bases for preparations and models. In this period began photography. Remained without interruption in Rome until 1896.
In 1898, assistant to Professor Ernst Ewald at the Royal School of Art in Berlin, teaching the model making class. Married Maria Plank.
1 October 1899, became a lecturer at the Royal Industrial Museum in Berlin, specializing in models of living plants. First photographs of his own plant preparations. Director of the school was Professor Bruno Paul. 1900, constructed a 13 x 18 cm plate camera and began to photograph plants systematically. From his photographs he made slides to illustrate his lecture material. 1921, Professor at the Royal Museum of Arts and Crafts (to 1930/31). Publications: 1928, *Vorformen der Kunst* (Forms preliminary to art) edited by W. Benjamin. 1932, *Wundergarten der Natur* (Nature's Garden of Miracles).

Bradley, William H. (1868 Boston – 1962 La Mesa)
Taught by his father, Aron Bradley. 1895, set up a publishing business; associated with the journal *Pan* in Berlin (1895-7). 1907 to 1916, active as director of different periodicals. Achieved great things in early poster printing (colour lithography); also a renowed commercial artist and book illustrator.

Brauchitsch, Margarete von (1865 Frankenthal/Rügen – 1957 Munich)
Active in Munich. 1897, founding member of the *Vereinigten Werkstätten für Kunst im Handwerk* (United Studios for Art in Handicrafts) in Munich.

Carabin, François Rupert (1862 Zabern (Savern) Alsace – 1932 Strasbourg)
Alsatian sculptor in wood, medallion maker, badge and plaquette artist, gem cutter, and worker in arts and crafts. Figures in ceramic, bronze, and silver. Began as gem cutter, pupil of Lequien. Together with Seurat, Signac, and Dubois-Pillet founded the Society of Independent Artists in Paris. From 1899 on exhibited regularly in the salons of the National Society. From 1920 director of the School of Decorative Arts in Strasbourg. "In the sphere of goldsmithing and figure work as well as ceramics Carabin is one of the pioneers of modern style."

Carriès, Jean (1855 Lyons – 1894 Paris)
In 1874, pupil of the sculptor A. Dumont at the Beaux Arts, Paris; then self-educated. In 1878, first encounter with Japanese pottery at the Paris Universal Exhibition; founded a large ceramics studio in St Armand-en-Puisaye as well as buying the château Monriveau (Nièvre) as a second place of work.

Christiansen, Hans (1866 Flensburg – 1945 Wiesbaden)
Painter, typographer, arts and crafts designer. About 1900 Christiansen was a member of the first Darmstadt Artists' Colony around Joseph Maria Olbrich and Peter Behrens. 1902, went to Paris to live. Occasionally worked on posters and arts and crafts designs.

Colenbrander, Th. A. C. (1841 Doesburg (Holland) – 1918 Arnheim)
Architect, porcelain and textile designer. Worked for the architect C. H. Ebersohn in Arnheim; 1869-70 for French architects in Paris. Back in Holland he worked from 1884 to 1889 for Rozenburg, manufacturers of faience, in The Hague, where he helped in the breakthrough to a new style. From 1895 on artistic director of a carpet manufacturing firm in Amersfoort.

Cranach, Wilhelm Lucas von (1861 Stargard (Pomerania) – 1918 Berlin)
Painter, interior decorator, goldsmith; descendant of the painter, Lucas Cranach. Studied in Weimar and Paris; from 1893 on active as a portrait and landscape painter in Berlin; designed the architectonic furnishings of the Wartburg in Thuringia and other castles in Silesia and Posen. Under the influence of the Russian Yulovski, designed in gold and silver, examples of which were shown at the Paris Universal Exhibition 1900 (Gold Medal for brooches) and the Great Berlin Art Exhibition of 1906.

Cuzner, Bernhard
Silversmith and jeweller, worked around the turn of the century for Liberty & Co (Cymric) Ltd. in London.

Cymric
Under the name Cymric a series of designs for the English hardware factory Liberty & Co. (q.v.) appeared which engaged the services of the following firms and silversmiths: William R. Haseler, Oliver Baker, Bernhard Cuzner, Reginald Rex, Arthur Gaskin, Archibald Knox, Jessie M. King, and Rex Silber. Strictly linear ornamentation adorned the silver objects, frequently decorated with coloured enamel inlay. Liberty was highly important in spreading the *modern style*, the English variant of art nouveau, not only in England but on the Continent. Even today, in Italy, the phrase *Lo stile Liberty* means English art nouveau.

Dalpayrat, Adrien Emile (1884 Limoges – 1910 Paris)
Ceramicist; worked with A Voisin-Delacroix; after his death (1903) with Madam Lesbros in Bourg-la-Reine near Paris. Towards 1910 he gained the cooperation of the designer M. Dufrene. His flamed stoneware vases with freely modelled figure decoration won him a Gold Medal at the Chicago Exhibition of 1893. From 1893 on the exhibitions of Société Nationale des Beaux-Arts presented his works frequently.

Daum Frères
French glassworks in Nancy. Founded around 1875 by Jean Daum. About 1890 the brothers Auguste (1853 – 1909 and Antonin (1864 – 1930), who inherited the glass factory, went over to the production of art glass along art nouveau lines. In 1891 they founded their *Ateliers d'art à la Verrerie de Nancy*. Besides using Gallé's techniques (high and deep cut, relief etching, enamel applications, and glass marquetry) they made their own discoveries: varying the colour of their glasses by the fusing in and on of powdered colours and ground glass, which endowed the pieces with a surprising expressivity. Along with floral and abstract decoration, favoured mood pictures, and

inclusions into glass of different materials. The shapes of their glasses after 1900 began to diverge from traditional form and take on a new look with floral design. Represented at the Chicago Exhibition of 1893 and the Paris Universal Exhibition of 1900. With Gallé, the Daum factory belongs to the artistically most significant representatives of the School of Nancy. The firm eventually discarded traditional types of vessel and chose models from nature, the bottle gourd being the most favoured object.

Debschitz, Wilhelm (1871 Goerlitz – 1948)
1891 in Munich. Primarily self-taught. Drew inspiration from, firstly, Schwind and Richter, later, from Morris and Crane. Soon became involved in illustrations and applied art designs. In 1901, together with Hermann Obrist, he founded, in Munich, the Studio for Training and Experiment in the Liberal and Applied Arts *(Lehr- und Versuchsateliers für freie und angewandte Kunst)* which became widely known as the Debschitz School. In 1906 he added a workshop for techniques in hand-weaving and, in 1907, a further one for ceramics. In 1906 the Debschitz School appeared as a group in the Bavarian Jubilee Exhibition at Nuremberg, winning the gold medal. From 1906 Debschitz, with H. Lochner, was director of an industrial enterprise in Munich, the Studios and Workshops for Applied Art *(Die Ateliers und Werkstätten für angewandte Kunst).*

Delaherche, Auguste (1857 Beauvais – 1940 Armentières)
1877 and 1879-1883, pupil at the School of Decorative Arts in Paris. 1888, he bought the Ernest Chaplet Studio in Paris. Spent the summers of 1890 to 1894 in Héricourt (Oise); 1890-1904, worked in Armentières. Gold medal at Paris Universal Exhibition in 1889. 1900 Grand Prix, Paris. With A. Dalpayrat and E. Lachenal most significant artist of Art-du-feu ceramics in France.

Delft, Porcelain Factory
Around 1900 the Delft Porcelain Factory experienced a resurgence. The old techniques (sharp fire and muffle painting, lead and lustre glazing) were reintroduced. In the last quarter of the 19th century, bizarre art nouveau forms deriving from Far Eastern models were introduced. At the same time severe stereometric vessel forms came into being. For a short period Th. A.C. Colenbrander was active at the Delft Factory.

Deutsche Werkstätten für Handwerkskunst (German Studios for Handicraft Arts)
The German Studios for Handicraft Arts are, first and foremost, represented in Dresden (Hellerau). In 1898, young specialists set up the studio and it developed into one of the largest in Germany. The Studios, which specialized in hand-crafted furniture, had branches in Hamburg, Berlin, and Hanover. Important workers there were Richard Riemerschmid, A. Niemeyer, von Beckerath, B. Scott, and E.H. Walther.

Eckmann, Otto (1865 Hamburg – 1902 Badenweiler)
Painter, graphic artist, and designer of art handicrafts. Attendance at School of Applied Arts and Crafts *(Kunstgewerbeschule)* in Hamburg and the Academy in Munich. From 1890 on, showed at the Munich exhibitions. In 1894, gave up painting, auctioning off all his paintings to date and changing to graphic arts and art handicrafts. From 1895 on, worked for the journal *Pan* in Berlin and *Youth (Jugend)* in Munich. From 1897, teacher of ornamental painting at the School of Arts and Crafts *(Kunstgewerbeschule)* in Berlin.

That year he also showed at the International Art Exhibition in Munich. He turned out designs for knotted carpets, linens, furniture fixtures, wallpaper, tiles, metal goods and furniture. He designed the study of the Archduke of Hesse in Darmstadt. He developed a new type face for the printing firm of Klingspor in Offenbach, and designed bookplates and posters for the publisher E.A. Seemann, Leipzig.

Eisenloeffel, Jan (1876 Amsterdam – 1957 Laren)
From 1892 attended the School for Teachers of Draughtsmanship *(Schule für Zeichenlehrer)* with part-time practical work in W. Hoecker's silverware studio, where he worked full-time from 1896. Perfected enamelling technique with stays in St Petersburg and Moscow; artist in metal and art craftwork; leading position in Holland. 1908, worked briefly with the United Studios for Art and Handicrafts *Vereinigten Werkstätte für Kunst und Handwerk)* in Munich. Main work in brass and silver, the latter chiefly with enamel inlays, strongly individual work with few geometric ornaments. Along with everyday and luxury items in silver, copper, brass and wrought iron, he undertook larger works such as fountains, fireplaces and long-case clocks. Handicrafts exhibitions in Turin (1903), Dresden (1904), Munich (1908). Preferred basic stereometric forms to bring out the structure of the metal; he achieved enhancement by means of geometric cloisonné enamel.

Endell, August (1871 Berlin – 1925 Berlin)
Architect and designer for arts and crafts. Began with the study of philosophy in Munich, changed – sponsored by H. Obrist – to architecture, arts and handicrafts. In 1896 he built the Studio Elvira in Munich, and in 1898 the sanatorium in Foehr. 1899, represented in the jewellery section of the "Munich Secession" exhibition. In 1901 he designed the Buntes Theater in Berlin, in 1910-11 the trotting track near Berlin; also planned and built many town houses and villas in Berlin and Potsdam. 1906, published *The Beauty of the Big City (Die Schönheit der Großstadt).* Later, Director of the Academy of Art and Handicrafts *(Akademie für Kunst und Kunstgewerbe),* Breslau.

Endell, Fritz (1873 Stettin – 1955 Bayrischzell)
Originally studied theology. Motivated by his brother August Endell and H. Obrist, opted for the life of an artist in Munich. About 1900, in Paris, specializing in woodcut. Entered the Académie Julien, where he was a pupil of Colarossi, with technical instruction by Quesnel. Artistically influenced by Lipère, Valloton, and Paul Colin. 1902, moved to Stuttgart for further studies with Max Weber and as star pupil of Kalckreuth. 1914-20, moved to America. Study and reproduction of antique vase paintings and mirror engraving. Concerned himself with the art of the North American Indians.

Engelhardt, Christian Valdemar (1860 Flensburg – 1915 Copenhagen)
Chemist, whose work, from 1895, gave the Royal Copenhagen Porcelain Factory the highest quality in crystal glazing. In close co-operation with Arnold Krog (q.v.), created masterpieces of porcelain art which can stand comparison with Far Eastern, particularly Chinese, models.

Feuillâtre, Eugène (1870 Dunkirk – 1916 Paris)
Goldsmith and enameller. Started with R.J. Lalique. First independent work at Paris Universal Exhibition, 1900. Worked in translucid enamel, glass and silver.

Feure, Georges de (1868 Paris – 1928 Paris)
Painter, stage designer, lithographer, engraver, handicraft artist and worker in glass. Professor of the decorative arts at the Beaux-Arts in Paris. First exhibited in Germany at the "Munich Secession".

Gaillard, Eugène (1862 Paris – 1933 Paris)
Architect and furniture designer; samples of his work in Paris Museum of the Decorative Arts; his combs show Japanese influence.

Gallé, Emile (1846 Nancy – 1904 Nancy)
Artist in glass. Began his career in the studio of his father, the Lorraine glassworker Charles G.-Reinemer. 1862-70, in Weimar studying the maufacture of glass. Returned in 1870 to his father's faience factory in St Clement. From 1871 in Paris, where he learned the art of working with glass, enamel and gems. In 1874 he founded his own studio in Nancy. In 1889 he had a complete pavilion at the Paris Universal Exhibition. Developed the so-called Gallé glasses, which are made of differently coloured layers of glass fused together. Inspired by Chinese deep glass cutting.

Glasgow School
Community of artists which supplied designs for architecture and every branch of handicrafts. Members: Charles R. Mackintosh, H. McNair, and the McDonald sisters (resident in Glasgow before 1900).

Gradl, Hermann (1883 Marktheidenfeld, Franconia – 1946)
Painter, etcher and handicraft artist. Attended the School of Arts and Handicrafts *(Kunstgewerbeschule)* in Munich and by 1900 was designing for the State-run porcelain factory in Munich-Nymphenburg. He studied to attain a naturalistic style, using an individualistic colouring with a preference for shades of green. In 1907 he was teaching weaving and ceramics at the Nuremberg *Kunstgewerbeschule.* From 1938, Director of the class in landscape painting at the State School of Applied Art *(Staatsschule für angewandte Kunst)* in Nuremberg.

Grasset, Eugène (1841 Lausanne – 1979 Sceaux)
Painter, graphic artist and handicraft artist. First studied architecture, but from 1867 was more concerned with ornamental statuary. From 1871 in Paris, where he started out as book illustrator; later active in every area of the applied arts where the French historicism of Viollet-le-Duc set the standard. 1884, successful exhibition in *Salon des Cents* (Salon of the Hundreds), and in 1906 in the Salon of Decorator Artists in the Pavilion of Marsan. Prominent in the field of black leaded opalescent glass; but aimed at new effects by inserting coloured double plates in addition to the traditional black and brown lead painting. In the 1890s he developed a style which is a combination of these techniques. This corresponds to art nouveau's obsession with materials, which saw the harmonizing of the contrasts of different materials as an essential task of the artist.

Habich, Ludwig (1872 Darmstadt)
From 1890 pupil of Kaupert at the Art Institute in Frankfurt am Main, then at the Academies in Karlsruhe under Volz and in Munich under von Rümann until 1900. 1900-06 in Darmstadt; member of the artists' colony there. From 1906 in Stuttgart, where he was appointed Professor at the Academy of Art.

Heine, Thomas Theodor (1867 Leipzig – 1948 Stockholm)
Designer, illustrator, painter and author. Originally pupil at

the Düsseldorf Academy under Janssen. From 1889 in Munich where he first worked as illustrator for *Fliegende Blätter* and *Jugend*. In 1896, with Albert Langen and Ludwig Thoma, founded *Simplicissimus,* to which he was one of the main contributors, along with O. Gulbransson and Heinrich Thony. Emigrated to Prague in 1933. Short stays in Brno and Oslo followed, and he settled in Stockholm from 1942.

Hoffmann, Josef (1870 Pirnitz, near Iglau (Moravia) – 1956 Vienna)
Studied architecture at the Vienna Academy under O. Wagner. In Italy as winner of the Prix de Rome. In 1898, took part in the founding of the Viennese Secession, whose Exhibition Building was erected by J. Olbrich. From 1899 Professor of Architecture at the Vienna School of Arts and Crafts. 1903, co-founder of the Wiener Werkstätte with K. Moser and H.O. Czeschka. In 1905 he left the Secession with the Klimt group and organized the 'Kunstschau'. 1912, President of the Viennese Secession. Founder and director of the Austrian Werkbund, which he left in 1920 to take over the direction of the "Gruppe Wien" (Vienna Group) of the German Werkbund. Closely involved in the installation and planning of international exhibitions in Buenos Aires 1909, Rome 1911, Leipzig 1913, Cologne 1914, Stockholm 1917 and Paris 1925. In addition to designs for architecture and interiors (Palais Stoclet, Brussels, 1905-11), designed furniture, carpets, table services, glass, light fittings, jewellery and small objets d'art, as well as film and theatre settings.

Jeanneney, Paul (1861–1920)
Potter. Jeanneney began to make stoneware because of his admiration for Carriès. After the latter's death he took over and continued to run the studio at St-Amand-en-Puisaye. His pottery is characterized by the influence of Chinese flammulated stoneware and the *trompe l'oeil* work of ancient Japan. Jeanneney himself had a celebrated collection.

Jensen, Georg (1866 Raavad, near Copenhagen – 1935)
Sculptor, gold- and silversmith. Goldsmith teacher from 1884; 1887-92 training as sculptor at the Academy. 1892, gold medal of the Copenhagen Academy. Visited France and Italy. On his return, designer of table-ware and potter (Paris Exhibition, 1900.) 1904, opened jewellery and silverware shop in Copenhagen. Made jewellery, vases, bowls with fantastic motifs, especially from the plant world.

Jerndahl, Aron (1858 Östervad (Möklinta) – 1936 Stockholm)
Sculptor and painter; 1886-8 at the Academy of Art in Copenhagen. 1888-91 in the studio of P.S. Kroyers. In 1891 took part in the execution of reliefs for the Uppsala cathedral choir. 1898-9, studied at the Technical Evening School in Stockholm and the School of the Swedish Artists' Union. 1901, created the half-figure of an old man *The Evening of Life*, in sandstone; 1902, chimney reliefs and a bronze relief, *The Carnival of Life*. Exhibited at the Swedish Artists' Union in Stockholm and exhibitions in Munich (1909) and Düsseldorf. Represented in pastel painting at an exhibition of the Swedish General Art Federation (1932-3).

Kayser, Engelbert (Kaiserswerth 1840 – Cologne 1911)
Son of a tin-founder (see below), designed a "modern"-style beer mug in 1894 and developed his workshops at Cologne into a school for the art of pewter. Participation in exhibitions at Paris 1900, Düsseldorf 1902 and Saint Louis brought him prizes. He developed the so-called Kayser pewter; it consists of block pewter, has a silvery gleam and acquires great strength by the addition of copper and antimony, and a clear sound.

Kayser, J.P., metalware manufactory
The firm had its seat in Krefeld-Bockum and Cologne. It was predominantly a pewter manufactory. In 1862 the tin-foundry was moved from Kaiserswerth to Krefeld-Bockum by J.P. Kayser and in 1855 it was considerably enlarged and modernized. Around 1900 Engelbert, his son, set up a studio for the art of pewter in Cologne where the designs and models for the foundry were produced. The foundry was under the exclusive direction of his brother, Johann Peter Kayser Jun., who insisted that Kayser pewter be exhibited at all international exhibitions. The Kayser foundry developed new sensational techniques of tin founding. This was the so-called 'Kayser pewter', which was characterized by an especially silvery sheen and took a splendid polish. It was made of block tin with large additions of copper and antimony. This alloy produced the silvery gleam and above all made the vessel walls much stronger. The numbering of individual pieces started from 4,000.

Kirsch, Reinhold (1850 Buir, near Cologne – Munich 1915)
Artist smith. After completing his studies and travelling, settled in Munich where he founded an art locksmith's workshop.

Koepping, Karl (1848 Dresden – 1914 Berlin)
Graphic artist and designer for skilled crafts. Switched from chemistry to art studies; from 1869 at the Munich Academy for etching technique, later with A. Waltner in Paris. 1876, meeting with M. Liebermann, Jettel, Munkácsy and Charlemont in Paris. 1878, illustrations for the periodical *L'Art.* Until about 1890, reproduction etchings after paintings by old and contemporary masters (Rembrandt, Munkácsy, Liebermann and others). From 1890 director of the master studio for copper-plate engraving and etching at the Berlin Academy. 1892 – 1893 etchings of his own work: landscape motifs, nudes and still-lifes. Also devoted himself to the production of new-style glass and coloured glazes streaming into each other in the Japanese style. From 1896, senior writer on the review *Pan.*

Kok, Juriaan (1861 Rotterdam – 1919 The Hague)
Architect and designer. 1894-1913, Director of the Rozenburg Faience Factory at The Hague; under his direction mainly porcelain production 1899-1900. After 1900 he favoured the faience technique of quasi- or eggshell porcelain. Influenced by Javanese batik patterns.

Krog, Arnold Emil (1856 Fredriksværk – 1931 Tisvilde)
1874-1880 Copenhagen Academy; architect's degree. 1881-82 travelled to Italy. 1885 Director of the Royal Copenhagen Porcelain Factory. Universal Exhibitions 1899 and 1900, Paris; reintroduced painting under glaze. Influenced by Japanese woodcuts.

Lachenal, Edmond (1855 Paris – 1930)
Potter, sculptor and painter. 1867, worked in a pottery in Paris. In 1870 he changed to the studio of Th. Deck in Paris and from 1873 he was Director of the Deck firm's painting studio. 1880, opened his own faience workshop at Malakoff, near Paris. Around 1887 he installed his celebrated studio at Châtillon-sous-Bagneux. About 1896, began to work with stoneware and had great success in that field. 1900-1, created a highly differentiated range of glazed faience ornaments as applications for furniture and faience vases, which combine with gold and silver ornaments, in *métallo-céramiques.* In 1914 his son Jacques took over the workshop. From 1873 Lachenal was represented at all exhibitions. He is looked on as

the inventor of *émail-mat-velouté,* a velvety glaze, which he preferred to use in a light copper-blue with hints of green.

Lalique, René Jules (1860 Ay (Marne) – 1945)
Jeweller and glass artist; student at the Paris *Ecole des Arts Décoratifs.* From 1885 had his own jeweller's workshop in Paris. First sensational appearance 1895 in the Salon of the Champ de Mars; enthusiastically received at the Universal Exhibition of 1900. Motifs are plants and animals (mainly fishes and insects), figures and landscapes. He decorated semi-precious stones and glass in a kind of relief. Preferred subtle colour nuances for his pieces of jewellery. Besides gold and silver he combined every conceivable kind of material.

Larche, Raoul François (1860 St André-de-Cubzac – 1912 Paris)
Sculptor, pupil of Falguière. From 1884 represented at the *Salon de la Société des Artistes Français.* Numerous commissions for sculptures for public buildings in Paris, e.g. the statues 'Sap' and 'Spring' in ministries, 'Music and Poetry' in the Grand Palais, 'The Seine and its Tributaries' on a fountain in the Champs-Elysées. In addition produced countless models for the Porcelain Factory at Sèvres. 1920, Memorial Exhibition in the *Salon de la Société des Artistes Français.*

Léonard, Agathon (real name van Weydeveldt) (b. 1841, Lille) Belgian-French sculptor and skilled craftsman. Pupil at the Academy in Lille; later settled in Paris. Portrait medallions, decorative statuettes in precious metals, ivory and other materials. Apart from stoneware vessels and vases with flammulated glazes, he produced the famous fifteen-figure table service *Le jeu de l'écharpe,* executed in biscuit for the Sèvres factory. For this, he won a gold medal at the Universal Exhibition in Paris, 1900; the same figure service also in bronze. Complete example unknown.

Levallois, Louis (b. 1881)
Master pupil of the *Ecole de Céramique* at Sèvres. Worked for the Nymphenburg Porcelain Factory 1901-12.

Leveillé, Ernest (before 1900 Paris)
Glass artist, pupil of François Rousseau (q.v.), and his partner from the late 1880s. Like him, he added metal oxides to the glass melt and also gold and silver inclusions.

Liberty & Co.
At first a metalware factory in London, founded in 1875 by Arthur Lazenby Liberty (1843-1917). The firm mainly produced jewellery and silverware, but objects for interior decoration were gradually added. The diffusion of the 'Modern Style' acquired great importance in England and finally in Europe as well. In Italy it was called 'Lo Stile Liberty'. In 1901 they collaborated exclusively with the firm of H.W. Haseler. Among the designers, Archibald Knox and Arthur Gaskin stand out. From 1899 the firm's pewter production went under the name of 'Cymric' (q.v.), from 1912 under the name of 'Tudric'.

Lobmeyr, J.L. (Vienna)
Company trading in artistic glassware, founded 1822. Exclusive purveyor of glass to the Viennese Court. In the last quarter of the 19th century the firm represented Eisenmeyer, and later Mayrbach, and such well-known artists of the Vienna *Kunstgewerbeschule* as Bittlerlich, J. Hoffmann, Strnad and Loos. Many exhibitions, and prizes for table services, everyday and decorative glasses, vases etc. of crystal, and coloured glass with enamel, engraving, grinding and flashing.

Löffler, Berthold (1874 Nieder-Rosental, Bohemia – 1960 Vienna)
Painter, graphic artist and designer for art handicrafts. Studied at the *Kunstgewerbeschule* of the Austrian Museum.

Loetz, Jo., Witwe (Max Ritter von Spaun)
Glassworks in Klostermühle, Bohemia.

Loos, Adolf (1870 Brno – 1933 Vienna)
Architect and handicraft designer. Studied at the Technical High School in Dresden; study trip to Chicago, Philadelphia and New York. From 1896 in Vienna. 1898, designed the furniture and fittings for the Museum Café in Vienna; 1904, planned a vlla for Dr Beer on Lac Leman; 1908, a warehouse in Vienna; there follow several new-built and rebuilt Viennese private houses. His writings include *Ornament und Verbrechen* (1907), *Richtlinien für ein Kunstamt* (1919) and *Ins Leere gesprochen* (1921). In 1926 he drew the plans for Tristan Tzara's house in Paris.

Mackintosh, Charles Rennie (1868 Glasgow – 1928 London)
Architect, designer for handicrafts and graphic artist. 1884, studied at the Glasgow School of Arts, then with the architect John Hutchinson. 1897, planning of the new buildng of the Glasgow School of Arts. 1901, runner-up to Baillie Scott in the competition for the 'House of a Friend of Art' announced by the publisher A. Koch in Darmstadt. 1902, plans for the Scottish Pavilion at the International Exhibition in Turin. From 1913 he designed furniture, book bindings, posters, and patterns for printed textiles. In 1920 he retired to Port Vendres, France, and painted watercolour landscapes.

Majorelle, Louis (1859 Toul – 1926 Nancy)
Artistic craftsman. In 1879 he took over his father's ceramic factory and furniture workshop in Nancy, mainly producing pieces of furniture wholly in line with the floral tendency in art nouveau; wavy outlines with flower tendrils and intarsia work in various kinds of wood. From 1900, close collaboration with A. Daum for whose glasses and lamps he designed holders, bases and feet. Important representative of the school of Nancy.

Massier, Clément (1845 Vallauris – 1917 Golfe Juan, Cannes)
Potter. Learned in his father's pottery at Vallauris, and opened his own workshop in Golfe Juan, near Cannes, where he supplied the gardens of Riviera villas with vases. The Massiers made the technique of metal glazes on clay blossom again. They used reddish copper oxide glazes, which turned to mother-of-pearl with the admixture of silver, and ruby glazes. Clément softened the iridescent metal gleam by partial etching, and allowed the glazes to flow into each other with mixed earthen colours. He was represented at the International Exhibition, Paris, 1899, and regularly at the spring exhibitions in Paris.

Morris, William (1834 Walthamstow – 1896 London)
At first Morris was craftsman, poet and social politician. 1852-6 at Exeter College, Oxford, with Burne-Jones. 1854, Morris travelled to Belgium and northern France and founded the Brotherhood with Burne-Jones in 1855. This was a socially oriented group which wanted to get back to the origins of life. 1857, settled in London and painted under the influence of Rossetti. In 1858 *The Defence of Guenevere,* his first poem, was published, and made him celebrated. In 1859 he furnished his house at Upton and built the Red House in London. 1861, founded the firm of Morris, Marshall and Faulkner, Fine Art Workmen in Painting, Carving, Furniture and Metal. In 1868

his work was on show in the South Kensington Museum. In 1881 he transferred his workshop to Merton Abbey and in 1891 founded the Kelmscott Press for hand-made books. This workshop, too, was significant throughout Europe. He published various art-historical books, prose romances, narrative poems and Arthurian and Nibelung epics.

Moser, Koloman, usually Kolo (1868 Vienna – 1918 Vienna)
Painter, graphic artist and designer for handicrafts. Studied at the Academy and the *Kunstgewerbeschule* in Vienna. 1897, founding member of the Viennese Secession. From 1899, lecturer and from 1900 professor at the Vienna *Kunstgewerbeschule.* 1903, co-founder of the Wiener Werkstätte with J. Hoffmann. He also designed glasses for the art glass factory of E. Bakalowits and Sons, Vienna.

Nielsen, Ejnar August (1872 Copenhagen)
Figure, portrait and landscape painter, wood-engraver. Studied at the Copenhagen Academy 1890-3. From 1920, Professor there. Pictures of generous decorative stylization on naturalistic foundation, achromatic colouring.

Niemeyer, Adelbert (1867 Warburg – 1932 Munich)
Painter, architect and craftsman. Trained in Düsseldorf with P. Janssen and A. Krampf, from 1888 in Munich with W. Diez. Temporarily in Paris at the Académie Julian and with B. Constant. Study trips to Belgium, Holland, Italy, Turkey and Greece. Around 1900 in Munich made friends with Strathmann and A. Salzmann. From 1907, teacher at the State *Kunstgewerbeschule* in Munich, where he became friendly with Riemerschmid. From 1912, concentrated on pottery and glass engraving. Worked for the Nymphenburg, Berlin and Meissen Porcelain Factories.

Nymphenburg, State Porcelain Factory
Founded in 1747 by the Elector Max III Josef of Bavaria at Neudeck near Munich. Production began in 1753 and was transferred to Schloß Nymphenburg in 1761. In 1802 the old models were destroyed and not until 1862 did the factory receive a new state subsidy to develop a larger programme. At first the intention was to produce technical porcelain, which Ferdinand Scotzniovsky favoured. In 1888 Albert Bäuml took over the direction, and the factory's artistic sucess began. Around 1900, porcelain painting and design reached a peak. There was also a increase in animal figures and muffle painting. Art nouveau decoration was a big stimulus to the Nymphenburg Porcelain Factory. At this time, 1905-18, well-known artists worked for the factory, such as Joseph Wackerle and Theodor Kärner.

Obrist, Hermann (1862 Kilchberg, near Zurich 1927 Munich)
Studied science at Heidelberg; from 1888 studied at the Karlsruhe *Kunstgewerbeschule.* Designs for ceramic works for the Archduke of Sachsen-Weimar-Eisenach in Bürgel, Thüringen. Studied sculpture in Paris, and in 1892, without connections with any school, founded in Florence with B. Ruchet an embroidery workshop which was transferred to Munich in 1894. In 1897 represented at the VII Internatonal Art Exhibition in the Royal Crystal Palace in Munich by a range of textiles. Founding member and main collaborator of the 'United Workshops for Art in Handicrafts', Munich.

Oerley, Robert (1876 Vienna – 1939 Vienna)
At first, between 1889 and 1903, Oerley was active as a painter but also ran a school of cabinet-making which he closed in 1892. Oerley was a founding member of the Hagen Bund and a member of the Secession from 1907 until his death. He was

President of the Secession from 1911 to 1912. He was active as an architect specializing in interior decoration. He specialized in large-area decoration and in house furnishing and equipment. He was involved in the furnishing and equipment of the Auersperg Sanatorium, 1907, and in 1917 furnished the Carl Zeiss optical works in Vienna. In addition, he worked for Robert Bosch AG in Vienna until 1924.
Oerley was a highly individual furniture designer, working from the vernacular tradition and pioneering furniture designs which exhibited robust, movement-free elements. His primary points of reference were items of rural furniture, which he constructively refined. Oerley was always ready to carry out experiments and even took an early interest in moulded plastic furniture.

Ofner, Hans (1880 St Pölten)
Attended the general section of the Vienna *Kunstgewerbeschule* under Professor Schulmeister and from 1903 to 1907 Josef Hoffmann's School of Architecture. Ofner had early taken an interest in metal work and furniture. He especially favoured the simplified form, although it was enriched to some extent by struts and lattice-work. He learned the forming and embellishment of metal in Adele von Stark's experimental studio for enamel technique. In his home town of St Pölten he organized (1905-6) an art exhibition in which a dining-room, dressing-room and numerous individual objects were on show. In his furniture Ofner represents a stylistic tendency lying between Hoffmann and Moser, although he was ready to put experiments to practical use. An exhibition of his was treated in detail in the periodical *Hohe Warte,* 1905-6. *Die Kunst,* vol. 16, 1907, also has an article on Ofner's art with illustrations of the interior decoration of his home.

Olbrich, Joseph-Maria (1867 Troppau – 1908 Düsseldorf)
Architect and designer for arts and crafts. 1890, pupil of the Vienna Academy. Won the *Premio di Roma* for a stay in Italy and Tunisia. 1894, back in Vienna in Otto Wagner's studio. 1897, with G. Klimt founded the Viennese Secession *(Wiener Secession),* for which he built the exhibition pavilion in 1898. 1899, summoned to the artists' colony on the Mathildenhöhe in Darmstadt by the Archduke of Hesse.

Pankok, Bernhard (1872 Münster – 1943 Baierbrunn)
Architect and designer for artistic handicrafts. Attended the Academy in Düsseldorf and Berlin. 1892-1902 in Munich. Contributed to *Jugend.* 1897, participated in the VII International Art Exhibition in the Royal Crystal Palace in Munich with furniture. Co-founder of the 'United Workshops for art in Handicrafts'. 1899, took part in the Exhibition of the Munich Secession, showing the interior decoration of a room. 1900 took part in the Universal Exhibition in Paris, again with the interior decoration of a room. From 1902, worked in Stuttgart; from 1903 as Director of the teaching and experimental institutes. 1904, participated in the Universal Exhibition at St Louis with the furniture for a music room. 1913, Director of the State *Kunstgewerbeschule* in Stuttgart.

Paul, Bruno (1874 Seifhennersdorf in Lausitz)
1886-94, attended the *Kunstgewerbeschule* in Dresden. From 1894 at the Academy in Munich. 1897, co-founder of the 'United Workshops for Art in Handicrafts'. From 1907, Director of the teaching institute of the Museum for Arts and Crafts in Berlin. 1924-32 Director of the United State School for Liberal and Applied Art. 1933 resigned his post as Director of the master class.

Peche, Dagobert (1887 St Michael, Salzburg – 1923 Mödling, near Vienna)
Architect and designer of arts and crafts. 1906-10, studied at the Technical College; 1908-11 studied architecture at the Academy in Vienna. Installed a lady's boudoir in the Austrian Pavilion at the *Werkbund* Exhibition in Cologne, designed for Viennese textile and carpet firms and for *Wiener Keramik* (Viennese Pottery). From 1915, through the good offices of J. Hoffmann, worked with the Wiener Werkstätte, and ran its Zurich branch from 1917 to 1919. He made designs for interior decoration, silverware, jewellery, embroideries, ivory and leatherwork. Played a large part in the special exhibition of the Wiener Werkstätte *Kunstschau 1920*. Memorial exhibition in 1923 in the Austrian Museum, Vienna.

Plumet, Charles (1861 Cirey-sur-Vezouze – 1918 Paris)
Architect, pupil of A. Baudot; together with the architect T. Selmersheim, considered in Paris as the creator of art nouveau in house-building and interior decoration. Head architect of the Universal Exhibition 1900 and the International Exhibition of Arts and Crafts 1925 in Paris.

Powolny, Michael (1871 Judenburg – 1954 Vienna)
Designer for handicrafts and sculptor. 1891, attended the technical school for the clay industry at Znojmo (Znaim) and in 1894 the school of arts and crafts of the Austrian Museum in Vienna. With B. Löffler, founded in 1906 the *Wiener Keramik* (Viennese Pottery) studio which was transferred in 1912 to the *Gmundener Keramik* run by his pupil F. Schleiss. Like Löffler, he was appointed teacher in the school of arts and crafts, where he introduced a studio for glass grinding and cutting. In 1932 he transferred from the pottery class to the sculpture class. Designed for the Wiener Werkstätte, the Viennese Porcelain Factory and glass and stove firms. Ceramic figures after his designs exist in the Stoclet house in Brussels, a ceramic crib in Stift Klosterneuburg and a bronze tabernacle in St Georg near Cologne.

Prutscher, Otto (1880) (1882?) Vienna – 1949 Vienna)
Architect and handicraft designer. Studied at the School of Arts and Crafts of the Austrian Museum under the painter Fr. Matsch and the architect J. Hoffmann. 1903, became assistant in the Graphical Teaching and Experimental Institute and in 1909 teacher at the School of Arts and Crafts. He built villas at Baden and Mariazell, working-class housing in Vienna and the shop of the Austrian *Werkbund*. Designed for the Wiener Werkstätte, the Vienna Porcelain Factory, the *Wienerberger Werkstätten-Schule*, glass and stove factories, textile and leather firms.

Rheinische Glashütte (Rhine Glassworks), Cologne-Ehrenfeld
Produced hollow and flat glass and carried on a distinguished, wide-ranging trade in ornamental and functional glasses. It was founded by Philipp Michel in 1864. It was turned into a limited company in 1872 managed by F.O. Rauter. He directed the undertaking until 1898 and was constantly concerned with technical improvements. A new section for art glass was set up from 1879 to 1880 and around 1888-90 the firm had the reputation of being the most important glassworks in Germany. The factory worked with many techniques and experimented with historical formulas, especially from the Middle Ages and the Renaissance.
The Rheinische Glashütte is known for the production of Venetian glass and various rummer forms. Around 1900 it was given new creative impulses and Peter Behrens was employed as designer. E. von Kralik (1895-1912) also had a large

influence, and Kolo Moser and George de Feure were significant designers alongside Peter Behrens. In 1910 the factory added a department for flat glass. From 1916 there was a steady decline, until its closure in 1931.

Riegel, Ernst (1871 Münnerstadt – 1939 Cologne)
Goldsmith and craftsman. Apprenticed as goldsmith and engraver in Kempten. 1890-5 pupil of, 1895-1900 assistant to Fritz von Miller in Munich. In Munich until 1906. 1906-12 member of the artists' colony at Darmstadt. From 1912, Professor in the city *Werkschulen* in Cologne.

Riemerschmid, Richard (1868 Munich – 1957 Munich)
Architect, craft designer and painter. 1888-90, student at the Munich Academy. In 1896, designed the Riemerschmid residence at Pasing. 1897, founding member of the 'United Workshops for Arts and Crafts'. 1900, represented at the Universal Exhibition, Paris, with B. Paul and B. Pankok. 1910, interior decoration of the Munich Theatre *(Schauspielhaus)*. 1902-5, teacher at the Nuremberg Art School. 1912-24, Director of the School of Arts and Crafts, Munich. From 1926, Director of the *Werkschulen,* Cologne.

Rörstrand
Porcelain factory in Sweden, founded as a faience factory in 1726. Porcelain production from 1797. At first mainly influenced by England; towards the end of the 19th century adopted art nouveau forms and created an individual style.

Rousseau, François (1827 Paris – 1891 Paris)
Potter and glass artist. Started in 1867 as director of a pottery shop in Paris with designs for glassware and soon afterwards concentrated exclusively on producing glass. He coloured and cut crystal, mixing in metal solutions (gold and copper) and heating it several times so that he could model it repeatedly.

Ruskin, John (1819 London – 1900 Coniston)
Studied at Oxford. Pupil of the painters Copley Fielding and J.D. Harding. In 1840 he met J.M.W. Turner, to whom he dedicated the first (self-illustrated) volume of his *Modern Painters* in 1843. As well as watercolour architectural drawings from Italy and France, he made scientific drawings with geological, mineralogical, botanical and zoological motifs. 1849 published *The Seven Lamps of Architecture*. In 1851 followed an essay on *Pre-Raphaelitism* and in 1868 the celebrated lectures published as *Sesame and Lilies,* a Utopian social programme. Together with William Morris, Ruskin also produced designs for architecture and handicrafts and worked for a revival of English pottery. Slade Professor of Art at Oxford, 1870-9 and 1883-4. There Ruskin assembled a collection of landscape paintings, the Ruskin Art Collection, to which he added the Ruskin Drawing School in 1872. He endowed another collection of paintings, graphics, casts and minerals at Sheffield; with it he incorporated a night school for craftsmen, and a model co-operative for craft and industry, the St George's Guild. In 1887 Ruskin's private fortune was exhausted, which put an end to his foundations. Nevertheless, his social and artistic ideas were taken up by the whole of Europe.

Scharvogel, Johann Julius (1854 Mainz – 1938 Munich)
Scharvogel was a potter. At first he worked with the firm of Villeroy and Bosch in Mettlach. Later he set up his own ceramic workshop in Munich. He experimented with painting under glazes and was strongly influenced by Japanese pottery. 1906, appointed Director of the grand-ducal pottery at Darmstadt and returned to Munich in 1913. He preferred

lively, gleaming glazes in shades of brown with particles of gold, high-fired glazes on a hard ceramic base, possibly influenced in form by machine parts.

Schmithals, Hans (1878 Kreuznach – 1969 Munich)
From September 1902 attended the Obrist-Debschitz school in Munich. 1902-9, mostly designing furniture. 1909-11 in Paris; founded an exhibition association for the art of interior decoration together with W. von Wersin. 1914, *Werkbund* Exhibition, Cologne.

Schmuz-Baudiss, Theo (1859 Herrenhut – 1942 Garmisch)
Painter, draughtsman and decorative artist. Pupil of Lindenschmit at the Munich Academy. From 1896 intensely concerned with the artistic and practical problems of pottery. Took his decorative motifs mainly from the plant and animal world. 1897, founding member of the United Workshops for Arts and Crafts.

Schnellenbühel, Gertraud von (1878 Jena – 1959 Weimar)
Studied painting under Professor Frithjof Smith and from 1900 under Professor Angelo Jank in Munich. Switched to handicrafts in 1902 and joined the metal class at the Debschitz school. 1911, in the workshop of the silversmith Adalbert Kinzinger. 1914, represented at the *Werkbund* exhibition in Cologne.

Seger, Hermann (1839 Gnesen – 1893 Berlin)
Director of the chemical and technical experimental institute of the Royal Porcelain Factory, Berlin. Inventor of 'Seger porcelain' (a mixture fritting together as hard porcelain) which was particularly suitable for glazing experiments and made possible a smooth firing at low temperatures, appropriate for enamelling and coloured glazes *(couvertes colorées)*. This made it possible to bring back the beauty of Chinese and Japanese pottery and their glazes (Chinese red, celadon glaze).

Serrurier-Bovy, Gustave (1858 Lüttich – 1910 Antwerp)
Architect and craftsman. Studied architecture at the Fine Arts Academy in Lüttich. Influenced by William Morris, he went to England in 1884 and was extremely busy with craft work for modern interior decoration.
His aim was to include natural forms in his interior decoration and to design industrial products. Several exhibitions of his designs in England. Back in Lüttich he founded in 1884 the firm of Serrurier-Bovy for furniture and decoration, which later did a brisk trade with the Far East, like Liberty in London and S. Bicy in Paris. 1894, founded the *Libre Esthétique*. salons. 1897, set up a branch of the firm in Brussels and in 1899 in Paris (where it was called *L'Art dans l'habitation*. 1901, visited the exhibition of the artists' colony at Darmstadt, which had a profound influence on him. In 1910 he showed the last example of his designs at the International Crafts Exhibition at Brussels.

Siegel, Gustav
Gustav Siegel is a name often quoted in connection with Viennese furniture design. At the Universal Exhibition in Paris he had shown a dining-room and bedroom which he had designed for the bentwood firm of J. and J. Kohn. These pieces of furniture were technically advanced because the front legs and the rear supports were all bent out of one rod. The static structure was equipped with so-called stabilization supports. These were mostly spheres or ovoids which were screwed on to the furniture at the points subject to the greatest pressure and tension. It is known that Siegel was influenced by Otto Wagner and Josef Hoffmann but he refined those influences

artistically and technically. His work filled a gap in the development of Viennese art around 1900.

Tiffany, Louis Comfort (1848 New York – 1933 New York)
Painter and artist in glass. Began as painter in New York and Paris. Turned to artistic craftwork and in 1879 founded the Tiffany Glass and Decorating Company, which was responsible for the interior decoration of the White House, among other commissions. After chemical experiments with opalescent window glass (simultaneously with La Farge) he developed the so-called 'Tiffany Favrile glass', an iridescent glass mixed with metal, which was produced at Tiffany's own studios in New York in 1892 and won first prize at the Universal Exhibition at Paris (1900) and at Turin (1902). Went bankrupt in 1932.
Tiffany imitated Bohemian glass products; French glass painters had their works executed by him. In 1902 Tiffany took over his father's jewellery shop, Tiffany and Co., and personally designed gold pieces and items of jewellery. In 1918 he set up the Louis C. Tiffany Foundation for Art Students in his palatial home at Oyster Bay, Long Island, and bequeathed his collections to it; later the house was burnt down. In 1946 the collections were sold by auction.

Van de Velde, Henry Clemens (1863 Antwerp – 1957 Zurich)
Painter, architect and craft designer. Studied painting in Antwerp, Paris and Brussels. Under the influence of William Morris, turned to architecture and handicrafts in 1890. In 1895 he designed the building and interior of his house at Uccle near Brussels and in 1898-1902 the interior of the Folkwang Museum at Hagen. He formulated his ideas in *Kunstgewerblichen Laienpredigten* (Leipzig, 1902), and *Von neuen Stil* (Leipzig, 1907). From 1902, as artistic adviser to Archduke Wilhelm Ernst in Weimar, established and directed the craft teaching institutes there from 1906 to 1914. 1914, built the theatre of the German *Werkbund* Exhibition in Cologne. Founded the *Institut Supérieur d'Architecture et des Arts décoratifs* in Brussels in 1925, which became the *Ecole Nationale* after 1938. Designed the Belgian pavilions for the Universal Exhibitions of 1937 and 1939-40. In 1958 the Zurich Museum of Arts and Crafts devoted a comprehensive memorial exhibition to him.

Vierthaler, Ludwig (1875 Munich – 1967 Hanover)
Sculptor and designer. Active in Munich; worked for the Rosenthal Porcelain Factory at Selb. From 1921, Professor at the Technical High School in Hanover.

Voysey, Charles Francis Annesley (1857 London – 1941 London)
Architect and craft designer. From 1882, built country houses near London and designed their interior equipment (furniture, carpets, wallpaper and metalware); the firms making his furniture are Story and Co. and C.F. Nilson. 1884, member of the Art Workers Guild. 1893, 1899 and 1903, showed furniture at the Arts and Crafts Exhibition in London. 1936, appointed Royal Designer for Industry and in 1940 received the Gold Medal of the Royal Institute of British Architects.

Wagner, Otto (1841 Penzing near Vienna – 1918 Vienna)
Architect. 1857-60, at the Vienna Technical High School. 1860-1 at the Royal Building Academy in Berlin and 1861/63 at the Vienna Academy's School of Architecture; built flats and villas in the style of the Florentine Renaissance. 1893, prize-winning competition design for the General Regulation Plan for the municipal district of Vienna. Influenced by G. Semper, he justified his rejection of historicism in his book

Moderne Architektur (1896). 1897, designed the buildings for the Viennese metropolitan railway. In addition, supplied designs for furniture, textiles, ceramics, glasses, book bindings and silverware. 1894-1912, Director of the School of Architecture at the Vienna Academy. From 1899, member of the Viennese Secession. 1905, left the Klimt group. 1898-1901 and 1905, took part in the exhibitions of the Viennese Secession.

Wiener Keramik (Viennese Pottery)
This ceramic workshop in Vienna was founded by Bernhard Löffler in 1905 and, in addition to Löffler, Michael Powolny had a decisive influence on its production. At first the forms of international art nouveau were adopted, but the vessel bodies became increasingly 'concretized', acquiring constructive characteristics and tending towards stereometric basic forms which could often have been adopted from metal objects. The glazes are suitable for stoneware and a preference for hard glazes is characteristic of the frequently angular ribbed bodies of the vessels. The workshop was active until 1912; a year later the Wiener Werkstätte took over some of its models.

Wiener Werkstätte (the Vienna Workshop)
The Werkstätte was established in Vienna in 1903 by Josef Hoffmann and Kolo Moser as artistic directors. The first publication announcing the Wiener Werkstätte's programme appeared in 1905. The text explained that the designs were fundamentally executed by both artists. It was not the intention solely to produce individual pieces, but rather to comprehend the *Gesamtkunstwerk* (the work of art considered as having certain universal characteristics transcending place and time). Thus the workshop made a significant contribution to cultural development around 1900. Houses, industrial layouts and special installations were included in the programme of the Wiener Werkstätte and the internal design of buildings forms part of its architectural planning.
The main collaborators were C.O. Czeschko, Powolny and Klimt, among others.
The style of the early years is decisive inasmuch as a geometrizing of individual form and overall building guides decoration and form. The stylistic development of the Wiener Werkstätte was influenced by the Scottish designers Mackintosh, McDonald and C.R. Ashbee.
In 1908 Eduard Josef Wimmer became influential within the workshop in the realm of fashion, and in 1915 Dagobert Peche began to develop new stylistic forms foreshadowing the 1920s, forms mainly developed from the triangle and occupying a colour range between dull sulphur yellow, copper green, ice blue and cyclamen red. The Wiener Werkstätte supplied the stylistic stimulus for Viennese understanding of form.

Wytrlik, Otto (1870 Vienna – 1955 Vienna)
Wytrlik first distinguished himself in the preparatory class of the Vienna School of Arts and Crafts. Hermann Herdtle recognized his talent and in 1902, constantly encouraged by Herdtle, Wytrlik completed his studies at the Special School of Architecture at the Academy under Otto Wagner. From 1906 to 1908 was Professor at the State School of Arts and Crafts in Innsbruck and 1909-18 Professor at the Technological Museum of Arts and Crafts in Vienna.
1918-20, he was Professor at the State School of Arts and Crafts in Vienna and from 1920 chose the career of freelance architect. This period is very important for the genesis of his later works, for Wytrlik made no concessions in developing an animated Viennese furniture style. His primary concern was always the creation of forms with clear-cut lines dominated by the cube.

Zitzmann, Friedrich (1840 Steinach, Thuringia – 1906 Wiesbaden)
Teacher of glass-blowing at various technical high schools. Father of Julius Zitzmann, Cologne. Used the technique practised at Murano of glass blown at the lamp. Around 1890, produced ornamental glasses in historicizing styles. His technique spread throughout Germany, especially in the Bavarian Society for Arts and Crafts. 1895-6, collaborated with K. Koepping in Berlin for a few months. Refined his technique under Koepping's instruction and executed glasses after his designs in stylized plant forms. In Koepping's absence, and without his knowledge, he produced such glasses and sold them. Even after his return to Wiesbaden his glasses show Koepping's influence.

Notes

Plants and their Movement – an Art Nouveau Theme

1. Wilhelm Bölsche, *Weltblick, Gedanken zur Natur und Kunst*, Dresden, 1904.
2. August Endell, *Um die Schönheit – eine Paraphrase um die Münchner Kunstausstellung 1896*, Munich, 1896, p. 10 *et. seq.*
3. Hermann Obrist, *Neue Möglichkeiten in der Bildenden Kunst*, Essays, Leipzig, 1903 .
   Hermann Obrist, *Nachlaßschriften*, Munich, 1895/1901, State Graphics Collection, Munich.
   Hermann Obrist, *Programmatische Schriften*, Munich, 1895/1926. Private collection, unpublished.
   Exhibitions:
   Exhibition catalogue, Munich, 1958, Haus der Kunst, *Aufbruch zur modernen Kunst*, p. 198, 199.
   Exhibition catalogue, Munich, 1964, Haus der Kunst, *Secession, Europäische Kunst um die Jahrhundertwende*, pp. 60, 61.
   Exhibition catalogue, Berne, 1967, Museum of Art, *Hermann Obrist, Louis Soutter, Jean Bloé Niestlé, Kurt Seligmann*.
   Exhibition catalogue, Zurich, 1976, Kunsthaus, *Neue Kunst in der Schweiz zu Beginn unseres Jahrhunderts*, pp. 28-31, 75-78.
   Details of his life from contemporary newspapers and monthlies (posthumous material).
   Lampe-von Bennigsen, Silvie, *Hermann Obrist, Erinnerungen aus seinem Leben.*
4. *Ibid.*
5. Siegfried Wichmann, 'Das gesockelte Gefäß in Ostasien und Europa' in *Japonismus*, Herrsching, 1980, p. 314 *et seq.*
6. *Siegfried Wichmann, Hermann Obrist, Wegbereiter der Moderne*, catalogue, Munich, 1968, no. 13.
7. Ibid., no. 10.
8. Gerlach had a great success with his portfolios *Formenwelt aus dem Naturreiche* (1904). At first Martin Gerlach took his own photographs. When the demand for his portfolios increased, he commissioned plant photographs from well-known photographers.
   On the basis of comparisons, Karl Blossfeldt, too, must have given Gerlach photographs. This probability is still being investigated.
9. Siegfried Wichmann, *Hermann Obrist, Wegbereiter der Moderne*, catalogue, Munich, 1968, no. 31.
10. *Programmatische Schriften*, 1896-1925, private collection Munich, p. 36 *et seq.* and Ernst Haeckel *Kunstformen der Natur,* quoted by Hermann Obrist in *Pan* 1, 1895, p. 319.

The Lamp as Sculpture and the Lamp as Flower

1. Felix Poppenberg, *Das Lebendige Kleid*, Gera (1st edit. 1904), 2nd edit., 1910, p. 60.
2. Felix Poppenberg, *op. cit.*, p. 51 *et seq.*
3. Paul Scheerbart, *Glasarchitektur*, Berlin, 1913, p. 11.
4. G. Pazaurek, *Moderne Gläser*, Leipzig, 1901, p. 43.
5. *Nachlaßschriften II*, 1896-1925, private collection, Munich.

Geological and Submarine Motifs and Themes

1. Ernst Haeckel, *Kunstformen der Natur*, Jena, 1904, supplement 1904, p. 4.
2. Cf. note 1 in chapter 'Plants and their movement – an art nouveau theme'.
3. Ernst Haeckel, *Schöpfungsgeschichte*, Berlin, 1879, p. 403 *et seq.*
4. Gerhard Heberer, *Der Gerechtfertigte Haeckel*, Stuttgart, 1968, p. 87 *et seq.*
5. Felix Poppenberg, *Das lebendige Kleid*, Gera, 1910, pp. 15-16.
6. August Endell in *Berliner Architekturwelt*, 1902.

Plant and Floral Models and the Abstract Play of Line

1. Hermann Obrist, *Nachlaßschrift II*, 1895/1925, private collection.
2. Ibid.
3. Siegfried Wichmann, *Hermann Obrist, Wegbereiter der Moderne*, catalogue, Munich, 1968, Chap. II *et seq.*
4. Friedrich Naumann, *Deutsche Gewerbekunst*, Berlin, 1908, p. 21.
5. Hermann Obrist, *Neue Möglichkeiten*, Leipzig, 1903, p. 109.

Bentwood Furniture: Form and Function

1. D'Arcy Thompson, *On Growth and Form*, CUP, 1966, chap. VIII, 'On form and mechanical efficiency', section on bone structure, p. 230.
2. Ole Bang, *Thonet Geschichte eines Stuhls*, Stuttgart, 1979, p. 42 *et seq.*
3. *Ibid.* (However, it should be added that high concentrations of glycerine have been found in bentwood furniture. Apparently glycerine prevented surface rippling. The extent to which glycerine affected the bending process under heat has not yet been mechanically and chemically explained.)
4. The mechanically obtained curvature of bentwood furniture is not lasting in the long term. In the absence of opposing pressures and tensions, unrestrained bentwood shapes gradually return to their original form.
5. This observation was immediately adopted in the process of making Thonet furniture.
6. The flattened strip of wood which was a 'refinement' of the round rod was more or less forced on the Thonet and Kohn programme. A genuinely formal system was first worked out from these principles by Otto Wagner, who in turn influenced Hoffmann and Moser.
7. Martin Gerlach, *Formenwelt aus dem Naturreich*, Leipzig-Vienna, 1904, I-XII.
8. Wilhelm Bölsche, *Weltblick, Gedanken zur Natur und Kunst*, Dresden, 1904, p. 26 *et seq.*
9. Karl Blossfeldt started to take his plant photographs around 1900. After a perusal of scientific works, Blossfeldt's photographs stand out because of his individual vision of the object. A rough chronology of early Blossfeldt photographs can be established by reference to contemporary periodicals, which Hermann Obrist also made use of.
10. These technical and artistic phenomena had not been researched before. They are stylistically and functionally important for 'constructive art nouveau'.

The Aesthetics of the Machine

1. N. Pevsner, *Pioneers of Modern Design*, pp. 25, 27.
2. Ernst Haeckel, *Natürliche Schöpfungsgeschichte*, Berlin, 1879, p. 2
3. Gottfried Semper, *Industrie und Kunst*, Brunswick, 1852, p. 9 *et seq.*
4. Fritz Hoeber, *Peter Behrens*, Munich, 1913, p. 227.
5. Henry van de Velde, *Die Renaissance im modernen Kunstgewerbe*, Berlin, 1901, p. 103.
6. Heinrich Tessenow, *Hausbau und dergleichen*, Munich, undated (1906) 3rd edit., p. 14.
7. Felix Poppenberg, *Das lebendige Kleid*, Gera (1st edit. 1904), 2nd edit. 1910, p. 16.
8. Adolf Loos, *Ins Leere gesprochen*, 1897-1900, Zurich, p. 62 *et seq.*
9. Hermann Muthesius, *Stilarchitektur und Baukunst, Wandlungen der Architektur im 19. Jahrhundert und ihr Standpunkt*, Mülheim-Ruhr, 1902, p. 41.
10. *Ibid.*, p. 58.
11. Josef Hoffmann, *Das Interieur II*, 1900, 'Einfache Möbel', pp. 196-7.
12. *Ibid.*, pp. 201-2.
13. *Ibid.*, p. 204.
14. Otto Wagner, *Moderne Architektur*, Schroll, Vienna, p. 29.
15. *Ibid.*, p. 56.

Cube and Square: a Functional Design Unit.

1. Felix Poppenberg, *Das lebendige Kleid*, Gera (1904), 2nd edit., pp. 21-22.
2. Bertha Zuckerkandl, *Zeitkunst, Vienna, 1901-1907*, Vienna-Leipzig, 1908, p. 3.

237

Photographic credits

Sophie Renate Gnamm
Munich

Photographic Department
Bavarian National Museum

Photographic Department
Austrian Museum of Applied Art, Vienna

Photographic Department
Stuttgart, Württemberg Landesmuseum

Photographic Department
German National Museum, Nuremberg

Photographic Department
Museum of Arts and Crafts, Cologne

Photographic Department
Art Museum, Düsseldorf

Photographic Department
Bavarian State Art Collections, Munich

Foto Himpsl
Munich

Foto Tippmann
Kronberg/Taunus

Foto-Studio Ossi Baumeister
Munich

Foto Hansmann
Stockdorf, near Munich

Foto Schnock
Berlin

Marlen Perez
Embach/Switzerland